BLACK MOODS

*A list of books in the series
appears at the end of this book.*

UNIVERSITY OF ILLINOIS PRESS • URBANA AND CHICAGO

Frank Marshall Davis

black moods

COLLECTED POEMS

Edited by John Edgar Tidwell

© 2002 by the Board of Trustees
of the University of Illinois
All rights reserved
Manufactured in the United States of America
C 5 4 3 2 1

♾ This book is printed on acid-free paper.

Library of Congress Cataloging-in-Publication Data
Davis, Frank Marshall, 1905–
Black moods : collected poems / Frank Marshall Davis ;
edited by John Edgar Tidwell.
p.   cm. — (The American poetry recovery series)
Includes bibliographical references and index.
ISBN 0-252-02738-8
1. African Americans—Poetry.
I. Tidwell, John Edgar.
II. Title.
III. Series.
PS3507.A727A17   2002
811'.52—dc21   2001005616

Frontispiece used with the permission of the Frank Marshall Davis family.

To the memory of
Helen Canfield Davis, 1923–98

CONTENTS

I Am the American Negro (1937)

Uncollected and Unpublished Poems, 1948–84

ACKNOWLEDGMENTS

In some ways, this collection might be more accurately viewed as a wide-ranging collaboration. Instead of an editor, I see myself as more akin to a facilitator, orchestrating the vested interests of a number of scholars, friends, and family of Frank Marshall Davis into a volume that collects and preserves his poetic expression. This book would not be possible without their support and encouragement.

At Miami University, I found cheerful assistance from colleagues in the English Department, especially Frances Dolan and Keith Tuma. A Grant for Research Graduate Assistant from the Graduate School made it possible for me to hire Carmiele Foster to help collect background information on Davis.

When I moved to the University of Kansas in 1999, I was greeted with an enormous outpouring of collegiality and support. To Chancellor Robert E. Hemenway, I cannot express enough my gratitude for the manner in which he facilitated this project. The English Department, now chaired by James Hartman, provided funding that enabled me to hire two especially conscientious research assistants: Vibha Shetiya and Tina Evaristo. Members of the department's Ad Hoc Committee on African American Literature were indispensable as they read with rigor drafts of my introduction. I am especially grateful to Maryemma Graham and Joe Harrington for their sage advice, rendered generally when I was most exasperated and in need of a way out of no way. The patience and expeditious work of Lynn Porter, Paula Courtney, and Pam LeRow of the College of Liberal Arts and Sciences Word Processing Center made working on this project an absolute joy. Their cheerful advice and thoughtful recommendations easily saved me time and labor. For their extraordinary proofreading, I wish to thank Kristyn Westphal and Nathan Poell. *Extraordinary* is a term I also use for Willis Regier, the director of the University of Illinois Press, for deftly ushering this project through its several stages of development and production.

The National Endowment for the Humanities, through a summer stipend, made it possible for me to explore Davis's papers at the Chicago Historical Society, where Linda Evans and Archie Motley provided superb guidance. This same support and expert direction were also given to me by William Crowe, director of the Spencer Research Library at the University of Kansas, and by the staff of Spencer's Kansas Collection, especially Deborah Dandridge. Less formally, but by no means less significantly, Irma Wassall and Fred Whitehead provided important resources and encouragement for this project.

In the midst of the frantic hustle and bustle to meet deadlines, my mother, Verlean Tidwell, always seemed to be the supreme voice of calm, confidence, and reason. Her intercessory prayers, like those of all mothers, worked wonders for me. More personally, I have received reassurance from Carmaletta M. Williams about the efficacy and necessity of my work. Her disarming intelligence, charming persuasiveness, and ebullient spirit have been mainstays during the process. She was and continues to be a bridge over troubled waters.

Arguably my greatest debts are to Cary Nelson and Beth Charlton. Cary's vision was broad enough to see the centrality of Frank Marshall Davis's verse in refiguring the significance of sociopolitical poetry in the canon of American literature. Even before I approached him with a proposal, he had already seen the need to reinsert Davis into these important discussions. For his vision and for including me in it, I'm deeply grateful.

In every family, the mantle seems to fall on one to be the custodian of its history and legacy. For the family of Frank Marshall Davis, that person is Beth Charlton, one of his daughters. Her tireless work and self-sacrifice were simply invaluable in preparing this book. In her efforts to preserve her father's life and work, she was matched only by her mother, the late Helen Canfield Davis. An artist, a poet, and a music aficionado, Helen Davis graced her husband and children with a sense of ineffable delight in language, life, and love. I can think of no better tribute to Frank's magnificent voice, Beth's dutiful labor, and the Davis family as a whole than to dedicate *Black Moods* to Helen.

CHRONOLOGY

1905	Born 31 December in Arkansas City, Kansas.
1906	Parents divorced.
1909	Mother remarried to J. M. Boganey.
1923–24	Graduated from Arkansas City High School and moved to Wichita, where he took classes at Friends University and worked.
1924–26	Studied journalism and began writing poetry at Kansas State College (now Kansas State University).
1927	In January moved to Chicago, where he first hacked out short popular fiction for *National Magazine* in issues published between May and August. From April to circa August he was night city editor and columnist for the *Chicago Evening Bulletin,* in which he published several short stories under the name Frank Boganey.
1928	Wrote for the *Chicago Whip* from January to September before moving on in October to the *Gary (Indiana) American,* for which he was a reporter, editor, editorial writer, and regular columnist. Wrote under pseudonym Raymond Harper, which he revealed in the 2 August 1929 issue. Also "Jazzin' the News," a very brief jazz riff on news of the day, first appeared here.
1929	Left the *Gary American* in August and returned to Kansas State on a Sigma Delta Chi perpetual scholarship, ending his tenure at the *American* in August.

1930   Returned to *Gary American* in the fall and stayed through December. Reprised "A Diplomat in Black," a column he first wrote for the *Kansas State Collegian,* a student newspaper.

1931–34   In January, W. A. Scott recruited him for the *Atlanta World,* which was being published twice weekly. As managing editor, Davis increased it to a thrice weekly paper before bringing it out as a daily on 13 March 1932. He also wrote a column entitled "Touring the World," reprised "Jazzin' the News," and penned a series of editorials on such controversial subjects as the unwarranted lynching of Black people. Some of these appeared under his own name on the front pages because Davis intended to direct all criticism directly to him and not to the paper as a whole.

1934   Left the *Atlanta World* in midsummer 1934 and returned to Chicago. Upon his arrival, he went back to the *Gary American* on a part-time basis and reprised the name Raymond Harper. Under the pseudonyms Frank Boganey and "The Globe Trotter" he wrote sports columns.

1935   *Black Man's Verse* appeared in October. In September, he joined the Associated Negro Press as features editor and eventually worked his way up to managing editor. He wrote a theater column under the pseudonym Franklyn Frank; regular jazz reviews (from 1939 to 1948), under various titles, including "Rating the Records" and "Rating Hot Records"; and an editorial column, "Behind the Headlines."

1937   Awarded the first Julius Rosenwald Fellowship for Poetry in May. His second volume of poems, *I Am the American Negro,* appeared.

1938   *Through Sepia Eyes* (later included in *47th Street*) appeared as a Christmas remembrance.

1944   "My Most Humiliating Jim Crow Experience" appeared in *Negro Digest* in the September issue. (Others who wrote for this series included Langston Hughes in May 1945, the eminent historian Rayford W. Logan in March 1945, the renowned sociologist E. Franklin Frazier in November 1945, and the NAACP official Walter White in December 1945.)

1945   Taught one of the first history of jazz courses in the nation at Abraham Lincoln School in Chicago. Briefly served WJJD in Chicago as disc jockey, playing jazz records for a show he entitled "Bronzeville Brevities."

1946   Cofounded and served as executive editor of the *Chicago Star,* a citywide labor weekly, beginning on 4 July until its sale on 4 September 1948. The editorial column "Frank-ly Speaking" began here.

"Negro America's First Daily" appeared in the November issue of *Negro Digest,* and Davis is also listed as "contributing editor."

1947   Received pressure from Rankin's House Un-American Activities Committee.

1948   *47th Street: Poems* appeared. Moved with second wife, Helen, to Hawaii on 7 December. Sent a series of Associated Negro Press articles from Hawaii.

1949   Reprised "Frank-ly Speaking" weekly for the *Honolulu Record,* a newspaper affiliated with the International Longshoremen's and Warehousemen's Union, and continued to write until 1958.

1950   Poems published in special issue of *Voices,* edited by Langston Hughes. In February started his company Oahu Papers, featuring printing, writing, duplicating papers, and supplies, especially mimeograph paper.

1951   Wrote a formal response to the increased pressure from the House Un-American Activities Committee. A fire of unknown origin burned down Oahu Papers on 26 March. He denied it was sabotage, but a paper shortage hampered his efforts to get back in business.

1953   White Southerners mounted stiff opposition to Hawaii's statehood because of the territory's "racially mixed" composition and also because two senatorial votes would be added support for civil rights legislation.

1956   Communism charges persisted. Gave up Oahu Papers and started selling advertising items (calendars, novelties, gifts) to business firms.

1959   Began Paradise Paper Company to sell paper and printer's supplies and to do some importing.

1963   Announced in 19 May letter to Associated Negro Press owner Claude Barnett that he had been working on autobiography, "Livin' the Blues," off and on for over a year.

1973   Returned to mainland for the first time in twenty-five years and read poetry at Howard University, Atlanta University, Chicago's DuSable Museum, the University of California at Berkeley, and San Francisco's African American Historical Society.

1974   Second return to mainland to read poetry, in Southern California's Orange County.

1976   Chapbook *Jazz Interludes: Seven Musical Poems* appeared.

1978   Chapbook *Awakening and Other Poems* appeared.

1987   Died 26 July.

1992   *Livin' the Blues: Memoirs of a Black Journalist and Poet* appeared posthumously.

INTRODUCTION

Weaving Jagged Words into Song

Forewarning
Fairy words . . . a Pollyana mind
Do not roam these pages.
Inside
There are coarse victuals
A couch of rough boards
Companions who seldom smile
Yet
It is the soul's abode
Of a Negro dreamer
For being black
In my America
Is no rendezvous
With Venus . . .
—Frank Marshall Davis

I do not advocate art for the sake of propaganda. I demand a proper subordination and the observance of good taste. An example of the violation of the limitations I place upon this requirement may be seen in the poetry of Frank Marshall Davis. His propaganda, though based on sound critical analysis, is so blunt and militant that it has little chance of winning sympathetic consideration. In addition, much of it offends good taste.
—Nick Aaron Ford

When [Davis's] poems are poetry, they are powerful.
—Langston Hughes

Rarely in African American literary history has one poet been made to serve the interests of *two* movements, especially when the ideologies driving them so widely diverge. Such a moment occurred when both the New Negro Renaissance and the Black Arts Movement looked to Frank Marshall Davis

(1905–87) for inspiration and studied example. Shortly after the 1929 Stock Market crash, the irrepressible Alain Locke, self-professed "midwife of the younger group of Negro writers,"[1] found himself without the allegiance and dutiful following of his first generation of literary progeny: Langston Hughes, Countee Cullen, Claude McKay, and Jean Toomer. Although he had vigorously promoted their talents and accomplishments via publishers, patrons, and literary prizes, he nonetheless became disillusioned with them when he believed they had failed to fulfill his vision for a folk-based cultural movement. In response to their apparent intransigence, Locke accused them of waning abilities and "fired" them.[2] Locke's withdrawal of support led to his search for "replacement" cultural workers—a search that culminated in his discovery of Sterling A. Brown, Richard Wright, and Frank Marshall Davis. Ultimately, of course, this second generation would disappoint Locke too, although not because they lacked talent. Temperamentally, each of his new discoveries—like his previous ones—was unsuited to the role of chick to Locke's mother hen. More crucially, though, they resisted Locke's desperate effort to keep alive a racially based notion of the folk that changing times, initiated by the onset of the Great Depression, had transformed into a more proletarian cultural moment. In effect, he suffered from cultural lag. Unlike Brown, Wright, and Davis, Locke found himself out of step with current literary and cultural development.

Nevertheless, Locke proved indefatigable in his role as cultural promoter. In a review of Davis's first collection of poems, *Black Man's Verse* (1935), he proclaimed that Davis "brings fresh talent and creative imagination to this waning field [of poetry]."[3] This exuberance was shared by Harriet Monroe at *Poetry: A Magazine of Verse* and William Rose Benét, from his "Phoenix's Nest" at the *Saturday Review of Literature,* who, respectively, found Davis's poetry to evince "authentic inspiration" and "natural dignity . . . and intelligence."[4] The Julius Rosenwald Fund affirmed this high praise by awarding Davis its first poetry prize in 1937. As a result, he brought out *I Am the American Negro* (1937) and the Christmas remembrance *Through Sepia Eyes* (1938), a chapbook later incorporated into his *47th Street: Poems* (1948).

Despite this early acclaim, Davis virtually disappeared from American literary history after 1948; in 1973, he again found himself the subject of adulation, this time by members of the rebellious Black Arts Movement, and was led to publish two more chapbooks: *Jazz Interludes: Seven Musical Poems* (1976) and *Awakening and Other Poems* (1978). The insurgency that characterized the politics and art of sixties Black Power advocates became manifest in their sense of being sui generis: that tradition in literature and culture was only as old as the birth of their movement. Cultural "elders" Margaret

Burroughs, Dudley Randall, and Stephen Henderson thus "rediscovered" and "introduced" Davis to younger Black aestheticians. In Davis's sturdy poetics and uncompromising racial assertion, the "New Breed," as the essayist Peter Labrie called proponents of the Black Arts Movement in *Black Fire*,[5] located a literary forefather, whose idea about racial pride they contorted into matching their own political and poetic sensibilities. As a consequence, on a 1973 tour of selected Black colleges, Davis was enthusiastically greeted by writers and students as "the long lost father of modern Black poetry" who had been "twenty years ahead of his time."[6] Thus, a presumably shared aesthetic erased the boundaries erected by age, and the younger group found ideas and inspiration in Davis's robust thematics of urban life, fierce social consciousness, strong declamatory voice, and almost rabid race pride.

And yet despite a new literary reputation—augmented by such newspaper positions as editor, managing editor, executive editor, feature writer, editorial writer, correspondent, sports reporter, music and theater critic, contributing editor, and fiction writer for the *Chicago Evening Bulletin,* the *Chicago Whip,* the *Chicago Star,* the *Gary (Indiana) American,* the *Atlanta World,* the Associated Negro Press, and the *Honolulu Record*—that can be read as a palimpsest of the first, Davis has not enjoyed the canonical status accorded his more celebrated contemporaries, including Langston Hughes, Margaret Walker, Melvin B. Tolson, Gwendolyn Brooks, Robert Hayden, and Sterling A. Brown.

Black Moods: Collected Poems seeks to correct an oversight in African American literary tradition by restoring Davis to his rightful place in the historical narrative. Given Davis's history, this is not simply another "recovery effort" of a previously well-known writer who had descended into obscurity. Instead, this collection reopens an important but neglected discussion of poetry from the 1930s and 1940s, proposes new ways of considering its importance, and, using Davis as an example, provides fresh perspectives on the writing of literary history. Although Davis's commitment to social causes often led him to subordinate aesthetic concerns to political issues, he nevertheless wrote four kinds of poetry: social realism, jazz poetry, social satire, and lyric and love poetry. By recovering the variety in Davis's poetic expression, we not only debunk the myth that his verse was one undifferentiated body; we also participate in what the cultural critic Cary Nelson describes as redefining "the cultural function of poetry, the cultural space it occupied, and its relation to all the other discourses of the day."[7] In so doing, we identify for readers today what is most valuable about recovering Davis's verse: revealing a fuller, more inclusive history of African American poetry; forging a convincing nexus between the New Negro Renaissance and the sixties Black Arts Movement; and repositioning the significance of the social, the cultural, and the political in the historical narrative of African American poetry.

Reconstructing a Blues Life

To understand more fully the tensions in Davis's poetry, it is necessary to revisit the public self he constructed in his posthumously published *Livin' the Blues: Memoirs of a Black Journalist and Poet.*[8] By recovering some of the biographical background to the poems, we gain a sense of how Davis dealt with material from his life because writing poems, for him, was an alternative form of self-expression. As a practicing journalist, Davis felt burdened emotionally by the weight of lynchings, discriminatory practices, and other racism-induced conditions. Reporting these omnipresent events as news items required what he termed "objectivity"; yet, his spirit and soul suffered as well, which propelled him into responding in poetry, a more "subjective" medium. Many of these tensions were shaped initially by the geography and demographics of his life in south-central Kansas, from 1905 to 1923.

The life he retraces began inauspiciously in Arkansas City—"a yawn town fifty miles south of Wichita, five miles north of Oklahoma, and east and west of nowhere worth remembering" (*Blues* 3). Underlying this portrait of somnolence, however, is a subtext of horror and despair—at least for African Americans. The source of this dispiriting account is the effort made by whites to inculcate a feeling of racial inferiority into him. In this narrative of conflict and contradiction, Davis sketches a sociopolitical context that would later force him to confront the racist onslaught that attempted to rob him of his humanity.

One poignant example of the process of instilling self-hate into Davis reveals how worthless white individuals and institutions considered African Americans to be. When Davis was five years old, a group of white third graders, with curiosities piqued by overhearing their parents discussing lynching, selected Davis for an experiment:

> I was on my way home alone, crossing a vacant lot, when these white boys, who had been lying in wait, jumped me. They threw me to the ground and held me down while one lad produced a rope and slipped it over my head. I kicked and screamed. Just as one started to snatch the noose tight around my neck, a white man appeared. He took one look, chased the boys away, freed me, and helped brush dirt and trash off my clothes. . . . I never learned who he was, nor could I single out the embryo lynchers at school next day.

Naturally, school officials did not push their probe. I was still alive and un-harmed, wasn't I? *Besides, I was black.* (*Blues* 13; emphasis added)

Part of Davis's narrative purpose in beginning his memoir with this incident is simply rhetorical. The writerly strategy forces readers to confront the representation of a world in which Black life is tenuous, insignificant, and often brief.

But this tack also introduces themes, ideas, and controlling metaphors that inform his six collections of poetry and a career as a journalist for more than forty years. In *Livin' the Blues,* Davis meditates in prose on ideas discursively presented in his poetry: themes affirming humanity, advocating sociopolitical change, and raising consciousness—reflections that grow out of the failure of social institutions to grant all people life, liberty, and the pursuit of happiness, as urged in the Declaration of Independence. For instance, his reflections about the educational system of Arkansas City schools enable us to understand ideas and arguments that will appear in both his journalistic writings and such representative poems as "What Do You Want America?" and "Give Us Our Freedom Now!"

Turn-of-the-century Arkansas City participated in a contradictory state policy that supported racially integrated schools while simultaneously permitting racial segregation.[9] In effect, Arkansas City was trapped between de jure and de facto social relations, between principle and practice, and between illusion and reality. About the curious form of racially integrated education, he writes: "I have completed twelve years of formal study that prepares none of us, white or black, for life in a multiracial, democratic nation. This is a mixed school—mixed in attendance, mixed-up in attitudes" (*Blues* 3). Not uncommonly, then, Davis would write about the diverse racial makeup of the United States as a way of coming to terms with questions of racial inequality, constitutional contradiction, and personal rights. His recollection indicts this public education system not only for its exclusionary practices but also for the confused ideological assumptions supporting the goal of social "inclusion." The life thus represented in *Livin' the Blues* is shaped by a difficulty reconciling the contraries, the contradiction between *principle* and *practice:*

What embittered me most was flagrant white hypocrisy. Virtually all aspects of daily life were geared to maintaining white supremacy. And yet, teachers, newspapers, and speakers solemnly preach the doctrine that all men are created equal as they proudly pointed toward the Declaration of Independence and the Constitution. . . . Obviously, the establishment intended to maintain the status quo until eternity. But why did they lie? Why did they not come out and say flatly what was in their hearts: equality was not for black people? Why did they teach about democracy and then shove me back when I sought my just share? Why is hypocrisy a strong national trait of American whites? (*Blues* 55–56)

As a counterbalance to the omnipresent de jure and de facto segregation, Davis discovered self-preservation in cultural activities and practices that also enabled other African Americans to survive. For instance, the annual Emancipation Day celebrations brought Blacks together to commemorate, in an unofficial holiday, Abraham Lincoln's issuance of the Emancipation Proclamation on 1 January 1863. The Baptist church has traditionally been a sanctuary for African Americans; Davis, however, was less moved by the church's spiritual value than by its sense of community. And like Audre Lorde, Richard Wright, and Frederick Douglass, he discovered a new world in the public library, first in the juvenile fiction section and, having exhausted it, then in the adult area.

At age eight, though, Davis made a discovery that would ultimately prove to be his most significant source of personal salvation: the blues. He recalled: "The blues? We were formally introduced when I was eight; even then I had the feeling we weren't strangers. So when the blues grabbed me and held on, it was like meeting a long-lost brother" (*Blues* 27). Although the blues emerged from such progenitors as ragtime, minstrelsy, Tin Pan Alley, and vaudeville via Williams and Walker, Scott Joplin, and Mamie Smith, Davis's early introduction to this art form came by way of many lesser-known touring two- or three-member combos, usually from Kansas City. Their influence, while tentative, fostered enough of an emotional or spiritual kinship to sustain him until he reached Kansas State College (1923–27), where his inchoate cultural urges began coalescing into a mature aesthetic.

In his quest for self-fulfillment, Davis at Kansas State discovered that free verse suited his aesthetic sensibility. He felt free verse was unconventional and iconoclastic, two features he considered poetic equivalents of the blues and jazz:

When I heard my first blues and early jazz at the age of eight years, I felt the same kind of exultant kinship with this music that I felt when I read my first free verse in college. I am by nature an intellectual rebel, and I felt emotionally akin to those musicians who emancipated themselves from the rigid traditions of Western music. The improvisation and freedom from rigid rules which made the blues and jazz so revolutionary appealed immediately to me, just as did the break with tradition and the freewheeling which are basic ingredients for free verse.[10]

Davis never found the modernist avant-garde poetic practices of Ezra Pound and T. S. Eliot engaging, but instead inflected his poetic practice with "Black moods," especially in his jazz forms.[11] In this self-described aesthetic, Davis located himself in a poetic tradition—including such practitioners as Hughes, Brown, and the lesser-known Waring Cuney—that resists the stereotypical characterization of the blues as an extended moan over lost love. Here is no expression of what the folklorist Alan Lomax once described as self-pity; instead, it is a profound assertion of self. For Davis, the ontological axis turned on how the self responded to hardship, pain, denial, and suffering. The response he found most often was not defeatism but transcendence over difficulty and therefore triumph. Kansas, then, provided Davis with the basic intellectual and aesthetic training that enabled his writing to be like the fabled ram's horn—his means for blasting away at the walls constructed to maintain the boundaries of racial difference.

The political and aesthetic rebelliousness inculcated at Kansas State College came to define a life in which freedom against racial and class oppression would be the *raison d'etre*. In the years 1935–48, his most productive period as a poet, Davis's tireless struggle for social, intellectual, political, and aesthetic freedom led him to new epiphanies. His outrage at the exceptionally heinous lynching of Cleo Wright in Sikeston, Missouri, in 1942, and the infamous Detroit Riot of 1943 forced him to abandon his "lone wolf" strategy of decrying social injustice. "The establishment," he writes in *Livin' the Blues,* "tolerates the solitary protester. It smiles and points to him as proof that free speech *does* exist in America. The unwritten rule is that you can yell as loudly as you please—by yourself. But when two or more of you get together you become a threat even though you speak only in whispers" (276). The decision to seek allies brought Davis to this understanding: that, whether real or perceived, his protestations would be considered those of a Communist. The war years, as Davis clearly knew, demanded a certain obeisance to maintaining the sociopolitical status quo. To rail against the urgent demand to close ranks would automatically brand one a subversive. Undeterred by the risks, Davis ventured out. "For the first time in my life," he writes, "I quit being a loner. I [decided to work] with all kinds of groups" (*Blues* 276).

Although occurring later, Davis's decision answers the call issued in 1937 by Richard Wright for Black writers to break down the isolation among themselves as well as between African American and white writers.[12] Wright characterized this movement as a need to establish collective work. Davis answered this call in two ways. First, he actively allied himself with such prominent white Chicago writers as Jack Conroy, Nelson Algren, Stuart Engstrand, and Meyer Levin. Next, through associations with these "socially conscious 'proletarian writers'" (*Blues* 245), Davis developed a progressive vision and resolved to work with such ideologically diverse groups as Communists, Socialists, and liberals (*Blues* 278). For him, there was no distinction between them: "My sole criterion was this: Are you with me in my determination to wipe out white supremacy?" (*Blues* 278).

"Passing Parade," an Associated Negro Press column he published intermittently in 1943 and 1944, can be read as his attempt to implement a collectivist vision. In this series, he registered his most blistering prose critique of American domestic and international relations. We now know that he expressed his views just as passionately in another, less visible, way. Sometime during the middle of the war, he joined the Communist party. His attraction no doubt derived from what he perceived to be the Party's determination "to use any and every means to abolish racism" (*Blues* 276). Of course, the Party was not perfect. Like many other converts, he felt betrayed when Stalin signed the infamous nonaggression pact with Hitler on 24 August 1939. But Stalin's later agreement to join the United States in conducting an all-out war on the Axis restored a measure of Davis's confidence in the USSR. Ideologically, then, Davis was persuaded by the Popular Front's integrationist and anti-Fascist beliefs. This group attempted to foreground the role of Black culture as both unique and typically American. Davis saw his own ideas reflected in this thinking, which encouraged his writing of the poem "To the Red Army."

Yet, it was Davis's public effort to force a more inclusive participatory politics that ultimately put him on a collision course with such guardians of the status quo as the House Un-American Activities Committee and the Federal Bureau of Investigation. For in the years 1935–48, Davis boldly fashioned his journalism into a catalyst for social change. In a variety of editorial positions at the Associated Negro Press, Davis helped to shape what many Black newspapers came to agree was their central purpose: to give "the widest possible publicity to the many instances of racism and the dissatisfaction of Afro-America with the status quo" (*Blues* 272). The pragmatic function of this gesture called attention to the need for a press to counterbalance the welter of misinformation reported in the white media. For instance, while national public policy sought to "close ranks" and ignore domestic social problems in favor of promoting a unified war effort, the African American press conducted its "double-V" campaign—victory abroad and victory at home.[13] This campaign was committed to guaranteeing that the freedoms African American soldiers fought for in the European, African, and Asian theaters would also be granted to them at home. One part of this struggle was to dismantle the codes and practices that sustained racial separation in the armed services, in effect showing how a desegregated military could serve invaluably in desegregating American society.

A bit less consequential for the direct, progressive political vision Davis developed but no less significant for his poetry was his running commentary on Black cultural matters. In his "Rating the Records" column, Davis reviewed the newest recordings of swing or "hot jazz." "Things Theatrical" provided him a venue for sharing his observations of live musical theater. "The World of Sports" enabled him to report on the many African American participants in boxing, football, basketball, and other athletic activities. In addition to these regular columns, Davis wrote over thirty-five book reviews. But even these pieces had their political resonances. The critic John Gennari was moved to observe that jazz, for Davis, "was primarily a protest music."[14] Of the several sports topics Davis routinely followed, his Joe Louis "watch" carefully reported on the movements of the heavyweight boxer and even offered marital advice intended to caution Louis from falling into the same pitfalls that caused the undoing of Jack Johnson—an earlier Black heavyweight champion. Even some of the book reviews—most notably those written about Richard Wright's works—functioned to promote a literature that would assist in attaining the hoped-for goal of racial integration.

From the multiplicity and implicit radicalism of these editorial tasks at the Associated Negro Press, Davis's political engagement is obvious. In his role as a journalist-activist, Davis found himself swept up in a vortex of political activism—much of which took the form of critique leveled at such differential treatments as racial segregation, anti-Semitism, and exploitation of labor workers. In the years 1944 through 1946, Davis seemed to draw from an endless fund of energy and commitment as he involved himself in an astounding number of organizations and committees. Among these, he expressed his commitment to labor causes by cofounding the *Chicago Star,* a labor newspaper. He worked for the Republican and Democratic parties as well as for the Progressive party's Henry Wallace, who campaigned as an independent presidential candidate in 1946, and for the National Committee to Combat Anti-Semitism, the Chicago Civil Liberties Union, and the National Civil Rights Congress (*Blues* 295–97). Davis's membership or participation in these groups was enough to pique the interest of the FBI. But the agency's interest became much keener when, relying on confidential informants, officials determined that he was at least affiliated with the Carver Second Ward West Communist Political Association Club, the Dorrie Miller South Side Council (CPA), the South Side Cultural Group, and the Abraham Lincoln School.[15] Such poems as "To Those Who Sing America," "Peace Quiz for America," and "Nothing Can Stop the People" no doubt reflect the activism the FBI identified as subversive politics. Although Davis's FBI file is rather silent about the agency's coercive efforts to contain him, it is still possible to claim that the pressure on Davis to conform was enormous. Despite what Davis "officially" states as a planned vacation, I believe the actual reason for his departure for Hawaii is rooted in his capitulation to the governmental pressure of McCarthyism. On 7 December 1948, he and his wife Helen left the mainland for the rather quiescent sanctuary of the Territory of Hawaii.

Davis's move should not be misconstrued as either a retreat from the struggle for social justice and racial equality or an abrogation of social responsibility; he merely changed the venue, the site of conflict. A *malihini,* or newcomer, he learned quickly about the complex ethnic makeup of Hawaii, which he shared with mainlanders via an Associated Negro Press series entitled "Democracy: Hawaiian Style." Although the column lasted only four months in early 1949, its focus reminds us that Davis's political vision remained important to the poetry he wrote there. He came to see the proliferation of Filipinos, Samoans, Koreans, Japanese, Chinese, Puerto Ricans, Portuguese, full-blooded Hawaiians, African Americans, and whites as constituent parts of "a land of ethnic hash." Instead of a land teeming with tolerance for difference that would render the conventional modes of racial discrimination inoperable, Davis perceived the subtle persistence of ethnic tensions. Much of this feeling was directed toward the two most populous groups: whites and Japanese. The strong economic position enjoyed by the Japanese elicited from other groups an anti-Japanese bias. Anti-white feelings were precipitated by the influx of "'foreign' customs and ideas, by the Caucasians' economic strength, and by the contempt" whites showed for other groups.[16]

Despite the persistence of these prejudices, Davis was greatly encouraged by the possibilities for intergroup cooperation and tolerance for difference. This hopefulness became the basis of his argument for miscegenation and for his belief that the struggle for racial and class equality must be fought collectively by those who suffer the ill effects of discrimination.[17] But it was largely from the editorial pages of the *Honolulu Record,* from 1949 to 1958, that Davis registered his most important political observations.

At the *Record* he was especially vituperative in pointing out the disparity between labor and management. This newspaper, the organ of the International Longshoremen's and Warehousemen's Union, strongly argued for labor solidarity in an effort to obtain fair wages and benefits. In effect, Davis's editorial writing in Hawaii reconstituted his earlier campaign for fairness and equality. He felt that Hawaii, more than any area of the United States, had shown successfully "the possibility of integration with integrity" (*Blues* 318). What Davis meant was that, despite some ethnic strife, "various ethnic groups had been able not only to maintain group identity and pride but work together with other peoples of vastly different traditions and live side by side without noticeable tension" (*Blues* 318). The respect for cultural difference implied in Davis's view of Hawaii also informed his labor philosophy—that fairness and respect were due everyone, especially the worker, regardless of race or ethnic background.

In several memorable poems, Davis chose a more subjective means of responding to the variety of people, places, and activities he observed. Although he was often moved to lyrical expression, his social poetry captured a vision committed to exposing discriminatory practices and to revealing the humanity of the common people. For instance, "This Is Paradise" offers a contrast to the usual picture postcard or chamber of commerce boosterism of Hawaii. Beneath the placid surface of beach-front hotels, bikinis, and beach bums lay the complicated world of "the bright prismatic people." It is one shaped by the history of Captain Cook's invasion, the influx of Christian missionaries, the arrival of the Big Five pineapple growers, and the influx of tourists. The lives of the native Hawaiians, Davis reveals, have been distorted and destroyed by economic power and an exploitative variety of Christianity that transformed the purity of religious values into tainted belief. One exploited group is featured in an innovative collection of portrait poems, which he wrote sometime during the seventies, entitled "Horizontal Cameos." In these thirty-seven poems, Davis enabled women reduced by circumstances to prostitution to speak their lives.

Social Realism

The process by which some poets achieve the elite status of "major" while many more are either marginalized or even forgotten, according to Cary Nelson, is a heavily contested debate. Writing specifically about the years 1910–45, he reminds us that an important feature that until recently had gone unremarked in canon formation and recovery efforts was the diversity of American poetries that appealed to multiple audiences, including "black poetry, poetry by women, the poetry of popular song, and the poetry of mass social movements."[18] A casualty of these discussions was the poetry of Frank Marshall Davis.

A handful of reviewers, motivated by the need to prescribe the nature and relationship of literary and social matters in art, propounded the view that Davis's poetry was largely undifferentiated and identified its predominate tone as "bitter." It is precisely this misjudgment that ultimately jeopardized his place in the poetry canon. These critics, especially Nick Aaron Ford, roundly criticized him for exemplifying the worst excesses of "social realism" and "propaganda." It mattered little that these critics' definitions of "social realism" and "propaganda" were barely distinguishable. The absence of logically consistent evaluative standards resulted in a conflating of "isms" in which "propagandistic" became equated with "undifferentiated." Both descriptions of his work took their "authority" from a "bitterness" that certainly predominated in a few Davis poems.[19] As a result, this single quality came to be the part representing the whole of Davis's output. This characterization goes a long way toward explaining why Davis was eventually relegated to the historical anonymity of a "minor" poet—one whose achievement was marginal in the canons of both American and African American poetry. However, this oversimplification of his work contains two distinct, although at times overlapping, problems: it denies the rich variety of Davis's verse and it betrays an implicit conceptual uneasiness with the relationship of art to social causes.

In commenting about his own poetic theory, Davis proved to be unhelpful because his views exacerbated the antagonism with opposing critics:

> To me, poetry is a subjective way of looking at the world. All poetry worthy of the name is propaganda. Milton's *Paradise Lost* is Christian propaganda as is Joyce Kilmer's "Trees." But such works are not likely to be condemned as propaganda because the beliefs expressed in these and similar poems are shared by a majority of the population. . . . Since I take pride in being considered a social realist, my work will be looked upon as blatant propaganda by some not in sympathy with my goals and as fine poetry by others of equal discernment who agree with me. . . . Since I am blues-oriented, I try to be as direct as good blues. This implies social commentary.[20]

This definition of good poetry provided fairly elastic boundaries between the literary and the social. But Davis failed to demonstrate to his detractors a common ground between these impulses. As a result, his poetry and his place in literary history became vulnerable to critics' displeasure.

The issue of what it meant for Davis to be considered a social realist provides a poignant opportunity for examining the problematics of his place in literary history. In its own time, Davis's work clashed with the normative value of poetry as a discourse that could redefine the nature of human relations. For critics like Nick Aaron Ford, the cultural space occupied by poetry was intended to create interracial accord by offering proof of racial achievement, which was interpolated into a social sign of African American merit for entry into the amorphous American "mainstream." Thus a poetics of "good taste" and "sympathetic consideration" were fundamental principles intended to assure good will and interracial harmony.

But Davis's voice was capable of being strident and loudly critical, as his poem "Frank Marshall Davis: Writer" demonstrates in recounting the bluster of his negative reviewers:

> "He is bitter
> A bitter bitter
> Cynic"
> They said
> "And his wine
> He brews from wormwood."

The interpolation of "bitterness" into a critique of Davis's verse suggests condemnation of it as recalcitrant, bombastic, inartistic, and propagandistic. This assessment reveals the familiar critique of thirties social poetry as being little more than uncontrolled, unsystematic, and unconvincing proselytizing. Davis's verse, then, suffered the same fate experienced by thirties literature labeled "proletarian" and "naturalistic": it was considered second rate by some literary historians. This designation carried an additional burden: "The ideological and aesthetic baggage associated with these terms convey[ed] yet another implicit narrative: the predictable and dreary story about the tragic encounter between the creative writer and political ideology."[21]

From a retrospective glance, the criticism leveled at Davis's verse can be more clearly seen as having origins in anachronistic definitions of poetry. According to Cary Nelson, definitions of excellent poetry or poetic practice during the early part of the twentieth century often derived from an "apolitical modernism" or a "tired tradition of genteel romanticism."[22] Both are holdovers from a late nineteenth-century conception of art and are characterized by the creation of an idealized social arrangement in which the human condition is lifted up in lyrical lines above the muck and mire of a mundane world. As a proponent of such a view of poetry, Ford perceived no lyrical uplift in Davis's work and thus felt Davis had transgressed the boundaries of appropriate art. In language derived from genteel or popular poetics to articulate his thinking, Ford indicated that effective poetry could stir emotions but should never rouse them into uncontrolled reactions. To "move" readers to belief was preferable to propagandizing them in the name of changing their views. To win "sympathetic consideration" required the observance of the rather genteel notion of "good taste." It is no wonder, given these criteria, that writers like Davis, who articulated social necessity, were marginalized and had little hope of being canonized.

Today, however, the fundamental struggle between Ford and Davis can be viewed as a quarrel about the place of the social in literary idealization. As a concept, Charles Altieri describes *idealization* not as proposing propaganda but as the "writers' efforts to make the authorial act of mind or certain qualities in their fictional characters seem valuable attitudes with which an audience is moved to identify."[23] Cary Nelson is less sanguine about the positive effect implicit in Altieri's formulation, since idealization can be made to serve the cause of "both liberating and repressive projects."[24] As he concludes, "literary idealization is thus necessarily in dialogue with and embedded in all other idealizations by which our culture sustains and justifies itself."[25] The exclusive claim Ford lays to the rightness of his function of poetry fails to account for, in any protracted way, the multiple meanings of idealization and how they relate to social concerns. Despite its insistence on a skillful subordination of propaganda to art, Ford's approach highly values an arguably narrow focus on style and subject matter. In so doing, it pays short shrift to what Nelson describes as "the changing social functions poetry serves" and "all alternative efforts to define and co-opt the other social domains poetry addresses."[26]

Clearly, Davis's socially constructed verse directly challenges Ford's idealized function of poetry. The material conditions that created the great racial divide in the United States often appeared with less acerbity in the poetry championed by proponents of ideal social arrangements. Davis, though, could be more broadly ideological in his poetics. For instance, he pointed unwaveringly at the white race for its many hypocrisies, including its religion: "I aimed my eyes at the holy doors of a white man's church and I heard God's Servant say 'Niggers must be saved elsewhere.'" At the same time, the speaker submits African Americans to this same intense scrutiny: "I turned to what was called my own race . . . and I looked at a white man's drama acted by inky performers." Standing outside the cultural space that Ford and others defined for "appropriate" poetry, Davis transforms, in this instance, the site of religion from its usually reflective or meditative pose to a contested ground, where social, historical, and political implications are explored.

While the focus of Ford's critique is specifically on Davis's socially constructed poetry, it also prompts us to question its merits for determining the extent to which Davis's political engagement contributed to his radical persona. In some ways, any attempt to construe Davis as anything other than leftist might, at best, seem imprudent. His life and work are exemplary modes of "leftist" (small *l*), if not "Leftist" (capital *L*), experience. As the editor of the *Atlanta World*, he half-seriously lampooned African Americans in 1932 for a racial reticence to venture forth with the Communist party as a means for effecting social change. He remained actively involved in the Chicago chapter of the League of American Writers even though, as he found out later, the organization "was created following a decision by the Communist Party to close down the John Reed Clubs and establish a broad, united front organization among writers" (*Blues* 245). A contributor to the league's *Writers Take Sides* (1938), Davis confirmed his commitment to opposing fascism "because it is contrary to the American principles of freedom and democratic government, and because Negroes would not only suffer the plight of white Americans but would also suffer especial terror aimed at minority groups."[27] His association with the National Negro Congress, in 1936, brought him closer to communism via its first executive committee, whose members, including Ralph Bunche, Mande White, and James W. Ford, were either Party members or fellow travelers (*Blues* 363n8). That he taught possibly the first history of jazz class in the nation was lost in the designation of Chicago's Abraham Lincoln School, the location of this course, as a Communist-front organization by the House Un-American Activities Committee.[28] As a consequence of his involvement in these very public activities and the ceaseless attack he waged on Jim Crow in his Associated Negro Press newspaper work, Davis came under intense scrutiny of the FBI around 1945.

Despite Davis's public denials of his activities, the historical record indicates that the surveillance was not based solely on supposition. Davis's commitment to Communist ideology had begun even earlier and continued subtly in much of his writing until 1945. In an effort to recruit the extremely attractive, multitalented Kansan Irma Wassall to Party membership, Davis had confessed:

> I've never discussed this with you and don't know whether you share the typical American uninformed concepts of Marxism or not, but I am risking such a reaction by saying that *I have recently joined the Communist party.* I see in it the only movement that is actually conscious of social evolution and the meaning of the various forces at play in the world today. As a matter of fact, *I have had leanings in that direction since I was in college,* but it has been only in the past few months that I developed certain associations that caused me to view this movement with the proper critical appreciation. And, frankly, I think that you have some of the gentleness, the desire to help others.[29]

The file on Davis maintained by the FBI, from 1945 to 1963, reveals very little about the major ideological position that energized him: his passionate commitment to dismantling the legal and social stanchions supporting fascism abroad and Jim Crow at home. Influenced by what now reads as ideological blind faith, the FBI, the House Un-American Activities Committee, and the Senate Internal Security Subcommittee led a determined march to preserve the nation's racial and social status quo. Their preservationist tactics meant the use of their own variety of subversion in an effort to root out so-called dissidents and to maintain "the American way."

The extent of these efforts is too far-reaching to discuss here, but it bears mentioning that the typical government strategy of using confidential informants to elicit and compile information about a subject often proved unreliable because it forced the government to draw conclusions based on the authority of perceived associations. What makes this strategy particularly dubious in Davis's case is that no informant could actually confirm the government's allegation that he desired a violent overthrow of the government. In nearly all his pronouncements, Davis affirmed a commitment to democratic principles. The motivation for his rhetoric and much of his socially committed verse derived from a deep-seated need to guarantee a democratic way of life to those citizens who, at best, had only unequal access to those rights. According to its files, the FBI was reluctant to interview Davis because of his stubbornly uncooperative attitude and his refusal to identify other Party members. In this assessment of Davis's character, the FBI was correct. Despite the pressure that came from nearly twenty years of careful scrutiny— a pressure so intense that it probably caused his flight from Chicago to Hawaii in 1948—he never admitted his Party membership. In retaliation, much of Davis's file reads like a self-justifying report achieved by distorting his public pronouncements into statements that are open to interpretation as Communist propaganda.[30]

Arguably, Davis has the last laugh in this jousting with the FBI. It is true that he became a "closet" member of the Communist party. What remains unclear—and the FBI records are unhelpful here—is how long he stayed with the group. In *Livin' the Blues,* Davis carefully crafts a representation of himself as not just a Party outsider but as a bigger militant than most Communists. His long poem "War Quiz for America," published in the April 1944 issue of *Crisis Magazine,* he describes as potentially so volatile that most of the Party members shied away from him: "The irony of the situation is that this [poem] was far too militant for many leading Communists who belonged to what was generally labeled a subversive, radical movement, thus making [editor] Roy Wilkins and his associates at *Crisis* far more belligerent than the avowed Reds of that era" (281). Although it is difficult to separate fact from bravado in this statement, Davis obviously uses this anecdote to begin listing other reasons why the Party failed to sustain his interest as well as that of other Black people.

He refused to accept the Party's mandate that "the struggle against racism must be sacrificed on the altar of national unity." The issue of "self-determination for the black belt," he felt, ran counter to his personal goal for complete racial integration. Finally, the failure of the Party to maintain positive relations with the Black press resulted in its becoming "almost as violently anti-Communist as the general press" (*Blues* 282). In effect, then, Davis cast himself as an outsider by publicly disclaiming these ideological principles. Whether other Party ideas held his attention we simply do not know. He did admit to working with known and suspected Communists when their goals agreed with his. But it very well could be that the FBI invested a great deal of surveillance time on a suspect who had long since left the Party. Years later, he was moved to "apologize": "I can't help feeling guilty over taking up FBI time for so many years when apparently the Hoover gestapo needed agents to find the murderers of the black and white civil rights leaders in Mississippi, and the killers who threw the bomb in that Birmingham church and murdered those little children. I owe the FBI an apology for causing them a needless waste of so much energy on me" (*Blues* 327).

Poetry of Social Engagement

Black Man's Verse appeared in 1935—a pivotal year of the depression in which, among many crucial social changes, the U.S. Supreme Court upheld a Texas ruling outlawing Blacks from voting in white Democratic primaries; the Congress of Industrial Organization was organized, creating racially integrated unions in many industries; and escalating rumors about police brutality erupted into a full-scale riot in Harlem. Into this vortex of economic, social, and political uncertainty, Davis released his first poetry collection. An unlikely collaboration between an ultra-sophisticated Bohemian white woman and a former-sailor-turned-publisher made the publication possible. The Chicago socialite Frances Norton Manning, who lived a rather uninhibited life, introduced Davis to Norman Forgue, who had been a welterweight boxing champion in the Navy and whose post-military life found him indulging his passion for making beautiful books via his Black Cat Press. The book's title signified Davis's notions of racial pride, Black history, and race. Davis's uncanny ability to articulate these concerns, as in "Chicago's Congo" and "The Slave," simultaneously set him apart from his contemporaries and ushered in new ways of expressing a race-based poetry. His pro-Black assertions were defiant, if not downright arrogant. The fusion of Black history with conceptions of race made for a proudly distinctive poetic voice. In the end, it is in this way that the social realism poems in *Black Man's Verse* must be read—as Davis's contribution to an experimental phase of African American poetic practice during the depression years.

Black Man's Verse is like a Duke Ellington symphony: experimental, cacophonous, yet strangely harmonious. Presenting a variety of Black experiences, the collection is a virtual collage of lyrical moods, ranging from the tragic to the comic. "Chicago's Congo" aptly illustrates this fusion. Structurally, this poem shows Davis's penchant for experimenting with free verse, often using parallelism and some repetition to achieve the effects of oratory: "Sing to me of a warrior moon victorious in a Congo sky . . . show me a round dollar moon in the ragged blue purse of Chicago's heavens . . . tell me of a hundred spoil laden blacks tramping home from the raid . . . point me out a hundred brown men riding the elevated home on payday . . . pick me the winners . . . in Chicago? . . . in the Congo?" Parallel syntactic units help establish a theme the speaker has already introduced:

> *From the Congo*
> *to Chicago*
> *is a long trek*
> *—as the crow flies.*

For Davis, the history of the African in America was the narrative of this trek. Along the road, though, a unique race emerged—a "kaleidoscopic" people.

The effect of oratory is even more pronounced in a poem like "What Do You Want America?" because Davis uses rhetorical questions as structural and thematic devices. For instance, implicitly he asked what it means to be civilized when "Black scars disfigure / the ruddy cheeks of new mornings in Dixie / (lynched black men hanging from green trees)." Lynching, as poetic subject, had always been a difficult topic to treat, as writers as diverse as Claude McKay in "The Lynching," Sterling A. Brown in "Sam Smiley," and even Jean Toomer in "Blood Burning Moon" discovered. Davis also came to understand that exploiting the metaphoric range of poetic language has obvious risks when the subject is violence. In "Lynched," he locates the narrative strategy for resolving the problem in the poem's subtitle: "Symphonic Interlude for Twenty-one Selected Instruments." In this poem, invoking the idea of symphony, the hallmark of Western music, serves as an ironic commentary on civilization. The wind and string instruments he lists were, of course, capable of reaching the heights of lyrical expressivity—something completely at odds with the horrors of lynching. But here, their use both signifies on the idea of lynchers being civilized and rescues the poem from being consigned to mere bombast or propaganda.

Reviewers of *Black Man's Verse* unanimously sensed a charting of new territory by a Black writer. Many critics couched their excitement in comments like those of William Rose Benét: "There is not a trace of whining or maundering in this book. There is a natural dignity in the utterance, and intelligence."[31] Many would also agree with Harriet Monroe, who, at *Poetry: A Magazine of Verse*, found "a good deal of strength, much satirical club-bludgeoning over injustices to his race, some epigrammatic wit, and often touches of imaginative beauty."[32] Nearly all of them, however, concluded, that as much as Davis was "a poet of authentic inspiration," they had to follow Monroe, who felt compelled to "pass over the bitter things Mr. Davis has to say about lynching, and Scottsboro, and *Georgia's Atlanta* of chain gangs, breadlines, and the Ku-Klux Klan."[33] Even Ada Rice, the undergraduate teacher who set Davis on the course of writing poetry in 1924, was ambivalent about the social nature of Davis's first collection. She was delighted with "What Do You Want America?" and "Chicago's Congo." Still, she was apologetic but candid in saying: "I am sorry to note the bitterness that persists throughout the book in your observations on life, but I cannot blame you. Yet, I must remind you that the heroes of your race, as well as mine, have been those who rose above their handicaps and achieved victories."[34]

Given the poetic norm represented by Monroe, Benét, and Rice, it is surprising that more reviewers were *not* disturbed by the social nature of Davis's work. To Davis's credit, many others saw his direct, unapologetic approach as forward movement in poetry and in society too. These reviewers pointed with admiration to Davis's sharp wit and even sharper tongue. An unsigned review offered this typical African American perspective: "From the other side of the chasm which separates the realms of the black and white, Davis makes disclosures which are disquieting and original. Race-conscious as he is, and bitter, he often laughs derisively at his white neighbors. But he can sing, and best of all he can make pictures. . . . His poetry is of today, his free verse expressing contemporary themes in a modern world."[35]

In May 1937, Davis received the first poetry prize from the Julius Rosenwald Foundation, which enabled him to bring out *I Am the American Negro* that same year. It is easy to see why Alain Locke lamented that *I Am the American Negro* "has too many echoes of the author's first volume. . . . It is not a crescendo in the light of the achievement and promise of the author's initial volume."[36] In many of these new social realism poems Davis continues to experiment with ways of representing a racial consciousness in conflict with the dominant culture. The title page establishes the tone for the collection.

Its image of a Black man shackled with a ball and chain and bleeding from wrists and legs foregrounds racial oppression. As if to underscore the idea that idyllic or idealized notions of life are not the main bill of fare for this book, Davis uses the poem "Forewarning" as a preface to prepare readers for an unpleasantness not usually associated with poetry—a kind of "buyer beware":

> *Fairy words . . . a Pollyana mind*
> *Do not roam these pages.*
> *Inside*
> *There are coarse victuals*
> *A couch of rough boards*
> *Companions who seldom smile*
> *Yet it is the soul's abode*
> *Of a Negro dreamer*
> *For being black*
> *In my America*
> *Is no rendezvous*
> *With Venus . . .*

The strident criticism of racial discrimination, the diatribe against so-called civilization and progress, and the promotion of Black history continue themes developed in his earlier volume. The title piece, a "docudrama" in free verse and prose, inveighs against the "stones that formed the temple of America's Social System," his metaphor for the complex of Jim Crow laws that systematically denied Blacks a meaningful place in history and in society. What Langston Hughes would later say about *47th Street* applies to "I Am the American Negro": its structure represented a blurring of epic and dramatic poetry and oratory in its examination of the conditions of African American people living under white "civilizing" influences.[37] What Hughes finds problematic about this type of poetry is precisely what Davis proposes to make it do. As laid out on the page, the poem approximates a printed play, with extensive stage directions and indications of changes in scene. For example, directions for one sequence read this way: "*Great veins stand out in the giant's throat. His hands claw the air before him. His body rocks and sways. His hair mats against his forehead from the sweat that pours from his body and mixes with the small ooze of warm, red blood.*" These directions introduce the following lines:

> "I grin, I dance, I sing. I am the minstrel man for white America!
> I am a hodge-podge of paradox, a crazy collection of inconsistencies.
> Seldom to myself and before no whites dare I confess these traits.

Pity me, Lord, for there is none other like me ...
I am the American Negro!"

Davis never pretends that the racial problem is small; indeed, "I Am the American Negro" attempts to elevate African American experience into the realm of myth. It is in the large representational scale, as Hughes points out, that Davis found himself most vulnerable.

While "'Mancipation Day," "'Onward Christian Soldiers!'" and "Christ Is a Dixie Nigger" sarcastically portray the meaning that Christianity and freedom have for Blacks, "Modern Man—The Superman" registers the beginnings of a shift in poetic subject from racial to class concerns, a movement that reaches completion in *47th Street: Poems*. The poem—"A Song of Praise for Hearst, Hitler, Mussolini and the Munitions Makers"—with a keen sense of the ironic, invokes Nietzsche's philosophical doctrine of the superman. Those critics who found the poem wanting generally seemed incapable of making a distinction between Davis's biting irony and sarcasm. In his scathing denunciation of the profiteers whose weapons sustained the war, Davis makes an important comment on how war is promoted and conducted. As a way of building a bridge between content and form, Davis provides marginal notations for this poem too. While probably not intended for actual performance, these "stage directions" underscore the experimental nature of this poem. For example, the first such notation reads: "Eight airplane motors, each keyed to a different pitch, are turned on and off to furnish musical accompaniment within the range of an octave." But these sounds are not sweet, not melodious. Although keyed expertly to different pitches, such sounds become noise. And noise represents variations of the theme urged by war profiteers. If this is civilization, Davis seems to say, an appropriate coda for all these concerns might be the last line of "Note Left by a Suicide": "I am too brave to live!"

Davis's *47th Street: Poems* appeared in 1948, that moment when postwar America began to experience the hardening of international relations into the cold war and embarked, domestically, upon a course leading to the demise of de jure segregation. While the United States and the Soviet Union competed for world domination, Davis witnessed remarkable changes in domestic social policies, including President Truman's Executive Order 9981 ending segregation in the armed forces and all other areas of federal employment; the U.S. Supreme Court ban on segregation clauses in housing covenants; the state miscegenation law in California ruled unconstitutional; and the Progressive Party nomination of Henry Wallace for U.S. president, whose motto—"This is the century of the common man"—blended, for many people, the right proportion of labor rights, civil rights, and international human rights.[38] Having come to the issues Wallace campaigned on via his earlier political experiences, Davis shifted his ideological focus from issues of race to those of class. The collection *47th Street: Poems* represents the culmination of Davis's thought and poetic development.

In an unusual gesture, Davis introduces the collection with a long foreword laying out the terms for his shift in focus. The concept of race, he argues with a remarkably contemporary logic, inadequately describes groups of people because it bases distinctions primarily on skin color and political necessity. The concept of culture, however, with its basis in "customs" and language, more accurately categorizes people since it emphasizes milieu. In making this claim, Davis serves as a precursor for such contemporary historians and theorists as Anthony Appiah and Amy Guttman, who have pushed the discussion well beyond skin color.[39] Davis is nevertheless a "realist." He finds that he is prevented from being anything except Negro when he writes. That is, living in America means for him living a racially proscribed life, which "produces certain distinct ways of thinking." Although many of his themes concern the effects of racial discrimination on him, Davis considers himself one of the common people, subject to domination by the world's economic rulers. Thus *47th Street,* while filled with portraits of Black life, must be seen as an expression of class, not racial consciousness. He concludes his foreword with a testament to the way in which race and class influence his work: "I am not an escapist running to an ivory tower to blot out life. I am not an embittered black nationalist. I am a realist, and so I write primarily of the impact of discrimination upon me and the others singled out for this specialized treatment. But since I am also one of the common people . . . I write of all the common people, even though I know that many of another color and culture in their confusion consider me foe instead of friend."

The shift to a class and an international focus in Davis's poetry can be easily demonstrated by referring to his poem "For All Common People":

Let us the common people reclaim this earth;
We who are yellow in Asia, black in Africa, white in Europe, kaleidoscopic
    in the Americas;
We who have worked and fought and died to transfuse more power to the
    already powerful;
We who have been fed the burned bread of race hate to keep us apart;
We who have bloated our bellies on the brackish broth of superiority to
    others such as we;
We who are rival divers for pennies in a wide pool rich with handfuls of
    gold for everybody;

We who are the workers, the doers, the builders—
We the common people!

This poem resonates with some of the sense and sensibility of Margaret
Walker's preacherly oratory, found especially in the last stanza of her remark-
able poem "For My People." In defining "the common people," though,
Davis extends Walker's subtle suggestion of workers into a forthright expo-
sition of the manner in which the workers have been exploited. Its focus on
relations among the proletariat is a history writ small of their victimization,
exploitation, and divisiveness.

"Snapshots of the Cotton South" is both indictment and challenge; it con-
demns prevailing racist institutions and social behavior, but it also exhorts
starving Black and white southern sharecroppers to unite against a common
economic oppressor. Add to this poem "Peace Quiz for America," "War Zone,"
"Nothing Can Stop the People," and "Peace Is a Fragile Cup" and a series of
poems emerges that remarkably presents an antiwar sentiment, a call for union
of all workers, and a powerful critique of capitalism. Together, they question
the meaning of democracy and urge the rise of common people. The idea of
progress and civilization found in "Pattern for Conquest," "Egotistic Runt,"
and "Chicago Skyscrapers" ironically contrasts with the urban destitution in
"Tenement Room." Mojo Mike's Cafe in "Black Weariness" provides tempo-
rary surcease from the battle to make America live up to its ideals.

One discomfited reviewer said the collection seemed to result in propa-
ganda, not poetry, because he was left with the uncomfortable feeling of
"having shared almost too painfully the author's sense of injustice."[40] While
there is much to commend this reviewer's observations, they fail to account
for the public, rather than private, nature of Davis's verse. His intent was to
raise consciousness in rather bold and disturbing ways. Because his choice
was to depict injustice, he did so in formal ways that forced readers to con-
front their own participation in the exploitation he described. Not everyone,
therefore, agreed with the position Davis urged; but they had to deal with
what he said. For some, during this era of McCarthyism, it meant removing
his books from the shelves of their libraries and schools. Ironically, several
Davis poems were banned in the United States, but abroad, they were trans-
lated into Polish, German, Dutch, Czech, Serbian, French, and Spanish.[41]

Jazz Poetry

Defining the precise nature of jazz poetry is as difficult as finding a defini-
tion of jazz that everyone will agree to. As a genre, jazz poetry should satisfy

certain expectations and thus enable a degree of predictability about formal qualities and possibly content. In *Jazz Poetry: From the 1920s to the Present* (1997), arguably the most definitive study of the subject, the jazz historian Sascha Feinstein illustrates the difficulty inherent in this task: "A jazz poem is any poem that has been informed by jazz music. The influence can be in the subject of the poem or in the rhythms, but one should not necessarily exclude the other."[42] This working definition, of course, is imprecise, opaque, and simply too broad. At the same time, it is possible to argue that this failure to prescribe set rules, that this very imprecision, gives jazz poetry its synergy, its force. In any case, the idea of jazz poetry problematizes a number of questions. For instance, what makes a jazz poem a poem: free verse, theme (with variations of it), scene (cabaret, locale, setting), or subject matter (imagery dealing with music)? Is there a true jazz poem? Or is jazz poetry simply a synthesis of music and poetry? In short, is it idiom, milieu, theme, characters, form, images, subject matter, rhythmic pattern, or words seeking to imitate music?

Unlike his contemporaries Langston Hughes, Countee Cullen, and Alain Locke, Davis was silent about the generic qualities of jazz poetry. Hughes provoked the ire of a number of people when he wrote in his 1926 essay "The Negro Artist and the Racial Mountain": "Most of my own poems are racial in theme and treatment from the life I know. In many of them I try to grasp and hold some of the meaning and rhythms of jazz."[43] These comments tell us a great deal about the young man who attempted to locate himself within an expressive medium that derived from "the people farthest down," as he called Black folk.[44] In part, the twenty-four-year-old poet was a maverick in that he eschewed the conventional poetic forms that more "conservative" Black writers highly esteemed. But in the postwar era, during which Victorian and other values were jettisoned in favor of greater joie de vivre, Hughes found himself floating in a big sea of conflicting views about jazz, many of which produced racial and sexual anxieties. The pervasive idea that jazz was hysteria and shrieking convinced many to answer affirmatively the question posed by the *Ladies' Home Journal* in 1921: "Does Jazz put the Sin in Syncopation?"[45] This reduction of jazz to a form of primitivism, which put Hughes in the company of such white poetic experimenters with jazz as Carl Sandburg, Vachel Lindsay, and E. E. Cummings, appealed especially to Carl Van Vechten and later to that suffocating patron of Black arts, Charlotte Osgood Mason. *The Weary Blues* (1926), a collection containing one section of blues and jazz verse, nevertheless propelled Hughes to the top of the list of Black experimenters with jazz poetry. Even though Hughes would have to wait until the 1961 publication of *Ask Your Mama* before reaching the technical maturity that might define this genre, his early efforts were pivotal in the innovation of this form.

By contrast, Cullen, in a review of *The Weary Blues,* expresses a less than enthusiastic endorsement of Hughes's inclusion of jazz poems: "Never having been one to think all subjects and forms proper for poetic consideration, I regard these jazz poems as interlopers in the company of the truly beautiful poems in other sections of the book."[46] Cullen complains that Hughes's jazz poems move with the "frenzy and electric heat" of a Baptist or Methodist church revival. It is the alternate "chills and fevers of emotion" that lead him to wonder, somewhat like William Wordsworth, "if the quiet way of communing is not more spiritual for the God-seeking heart."[47] And in his most damning statement of all, Cullen muses: "I wonder if jazz poems really belong to that dignified company, that select and austere circle of high literary expression which we call poetry."[48]

It is possible to argue, as Gerald Early does, that Cullen "believed jazz to be an insufficiently developed, insufficiently permanent art form to use as an aesthetic for poetry."[49] However, Cullen's reluctance more likely betrays an unwillingness to accept the viability of racially derived art forms as a basis for good poetry. His study of versification at Harvard under Robert Hillyer, who would later win the 1934 Pulitzer Prize for poetry, fostered in him an aesthetic sensibility that privileged European formalism. This no doubt accounts for Cullen's view of race identification and racial consciousness, in Early's words, as "an exhibitionist display of emotion" while others, like Hughes and Davis, would disagree that this display was "a belief in his or her superior naturalness."[50] Nevertheless, Cullen concludes this review on a note sounding his familiar theme: "Taken as a group the selections in this book seem one-sided to me. They tend to hurl this poet into the gaping pit that lies before all Negro writers, in the confines of which they become racial artists instead of artists pure and simple. There is too much emphasis here on strictly Negro themes; and this is probably an added reason for my coldness toward the jazz poems—they seem to set a too definite limit upon an already limited field."[51] From this quote, it is easy to see why Cullen was probably Hughes's object of parody in "The Negro Artist and the Racial Mountain" as the Black poet who wanted to be white. In any case, Cullen represents the poet for whom race identification is a shackle. For true art, according to this position, transcends the individual and supersedes race.

Although Locke does not comment directly on jazz poetry, his discussion of jazz as a music form complicates, broadens, and extends the position taken by Cullen. Armed with the distinction of being the first Black Rhodes Scholar and with a Ph.D. in philosophy from Harvard, where he wrote a dissertation on axiology,[52] Locke's views projected a certain imprimatur. To us today, his position about the racial or cultural significance of jazz is a curious equivocation. But I think his voice is important for exploring certain questions about the intersection of race and class with jazz during the twenties and thirties. Writing in a 1927 essay, Locke has this to say:

> Even now, much of what is characteristically Negro is representatively American; and as the contemporary cultural and artistic expression of the Negro spirit develops, this will be so more and more.
>
> Unfortunately, but temporarily, what is best known are the vulgarizations; and of these "Jazz" and [its] by-products are in the ascendancy. We must not, cannot, disclaim the origin and characteristic quality of "Jazz"; it is an important racial derivative. But it does not follow that it is spiritually representative. It is in the first place not a pure Negro folk thing, but a hybrid product of the reaction of the elements of Negro folk song and dance upon popular and general elements of contemporary American life. "Jazz" is one-third Negro folk idiom, one-third ordinary middle class American idea and sentiment, and one-third spirit of the "machine age" which, more and more, becomes not American but Occidental. Because the basic color of the mixture is Negro, we attribute jazz, more largely than we should to Negro life. Rather we should think of it this way,—jazz represents Negro life in its technical elements, American life in general in its intellectual content.[53]

In this formulation, Locke prescribes a form of "cultural sharing" that has greater implications for unraveling the complexity of Lockean thought than it does for understanding the evolving history of jazz. First, Locke appears guilty of "second generation respectability" because he effectively sets forth a position that strives mightily to urge jazz's "universality" at the expense of its origins and significance. To him jazz is a vulgar form of Black musical expression that must be deracinated. In an effort to salvage jazz from its supposed disreputable past, Locke sought to invest it with a significance devoid of the sexual stigma marked by its birth in the bordellos of New Orleans. Minus this stigma, jazz, in his view, would cast no aspersions upon the race. This argument has implications for the larger context in which Locke worked: that of the New Negro attempting to reconstruct a racial image. The hybridity in Locke's argument is a curious blend of Negro folk sensibility, American white middle-class values, and Western thought. This combination perfectly describes the strategy Locke employs to document African American contributions to American cultural development in an effort to escape Black racial stigmas and stereotypes. What it also illustrates is an observation Sterling A. Brown once made about him: that when Locke's neighbors on R Street in Washington began playing their blues, Locke would pull his windows down and put on Bach or Beethoven. In Brownian humor, the message represents the best of his double entendres: on the one hand, it satirizes Locke's rather smug gentility in racial matters; on the other hand, it explains with full understanding how Locke's class status prevented him from being any different from what he was: the product of Harvard, Oxford, and Berlin. From this, we must conclude that Locke was intellectually attuned to the significance of jazz and blues but emotionally divorced from them.

Like Locke, Frank Marshall Davis had little to say about the genre of jazz poetry. Unlike Locke, though, he wrote with a full appreciation of the music's origins, historical development, social significance, and qualitative differences among individuals and groups. In November 1938, as an editor for the Associated Negro Press, Davis began perceptively surveying the current jazz scene and rendering discerning critical views for a column he entitled "Rating the Records." What emerges from Davis's pen, though, is a sense of how he combines the art of jazz with social and historical concerns, thus making jazz into a weapon of social change.[54] Surveyed in whole, Davis's topics could be assigned to one or possibly two of the following categories: Blues; New Orleans and Dixieland styles; Swing and Hot Jazz; Chicago and Kansas City styles; Boogie Woogie; Bop, Be-Bop, and Re-Bop; folk music; exemplary practitioners; and the history of blues and jazz. The last category has the greatest relevance for the poetry Davis would write.

Davis would never claim to be a jazz critic because such naming suggested a depth of inquiry or perspective that exceeded his ability as a journalist to communicate within the confines of newspaper columns intended for general readers. Nevertheless, Davis writes with a full understanding of European-American cultural hegemony. From the columns he wrote for nearly twenty years, we can comfortably deduce that his response to power was, in part, personal. Davis felt, as he writes expansively in *Livin' the Blues,* the need to exorcize feelings of inferiority imposed by a racially hostile world that regarded African American life as insignificant or even meaningless.

But part of his response to power—that which relates most specifically to his poetry—was historical revisionism, in that he sought personal liberation in the complex of African expressive cultures. Unlike Locke, who was most comfortable in sharing the origins of jazz in order to avoid stigmatizing the race, Davis found racial pride in its complicated, multifaceted development. In a remarkably cogent historical analysis, Davis commented: "Jazz was born of the musical experience of the Negro people in America. Into it went the highly complex rhythmic patterns and musical conceptions native to those sections of Africa from which the black man came; the spirituals, blues, and secular music developed in America following contact with European music patterns in the New World, and the social and psychological experiences of a minority group struggling for equality."[55] Notice how Davis conceives the nature of cross-cultural contacts. Like most of his generation, he felt that "the Negro" was a unique creation, a coalescing of social, political, and psychological forces to engender a new human being who still maintained cultural ties to Africa. Drawing from the social science "authority" of Melville J. Herskovits's *The Myth of the Negro Past* (1941) and Gunnar Myrdal's *An American Dilemma* (1944), Davis argues that these vestigial ties binding native and diasporic Africans provided the original bases of jazz. From the joining of complicated polyrhythmic and polyphonic patterns of African music with features of other music forms came a musicological "gumbo" he offers as proof of an African American cultural contribution. This music, formed in a crucible of debasing, dehumanizing economic conditions, represented for him a mature emotional response to horrific circumstances. He would be untroubled by what we today would term the essentialist character of his position. Instead, Davis found it necessary to counter the pervasive charge that African Americans were cultural foundlings by grounding his argument about the emotional basis of jazz in a belief in the intense struggle Africans in America waged for their very humanity.

The balance between emotional need and political necessity finds expression in what Davis would consider the most important feature of jazz: its improvisation. To show how Davis's thought negotiates among different functions for jazz, I use *improvisation* to suggest a malleability, a floating signifier merging psychological, political, historical, and aesthetic meanings. In Davis's theory, improvisation is an essential feature of jazz that derives from the blues, in particular the classic or standard blues form in which the stanzaic pattern is AAB: "I'd rather drink muddy water, sleep in a hollow log; / Said I'd rather drink muddy water, sleep in a hollow log, / Before I'd stay in Mississippi, treated like a dirty dog."[56] The first line sets forth a "problem" to be resolved, a premise, or a condition to be understood. The second line is "worried," or repeated, enabling the singer to think up a response to the problem posed in line one. It is in this mental pause, or what Albert Murray calls a "break," that improvisation takes place.[57] The third line offers the resolution. Davis's poetic praxis, though, extends this notion into areas beyond the narrowly musical. Whether in subject matter, theme, technique, or style, improvisation figures in Davis's poetic praxis as a rebellion against the Western tradition in music, just as free verse symbolized a break with regular rhythm and rhyme in poetry. The spirit of protest in jazz and free verse is manifest in a poetry that forcefully declaims against racial injustice and repression of all kinds.

If much of the foregoing can be said to imply a "theory" of jazz and jazz poetry, Davis's poems that qualify as members of this genre are interesting in how they conform or depart from it. There is good reason to agree with Harriet Monroe's assessment that "Cabaret" is "the best built and most successful of the longer pieces [in *Black Man's Verse*]."[58] As improvisation, it plays with a number of issues he explores discursively in his reviews and criticism of jazz. The opening stanza certainly introduces the wind and brass instruments, the piano, and drums as crucial instruments in the jazz band. But in personifying them into churchgoers, Davis marvelously converts the cabaret into hallowed ground. There even the swaying "dirt-brown woman" becomes an apostle, "a voice for hymns or blues." The hybridity of this singer resonates with the historical debate in Black music: "where do blues leave off and hymns begin"? For the "dancing dozens," the debate is inconsequential. Their "Grotesque gyrations / Rhythmic contortions" evoke the sense and sensibility of jazz mood and rhythms. In the entreaty to the band to "Weave for me a strange garment," the speaker summarizes and contextualizes the essential meaning of jazz. Unlike Sterling A. Brown's "Cabaret," which explores more directly the commodification of African American expressive culture, Davis's poem represents a life beset by sorrow but sustained by living. Here, jazz is a response to emotional needs in a highly complex, rapidly moving world. It represents a stay against confusion and becomes a pillar of strength against enervating forces.

Set slightly differently, "Dancing Gal" might have suggested the night club scene in New York during the heyday of the New Negro Renaissance if it had not evoked swing music and Chicago. In this poem, color imagery cascades into a collage of browns, yellows, reds, and blues. The very sensuousness of the collage resonates with a jazz motif. The speaker in the poem, drawn to the irresistible lure of her movement, nevertheless remains outside her private thoughts and is left wondering what drives her, what moves her, what impels her. But the collage also immediately invokes a favorite idea of Davis, expressed more explicitly in other poems: the notion of "blending" to signify Black cultural formation. For Davis, the distance between Africa and Chicago might appear to be a long way, but it is rather short when one looks into the faces of Black Americans and sees the faces of the Congo. Implicitly, the collage becomes an observation on cultural legacy: about the preservation of the ancestral past in cultural practices of the present, like jazz. Rhythmically, the young girl's dance, her very movement, is sweet music against the bitter, drab existence of humanity—much the way jazz is.

By contrast, "Mojo Mike's Beer Garden" is primarily concerned with scene and is only implicitly a jazz poem because its "room is an unscored symphony / of colors and sounds." Illuminated by the "Four fat white spiders" of light, the patrons of the beer garden take turns being described by the watchful eye of the speaker/observer. Somewhat like a Romare Bearden montage or collage, the scene recalls the beer garden in all its simple complexity. Holding it together are the "Two yellow gals [who] take 'em their beer and wine and gin."

"Jazz Band" is probably the most wildly jazz poem of the group since it both incorporates many strategies in "Cabaret" and makes explicit what the other two poems only imply. Eugene B. Redmond, writing in *Drumvoices: The Mission of Afro-American Poetry* (1976), remarks that this poem "anticipates the work of literally dozens of poets of the sixties ([Larry] Neal, [Stanley] Crouch, [Jayne] Cortez, [Don L.] Lee, [Amiri] Baraka, [Michael S.] Harper, the Last Poets, Carolyn Rodgers)."[59] Assuming this is true, it would not be inappropriate to look at Stephen Henderson's *Understanding the New Black Poetry: Black Speech and Black Music as Poetic References* for language to describe Davis's achievement in this poem.[60] Focusing principally on young Black Arts writers of the sixties, Henderson provided the first full-scale, serious analysis of jazz poetry, which had been summarily dismissed, trivialized, or ignored by mainstream literary critics. His was an effort to do for these Black insurgents what Cleanth Brooks and Robert Penn Warren did for white writers in *Understanding Poetry* (1938),[61] that towering monument to New Criticism.

The first stanza of "Jazz Band" opens with what Henderson calls the "jazzy rhythmic effect," which is achieved by recreating a hot jazz feel. The speaker's shouts combine seemingly incongruous images (e.g., skyscraper and jungle), all in a frenzy. From there, the music simply takes off. The instruments are nearly personified as each makes a distinctive sound, seemingly out of control. But the individual, improvising voices are connected and held in check by the onomatopoeia of "Plink plank plunk a plunk / Plink plank plunk a plunk." Invoking Chopin and Wagner reveals at once cross-cultural ties and cultural amalgamation. Stirred as it was in the gumbo of jazz, classical music was stewed and slow-cooked so that its distinctiveness blended with other forms to come out wholly transformed: "Chopin gone screwy, Wagner with the blues." All the world, from London to Sydney, embraced this new phenomenon. And all their gods caught the infectious madness, sending them marching "past in a high stepping cake walk."

The remaining jazz poems are all portraits—of Billie Holiday, Ella Fitzgerald, Louis Armstrong, Duke Ellington, and Charlie Parker. Because the figure being celebrated is more complex than a few lines can capture, Davis typically seizes on one feature to develop in these poems. A favorite strategy occurs in "Lady Day," which celebrates the sensuousness of Billie Holiday's voice via alliteration: "Her rum-brown rope of a voice / Fastens flannel strands / Around soft sides of staid notes / Sitting properly / On their oh so proper scale / She pulls / And the notes fall / Into her molten mold / Of flaming sound." Especially those sibilant sounds reinforce what Davis sees as the defining color of her voice: rich, rum-brown.

The sensuousness of Lady Day is distinguished from the artful scatting of Ella Fitzgerald in a poem that reads as if it is unfinished:

> Swing your hot hammer
> Gal
> Beat these shapeless songs
> Into fantasies
> For the hungry ear
> Pound these pale notes
> Into bright bracelets
> For the heart's wearing.

Although the alliteration is consistent with the idea of swing music and a hammering voice, this poem does not rise to the full-throated sensuality suggested by the silversmith and instead comes off a bit heavy-handed or labored.

"Louis Armstrong" is a wonderful homage that succeeds by invoking Armstrong's place in the pantheon of influential musicians. Playing off Armstrong's honor of being named King Zulu for the 1949 Mardi Gras, Davis declares that all players, old and new, bow to the best horn of all time. The one entitled "Duke Ellington" is a well-intentioned effort to praise the Duke's dignity and creativity. In collecting an array of totally different images to suggest the many indigo moods of Duke, Davis runs the risk of overwriting and therefore limits his effectiveness by forcing alliterations. But the poem "Charlie Parker" captures exactly the life and meaning of Parker. Here, Parker is no Yard Bird but a homing pigeon, one with no home to fly to. An Icarus without the pride, this homing pigeon flew to "Sky unlimited / Route uncharted / Eagle strong" until he scorched his wings—all while "feebler fowl / Looked up in awe / But played it safe." Instead of crashing into the sea, this homing pigeon tired and fell helplessly to the ground, where "He wandered aimlessly . . . / And he was trapped / And hooked / And cooked." In remembering Parker, Davis, in effect, uses him synecdochically to represent a lamentable history of musicians whose lives were tragically cut short by the excessive demands of their art.

Social Satire

Black Moods not only reverberates with various satirical takes on social and political ideas but also participates in the larger tradition of African American satire that has sought to provide a corrective to political and personal injustices. This tradition has employed a number of strategies, including such forms or stylistic devices as burlesque, parody, irony, and the comic. Beginning arguably with the poet Paul Laurence Dunbar and including Langston Hughes, Sterling A. Brown, James Weldon Johnson, and George S. Schuyler, African American writers have directly or indirectly expressed their concerns by diminishing a subject, making it ridiculous, and evoking toward it attitudes of amusement, contempt, scorn, or indignation.[62]

Although many of Davis's social realism poems wryly present an amusing or contemptuous attitude, the poems collected under the rubric "Ebony under Granite" specifically point to Davis's participation in the satirical traditions derived from both American and African American literatures. More than a few reviewers and critics have noticed the similarities between these works and Edgar Lee Masters's *Spoon River Anthology* (1915). When Masters first published his series of experimental epitaph poems, he demonstrated an astute ability to combine in unique ways the epigrams of *The Greek Anthology,* the dramatic monologues of Robert Browning, the narrative perspective of Dante's *Inferno,* and the free verse of Carl Sandburg. Because of his focus on small-town middle America, Masters was associated with the "revolt from the village" group of writers that included Sherwood Anderson with his *Winesburg, Ohio* (1919) and Sinclair Lewis with his *Main Street* (1920). But as the literary historian John E. Hallwas has perceptively shown, *Spoon River Anthology* was more than a critique of idealizations of small town life: "[It was] a depiction of the struggle for self-realization in a society that has lost contact with the great democratic vision that once gave purpose and meaning to American lives, and an account of the poet's quest to resolve his inner conflicts and to restore that vision."[63] In this interpretation, the act of rendering advice back to the living expresses a preoccupation greater than moralizing to them. Here, the more pressing need is to restore America to a sense of Jeffersonian democracy as captured in the Adamic myth of America as an unspoiled New World. The existential conflict proffered by the dead is how to achieve self-actualization in a world that materialism has caused to decline.

The Black tradition in satire has rarely been afforded the luxury of exploring Masters's concerns. Instead of seeking to restore America to its Prelapsarian innocence, African American writers have usually been charged with holding America accountable for its constitutional promises. Perhaps it is still hard to imagine the Paul Laurence Dunbar poems written "in a minor key" as satirical, rooted as many are in so-called Negro dialect. But the subversive humor that drives his "Ante-Bellum Sermon," for instance, barely conceals the poem's motivation as stated in its ending: "dat mighty reck'nin' day, / When we'se reco'nised ez citz'" (ll. 86–87). Much less situated in "dialect," James Weldon Johnson immersed himself more deeply in Black idioms and even echoes from Milton's *Paradise Lost* to write "Saint Peter Relates an Incident of the Resurrection Day" (1935). Before Langston Hughes, no one had envisioned a character in prose sketches so distinctive as Jess B. Semple (i.e., "just be simple"). In *Black No More* (1931), George S. Schuyler extended his Menckenesque voice into the first major novel to treat racial matters so distinctively satirical. But Sterling A. Brown was arguably the most artful of these distinguished writers. His series of Slim Greer poems combined in marvelous ways the tall-tale traditions of Mark Twain and the myriad and often unnamed African American "master liars" as well as the idiom of Black vernacular speakers. The result is a side-splitting but trenchant critique of the system supporting Jim Crow. Thus, Davis is heir to two satirical traditions. But while Masters was able to work out private agonies in an essentially public form, racial circumstances forced Davis to join his predecessors in working out group problems publicly.

The Davis poems formally grouped as "Ebony under Granite" in *Black Man's Verse* and *I Am the American Negro* and the fugitive ones either in *47th Street* or uncollected before now represent more than the Black dead speaking back to the world of the living. For them, the "democratic vistas" of Masters's speakers are not America in decline; instead, they are of an America that has failed to honor its promises of life, liberty, and the pursuit of happiness for all. Instead of seeking to restore America to an Edenic harmony, Davis's speakers point out the disparity between the ideal and the real for African Americans. To do so, Davis finds a useful narrative perspective in Masters's example. But the similarities end there.

Black sleepers under the headstones in the "Ebony under Granite" section of *Black Man's Verse,* like their white counterparts buried on the hill near Spoon River, represent a variety of faults, ironies, and strengths. Rev. Joseph Williams preserves the pursuit of truth in the Second Baptist Church by satisfying the women members sexually. Unlike her sisters, who trade virginity for comfort, marriage rights, and respectability, Goldie Blackwell collects two dollars and independence and keeps "respectability" to herself. Gambler Acey White loses the final pot to the "Big Dealer."

And yet, many of these same qualities are framed within an interracial dynamic, thus foregrounding tensions and holding them up to scrutiny. The financially successful Robert Whitmore dies of apoplexy when he is mistaken for a waiter from Georgia. Arthur Ridgewood, unable to decide between poetry and medicine for a vocation, dies

> from a nervous breakdown
> caused by worry
> from rejection slips
> and final notices from the finance company.

George Brown, who for forty years watched powerlessly as white Mississippi voters cheated at the polls, was sentenced to life in the Illinois state penitentiary when he voted five times in one congressional election. The plight of many Black writers is captured in Roosevelt Smith's bout with literary critics, whose sensibilities he could never please. As a result, he "traded conscience and critics for the leather pouch and bunions of a mail carrier."

Like the earlier collection, the "Ebony under Granite" section in *I Am the American Negro* explores fresh ways of critiquing intraracial as well as interracial matters. Here we find Moses Mitchell, whose Distinguished Service Cross saves his life from a sheriff's bullet; he is later hung by judicial decree. Sam Jackson, nearly dead from starvation, is shot to death by a police officer who sees him breaking into the Dew Drop Inn. Life sends unpromising writer Jonathan Wood a rejection slip. Neither Cleo Greeley, who earlier lived a promiscuous life and later married respectably, nor her sister Sarah, whose sexual inexperience causes her husband to seek pleasure from other women, is remembered by anyone. Benjamin Blakey, prominent Odd Fellow, church deacon, husband, and father, dies without learning from which of his six "kept" women he contracted his "fatal social disease." Nicodemus Perry, contemplating the sexual liberties white men took with his mother and sisters, is mortally wounded by several loiterers for "assaulting" a white woman whom he accidentally bumped. The snobbish, extremely color conscious Mrs. Clifton Townsend dies of shame when she bears a "penny-brown" son. Editor Ralph Williamson, who for twenty years waged unending warfare against racial discrimination, dies after dreaming "Of a perfect nation / Without prejudice or segregation." And as if anticipating the criticism of being bitter and cynical, Davis in "Frank Marshall Davis: Writer" pens what might prove his fitting epitaph:

> I was a weaver of jagged words
> A warbler of garbled tunes
> A singer of savage songs
> I was bitter

Yes
Bitter and sorely sad
For when I wrote
I dipped my pen
In the crazy heart
Of mad America
. . . .
But
I did not die
of diabetes . . .

Lyric and Love Poetry

Davis's lyric and romantic love poems have not received the proper critical scrutiny they deserve. Although his more directly political verse was appropriated by members of the Black Arts Movement, his love poetry was ignored by Lindsay Patterson, whose edition *A Rock against the Wind* (1973) virtually defined this kind of poetry. Nor have more recent historians, such as Nina Miller in her densely argued *Making Love Modern* (1998), found Davis's lyric or love poems grist for their interpretive mills. One possible reason for this oversight is that Davis's lyric verses, especially the early works, are rather conventional. But having said this, I do not mean to suggest that these poems are unimportant, uninspired, or uninteresting. Instead, critics have failed to see how Davis's lyric and love verses reveal another dimension of a profoundly complex writer and personality. Davis's lyric verse is important precisely because it situates itself within a more traditional poetic practice and becomes yet another indication of how broadly based his poetry is. Moreover, as an autobiographical act, it also uncovers much about the man, his life, and his loves—all of which have been shrouded in mystery and masked by his self-described poker-face expression.

As a small, but significant, portion of his writing, Davis's lyric poetry conforms to the concise, articulate definition of the genre provided by M. H. Abrams in his enduring *A Glossary of Literary Terms*. According to Abrams, lyric poetry, first of all, presents a speaker who expresses a state of mind or process of thought and feeling. This expression can vary from a brief mood to a complex explanation of a state of mind. The process of observation, memory, thought, and feeling can be organized in many different ways, such as a state of mind, an elaborate compliment of a lover, the deployment of an argument, a sustained meditation, and so forth.[64] But an emphasis on self-conscious expressiveness is an important feature of lyric and love poetry—a feature that is important but unremarked about Davis's verse.

The music in Davis's lyric voice fell victim to the long shadow cast by the husky, masculine, Sandburgian expressiveness of his social realism and jazz poems. Even Davis's wife of twenty-four years, the late Helen Canfield Davis, found him plagued by a persistent fear: that to be anything other than powerfully masculine would be considered effeminate or weak. Thinking more specifically about his autobiography, she felt that Davis acceded uncritically to this socially constructed view of a man by "not writing in contrast," in other words, by not acknowledging his inner fragilities and softness. The lyric and love poems, however, contradict this view. They provided him opportunities for expressing the very tenderness he otherwise sought to conceal. The love poems in particular reveal a vulnerability that, in the long run, make him appear stronger instead of weaker, more rounded instead of narrowly aggressive.

Thus Davis is not to be trusted when he distinguishes his news writing as "objective" and his poetry as "subjective." His idea of subjectivity broadly covers a number of issues discursively presented in his social realism verse. But just as his *Livin' the Blues* unwittingly allows tender moments to seep through the self-protective mask of memoir, certain of his lyric poems betray the softness he worked hard to conceal. Among the earliest of these efforts, "Kansas Winter" wonderfully represents a poetic strategy Davis would frequently employ. Here, the scene in nature is awash with liquid images, made fresh and vital by sibilant sounds. Unpunctuated, the pauses naturally assert themselves as reading time easily accords with breathing time. The vividness of the imagery is stunning and represents a profound engagement with winter in the nation's heartland. His use of free verse supports the mood and dominant images by shifting the burden of the poem away from the fashion of late-nineteenth-century Victorian expression, wherein the convention of personal utterance generally used poeticisms and clichés to develop themes of unrequited love, anger, self-recrimination, beauty, and self-doubt. Instead, the voice emerging from this poem rides a striking metaphoric range of language.

Even more revealing of the self Davis sought to obscure are his many love poems. Both *Black Man's Verse* and *47th Street* contain formal sections of such poems, while other poems are either scattered in *I Am the American Negro* or previously unpublished. In most of these, the connection between autobiography and personal utterance is difficult to determine. For example, "To You" reads like a generalized commentary about love. It distinguishes itself by appealing to nearly all the five senses, thus presenting the speaker's whole self to the subject of his affections. The poem proceeds by way of quite striking images and image patterns:

Gray haze of a summer afternoon
Green of the Pacific Ocean
Brown of oak leaves in November
and You—
These are lovely things.

Then Davis invokes a number of comparisons with nature to help bring about an ephemeral effect: "Your eyes—more beautiful than April rainbows / Your lips—sweeter than old wine from Bordeaux." But the body, like nature, is subject to the whimsy of change, of decay. So the speaker elevates the discourse to a higher, more spiritual, plane. And despite the poet's momentary lapse into rhetorical commentary, the poem foregrounds the changeless soul. For it is there that unending love abides.

"To Helen" represents one of the few poems in which Davis addresses a specific woman. Before their divorce in 1970, Helen Canfield Davis represented for him wife, mother of his children, lover, an older daughter, and much more. During a particularly conflicted moment in their marriage, Davis attempted to re-earn her undying love and affection by penetrating the hard shell encasing his emotions and revealing his own vulnerability. The result is "To Helen," both an homage to love and an attempt to express it to his wife. A beautiful poem, it celebrates the many physical attributes of Helen with arresting images and metaphors. By daring to invoke a Grecian goddess as the epitome of feminine beauty (perhaps mistakenly suggesting Helen of Troy), Davis risks clichéd expression and unimaginative development. But the poem is rescued by a clever shift to the life and love they share together:

I shall make you part of me,
My darling,
Fundamental as heart
Primary as mind
And to you I shall become
As the blood in your veins.

It is a love that is beyond strictures of time and space.

Revising Literary History

Although Davis spent a lifetime experimenting with jazz, satiric, and lyric verse, his social realism compromised his best chance for achieving the canonical space shared by so many of his contemporaries, including Richard Wright, Gwendolyn Brooks, Margaret Walker, Sterling A. Brown, and Robert Hayden. Too often the necessity to expose social ills limited the metaphoric range of his language, but what he lacked he more than made up for with vivid, realistic images of urban life and techniques that rivaled, if not surpassed, his predecessors Carl Sandburg and Vachel Lindsay. His use of wit, irony, and understatement reveal a remarkable ability to perceive human frailty and strength and provide insight into human nature. Langston Hughes beautifully summed up Davis's strengths and weaknesses: "When his poems are poetry, they are powerful."[65] The world in which Davis lived demanded a form of poetry equal to his reality. He found in free verse the perfect vehicle for effecting his liberation.

In my mind, the appearance at this time of *Black Moods: Collected Poems* is fortuitous. Since we have barely crossed over into the twenty-first century, bringing with us the baggage of debates about the (de)merits of racial and cultural diversity and the continuing contentiousness about the politics of art, Davis's voice has renewed importance. This collection's emergence coincides with the development of new critical and theoretical approaches capable of offering fresh interpretations of Davis's work. For instance, Davis's grounding in a social function of art lends itself wonderfully to analyses by the growing number of critics interested in performance theory. And his marriage of art and politics is ideally suited to the contextualism that now defines cultural studies as an academic discipline. Given the additional perspectives that have recently arisen on communism and literature, Davis's social realism can now be historicized within new modes of Marxist or socialist interpretation. Cary Nelson has this to say about the importance of literary revision: "Literary history is never an innocent process of recovery. We recover what we are culturally and psychologically prepared to recover and what we 'recover' we necessarily rewrite, giving it meanings that are inescapably contemporary, giving it a new discursive life in the present, a life it cannot have had before."[66] Recovering Davis's body of diverse poetry allows us to rewrite that part of African American literary history we were unprepared—intellectually or emotionally—to recover before now. This recuperative act, therefore, assumes a significance much greater than that of merely resurrecting the work of a formerly well-known writer. It is important because it leads to a revised, more inclusive history of African American letters.

It is in this spirit that Davis's collection also lends credence to the continuity of African American literary history from the New Negro Renaissance to the Black Arts Movement. To those rethinking the New Negro Renaissance, Davis's poetry forces a reassessment of such familiar questions as periodization, location, and interracial literary relations. In reconsiderations of the

Black Arts Movement, his poetry and his presence interrogate African American identity, intergenerational relations, the place of the historical in its conception of the past, and the multiplicity of political views held in an era seemingly dominated by a single, dogmatic belief. As a bridge connecting these two eras, *Black Moods: Collected Poems* represents Frank Marshall Davis's reemergence into these discussions. His will prove to be a significant voice—one as powerful as the enduring poetry that made it necessary.

Notes

1. Locke offers this self-description in a "psychograph," or autobiographical profile, appended to his essay "Values and Imperatives" in *American Philosophy Today and Tomorrow*, ed. Horace Kallen and Stanley Hook (New York: Lee Furman, 1935), 312.

2. This idea can be inferred from the following essay and book reviews Locke wrote in the 1930s: "Sterling Brown: The New Negro Folk Poet," in *Negro: An Anthology*, ed. Nancy Cunard (London: Wishart, 1934), ed. and abr. by Hugh Ford (New York: Frederick Ungar, 1970), 88–92; "Flaming Self-Portrait," rev. of *A Long Way from Home* by Claude McKay, *Christendom* 2 (1937): 653–54; and "Spiritual Truancy," *New Challenge* 2.2 (1937): 81–85. In his "Deep River, Deeper Sea: Retrospective Review of the Literature for 1935" in *Opportunity* 14 (Jan. 1936), Locke announces: "For the new notes and the strong virile accents in our poetry today, we must shift from Harlem to Chicago; for there are Willard Wright whose verse sees the light in the *New Masses* and other radical periodicals and Frank Marshall Davis, who really brings fresh talent and creative imagination to this waning field" (10). Locke was forced to correct himself in a subsequent issue by indicating he intended *Richard* Wright; *Willard* Wright, he explained, was a white writer of some renown.

3. Locke, "Deep River, Deeper Sea," 10.

4. Harriet Monroe, "A New Negro Poet," *Poetry: A Magazine of Verse* 48.5 (Aug. 1936): 293–95; William Rose Benét, "The Phoenix's Nest," *Saturday Review of Literature* 18 Jan. 1936, 19.

5. Peter Labrie, "The New Breed," in *Black Fire: An Anthology of Afro-American Writing*, ed. LeRoi Jones and Larry Neal (New York: William Morrow, 1968), 64–77.

6. John Edgar Tidwell, "An Interview with Frank Marshall Davis," *Black American Literature Forum* 19.3 (Fall 1985): 108.

7. Cary Nelson, *Repression and Recovery: Modern Poetry and the Politics of Cultural Memory, 1910–1945* (Madison: University of Wisconsin Press, 1989), 11.

8. Frank Marshall Davis, *Livin' The Blues: Memoirs of a Black Journalist and Poet*, ed. John Edgar Tidwell (Madison: University of Wisconsin Press, 1992). Subsequent references to this work will be given parenthetically in the text.

9. Kansas, in 1861, began statehood permitting racially integrated public education. But beginning with Reconstruction in 1867, state policy started vacillating between segregation and integration, based primarily on population size. More populous cities were permitted complete racial separation while smaller ones were forced into par-

tial integration. A number of excellent sources discuss this complicated history. See especially Nell Irvin Painter's *Exodusters: Black Migration to Kansas after Reconstruction* (New York: Alfred A. Knopf, 1977), 259n9.

10. Tidwell, "Interview," 108.

11. Davis has expressly denied adopting from Ezra Pound and T. S. Eliot any of the High Modernist habits he employs, including free verse, jagged rhythm, and fragmentation. Interestingly, his decision to write a poem instead of an essay to satisfy a class assignment led him to the library, where he discovered *Others: A Magazine of the New Verse*, a "little magazine" published from 1915 to 1919. This discovery, he explained in an interview, "had walloped me almost as hard as hearing my first jazz and blues some years earlier. I felt immediate kinship with this new poetry and felt I could write something in a similar vein" (Tidwell, "Interview," 105). Although Pound and Eliot published poems in *Others*, it appears their work was less appealing to him than was that of others. Later in that same interview, he acknowledged that Carl Sandburg ("his hard, muscular poetry") was his greatest influence, followed by Edgar Lee Masters, especially his *Spoon River Anthology*. In Vachel Lindsay, he found a pleasing "feeling of jazz and syncopation" (Tidwell, "Interview," 105). The poetry of E. E. Cummings produced "a kindred rebel spirit which I could not find in Frost or Eliot. To me they seemed lukewarm" (Tidwell, "Interview," 105). When asked specifically why Pound and Eliot were uninviting, he responded: "Their preoccupation with myth and ritual turned me off as I believe it did other Black poets. I think that rebellion is deep in the psyche of most Black poets and neither Pound nor Eliot and others of that type had this basic ingredient" (Tidwell, "Interview," 106). As an example of that spirit, Davis effusively praised Fenton Johnson, the Black Chicagoan, for pioneering "the free verse revolution" in the 1910s (*Blues* 131).

12. Richard Wright, "Blueprint for Negro Writing," *New Challenge* 1.1 (Fall 1937), rpt. in *Norton Anthology of African American Literature*, ed. Henry Louis Gates and Nellie McKay (New York: W. W. Norton, 1997), 1380–88.

13. This campaign is carefully delineated in several excellent sources, including John Morton Blum's *"V" Was for Victory* (New York: Harcourt, Brace, Jovanovich, 1976).

14. John Gennari, "'A Weapon of Integration': Frank Marshall Davis and the Politics of Jazz," *Langston Hughes Review* 14 (Spring–Fall 1996): 17.

15. Freedom of Information Act request, Federal Bureau of Investigation, File 100–15799, 22 June 1945, 1–6, editor's possession.

16. Frank Marshall Davis, "Democracy: Hawaiian Style: 'Land of Ethnic Hash,'" Associated Negro Press Feature Release, 12 Jan. 1949, Associated Negro Press Papers, Claude Barnett Collection, Chicago Historical Society.

17. Frank Marshall Davis, "Democracy: Hawaiian Style: 'Hawaii Students Study the Negro,'" Associated Negro Press Feature Release, 2 Feb. 1949, Associated Negro Press Papers. By definition, the concept of *miscegenation* refers to race mixing. At least since the nineteenth century, America has been preoccupied with the "one drop rule" and other legal machinations designed to determine the biological makeup and therefore the legal status of its citizens. As Eric Sundquist eloquently writes in his *To Wake*

the Nations: Race in the Making of American Literature, race mixing had profound implications for white property rights ("miscegenation law used blood 'to control the legal legitimation of social unions and the legal disposition of property to the children of these unions'" [Cambridge, Mass.: Harvard University Press, 248–49]). In writing about this concept, Davis is not concerned with the property rights and racial imperatives that consumed nineteenth-century America. Indeed, he is less scientific than Sundquist and is arguably very nearly romantic in discussing the matter. The race mixing he describes is couched in terms of "the dusky and sensuous beauty of the Oriental and Polynesian co-eds" who stand in beautiful contrast to the "washed out and unhealthy" look of the "haole" (the Hawaiian name for white people). When he concludes that the mixtures of these various ethnic groups is common, he refers quite specifically to a history of intermarriage and other interactions that produced not a single new ethnic group but new ethnic combinations. Davis therefore pins his hopes for a further decrease in racial tensions on the continued "cross-pollination" of the people. Because Davis wrote this column soon after his arrival in Hawaii, it is understandable that he is still developing a consciousness of the nuances of different intra- and intergroup dynamics. The achievement of this awareness is what informs the excellence of such poems as "Horizontal Cameos" and "This Is Paradise."

18. Cary Nelson, "The Diversity of American Poetry," in *Columbia Literary History of the United States,* gen. ed. Emory Elliott (New York: Columbia University Press, 1988), 913.

19. Nick Aaron Ford, "A Blueprint for Negro Authors," *Phylon* 11.4 (1950): 374–77. Ford (1904–82) emerged in the thirties as part of a coterie of academically trained African American literary critics, most of whom shared the belief that Black literature and criticism should promote the social integration of Blacks into the amorphous American mainstream—thus their designation as "Integrationist Critics." Among the more prominent names on this rather lengthy list are Jay Saunders Redding, Hugh Gloster, and Sterling A. Brown. Of course, W. E. B. Du Bois and Alain Locke were still active and quite influential during this period. Nearly all of them agreed with Saunders Redding, who described the development of Black literature, in his important book *To Make a Poet Black* (Chapel Hill: University of North Carolina Press, 1939), as a "literature either of purpose or necessity, and it is because of this that it appeals as much to the cognitive as to the conative and affective side of man's being" (xxix). Ford's critical contribution to this description bears directly on criticism of Davis's verse. In a revised M.A. thesis published as *The Contemporary Negro Novel* (Boston: Meador, 1936), Ford suggests the study's principal aim in his subtitle: *A Study in Race Relations.* Combining historical study with attitudinal analyses, he targets the principal audience for his book as the "[white] American citizens who are interested in Negro attitudes and viewpoints, but the press of business renders them unable to spend much time becoming familiar with the source material" (7). Thus when Ford, in his essay "A Blueprint for Negro Authors," argues that Black authors should use "social propaganda subordinated . . . skillfully to the purpose of

art," we can infer that he intends literature to facilitate harmonious interracial relations and not exacerbate racial tensions (374). Ford further clarifies this argument in his edited book *Language in Uniform: A Reader on Propaganda* (New York: Odyssey Press, 1967) and in a number of essays. Because of his extraordinary devotion to the issue of propaganda and art and because of the unusual acerbic attention he gives to Davis's verse, I use Ford's argument synecdochically for this period. It bears mentioning that Jean Wagner, in his *Black Poets of the United States: From Paul Laurence Dunbar to Langston Hughes* (1973), puts forth similar views about Davis's verse. He describes Davis as "undisciplined" and as an "untiring polemicist" whose "principal defect is a sort of bad taste which his journalistic activities did nothing to mitigate" (188). But coming as it did at the close of the Black Arts Movement, Wagner's comments represent a view not shared by Black aestheticians.

20. Tidwell, "Interview," 107.

21. James A. Miller, "African-American Writing of the 1930s: A Prologue," in *Radical Revisions: Rereading 1930s Culture,* ed. Bill Mullen and Sherry Lee Linkon (Urbana: University of Illinois Press, 1996), 79.

22. Nelson, "Diversity," 913.

23. Charles Altieri, "An Idea and Ideal of a Literary Canon," in *Canons,* ed. Robert von Hallberg (Chicago: University of Chicago Press, 1984), 46.

24. Nelson, *Repression and Recovery,* 260n30.

25. Ibid., 130.

26. Ibid., 129.

27. League of American Writers, *Writers Take Sides: Letters about the War in Spain from 418 American Authors* (New York: League of American Writers, 1938), 18.

28. *Guide to Subversive Organizations and Publications,* 82d Cong., 1st sess., H. Doc. 137, 14 May 1951, 9.

29. Frank Marshall Davis to Irma Wassall, undated letter, editor's possession, emphasis added. See "Note on the Text" for a discussion of his undated letters.

30. About the *Honolulu Record* and Davis's involvement in it, the FBI wrote: "On October 31, 1956, [name excised] Commission on Subversive Activities to the Legislature of the territory of Hawaii pointed out that DAVIS continues to write a weekly column in the 'Honolulu Record' entitled 'Frankly-ly Speaking'. [name excised] pointed out that subject's column in the 'Honolulu Record' is the most militant part of the paper and that during the last four months DAVIS has used his column to attack segregation, the Senate Internal Security Subcommittee, and to call for federal intervention to enforce integration. In March of 1953 the Territorial Subversive Activities Commission of Hawaii reported that the origin and purpose of the 'Honolulu Record', its editorial policy and the character of its personnel led the Commission to the inescapable conclusion that it is the journalistic mouthpiece of the Communist Party in the Territory of Hawaii" (Freedom of Information Act request, File HN 100–5082, 7 Nov. 1956, 3, editor's possession).

31. Benét, "The Phoenix's Nest," 19.

32. Monroe, "A New Negro Poet," 294.

33. Ibid.

34. Ada Rice, letter to Frank Marshall Davis, 8 Sept. 1935, Frank Marshall Davis Papers, DuSable Museum, Chicago.

35. "Critics Like Davis, First Reviews Show," Associated Negro Press News Release, Oct. 1935, Associated Negro Press Papers.

36. Alain Locke, "Jingo, Counter-Jingo, and Us," *Opportunity* 17 (Jan. 1938): 11.

37. Langston Hughes, "Chicago's South Side Comes Alive," rev. of *47th Street* by Frank Marshall Davis, Associated Negro Press Features Release, 18 Aug. 1948, 4, Associated Negro Press Papers.

38. We should also remember that Wendell Willkie's crusade for "One World" in the early forties was important for Davis's ideological movement from race to class. Defeated by Roosevelt in the presidential election of 1940, Willkie embarked upon a worldwide goodwill trip as a special envoy to Roosevelt. His mission was to demonstrate American unity abroad and to encourage a swift, secure end to the war. Davis was attracted by Willkie's effort to include China, the Soviet Union, and possibly Middle Eastern nations in a postwar coalition. Willkie describes his trip in his enormously popular book *One World* (New York: Simon and Schuster, 1943).

39. Of course, both Appiah and Guttman have more theoretically challenging comments to make about race. Indeed, their debate in *Color Conscious: The Political Morality of Race* (Princeton: Princeton University Press, 1996) represents a heady discussion about the implications of Justice Harlan's dissenting position in *Plessy v. Ferguson* (1896) that "the Constitution is color-blind." Appiah ultimately concludes that if the promise of individual freedom and equality is to be realized, "we shall have, in the end, to move beyond current racial identities" (5). Guttman, on the other hand, shows the flaws in the claims for "color-blindness" by arguing for a public policy that acknowledges "color-consciousness." Both Appiah and Guttman would probably find Davis's dismissal of race for "culture" troublesome, since culture generally assumes a body of commonly shared beliefs, values, and symbols, and not all members of a socially constructed group share these features equally. Still, Davis is rather far-reaching in his conclusions, even when he forces culture to become equated with class.

40. Unidentified news clipping, Davis Papers.

41. Dudley Randall, "'Mystery Poet': An Interview with Frank Marshall Davis," 23.3 *Black World* (Jan. 1974): 40. This interview is perhaps most important for recording the efforts of the poet Dudley Randall—along with those of Stephen Henderson and Margaret Burroughs—to reclaim Davis from the dust bin of historical anonymity. At the time of his 1973 reunion with Randall, Davis had had no real contact with his friends and fellow writers for nearly twenty-five years. In the course of this rather loosely organized, tape-recorded conversation, Davis mentions, without specifying, that his poems had been translated into Polish, German, Dutch, Serbian, French, and Spanish. In *Livin' the Blues,* he comments further on translations and establishes a tighter connection between his poetry of radical political expression and the censorship imposed by the McCarthyites: "With the rapidly deteriorating political situation and the growth of the witch hunts during the Joe McCarthy period, a number

of libraries removed my books from their shelves and stored them in the basement along with other controversial literature until the nation began returning to sanity. And while this was occurring at home, a number of European editors began translating some of my poems for use in foreign anthologies. I was 'safe' abroad but 'dangerous' at home" (304). In all this, we have no extant records confirming which specific poems were considered subversive, nor do we know the political persuasion of the foreign publishers who reprinted his work.

42. Sascha Feinstein, *Jazz Poetry: From the 1920s to the Present* (Westport, Conn.: Greenwood Press, 1997), 2.

43. Langston Hughes, "The Negro Artist and the Racial Mountain," *The Nation*, 23 June 1926, 694.

44. Ibid.

45. Quoted in Feinstein, *Jazz Poetry*, 18.

46. Countee Cullen, "Poet on Poet," rev. of *The Weary Blues* by Langston Hughes, *Opportunity* 4 (Feb. 1926): 73.

47. Ibid.

48. Ibid.

49. Gerald Early, introduction to *My Soul's High Song: The Collected Writings of Countee Cullen* (New York: Anchor Books, 1991), 51.

50. Ibid.

51. Cullen, "Poet on Poet," 74.

52. Axiology is the philosophical concept pertaining to values in ethics or aesthetics or the science of values. His dissertation was entitled "The Problem of Classification in Theory of Value" (1918), which was directed by the eminent Ralph Barton Perry.

53. Alain Locke, "The Negro in American Culture" (1927), rpt. in *Black Voices*, ed. Abraham Chapman (New York: New American Library, 1968), 524.

54. See Gennari, "'A Weapon of Integration.'" His is one of the most smartly argued discussions of this topic.

55. Frank Marshall Davis, "Frank-ly Speaking: Background of R & B," *Honolulu Record*, 2 June 1955, 8. Davis spoke most clearly in print on this issue in the fifties, as he offered, in effect, retrospective views about his thinking; however, these ideas can be gleaned from the columns he wrote in the late thirties through the forties for the Associated Negro Press. For much of his thinking, Davis draws on the work by the social scientists Melville J. Herskovits and Gunnar Myrdal, which he describes in *Livin' the Blues*, especially on 284 and 293.

56. Frank Marshall Davis, "Modern Jazz Is a Folk Music That Started with the Blues," *The Worker*, 25 Dec. 1955, rpt. in *The Negro in Music and Art*, ed. Lindsay Patterson (New York: Patterson, 1969), 108.

57. Albert Murray, "Improvisation and the Creative Process," in *The Jazz Cadence of American Culture*, ed. Robert G. O'Meally (New York: Columbia University Press, 1998), 112.

58. Monroe, "A New Negro Poet," 294.

59. Eugene B. Redmond, *Drumvoices: The Mission of Afro-American Poetry* (New York: Doubleday, 1976), 234.

60. Stephen Henderson, *Understanding the New Black Poetry: Black Speech and Black Music as Poetic References* (New York: William Morrow, 1973), 35.

61. Cleanth Brooks and Robert Penn Warren, eds., *Understanding Poetry: An Anthology for College Students* (New York: Henry Holt, 1938).

62. M. H. Abrams, *A Glossary of Literary Terms* (New York: Harcourt Brace Jovanovich, 1993), 166.

63. John E. Hallwas, introduction to *Spoon River Anthology* by Edgar Lee Masters (1915; rpt. Urbana: University of Illinois Press, 1992), 2.

64. Abrams, *A Glossary of Literary Terms*, 108.

65. Hughes, "Chicago's South Side," 4.

66. Nelson, *Repression and Recovery*, 11.

NOTE ON THE TEXT

Black Moods collects for the first time all of Frank Marshall Davis's poems known to be published either in book form or individually in serials and periodicals as well as his extant previously unpublished work. His books and chapbooks are *Black Man's Verse* (1935), *I Am the American Negro* (1937), *Through Sepia Eyes* (1938), *47th Street: Poems* (1948), *Jazz Interludes: Seven Musical Poems* (1976), and *Awakening and Other Poems* (1978). Except for facsimile editions of *I Am the American Negro* and *47th Street,* produced, respectively, in 1971 and 1974, his books have not been reprinted. Of the chapbooks, all of which were published in limited editions, *Through Sepia Eyes* was absorbed into *47th Street; Jazz Interludes* consists of three poems from *Black Man's Verse* and four new poems published in the February 1974 issue of *Black World;* and *Awakening* is culled entirely from *I Am the American Negro.* Given the rather limited availability of his work, Davis's notoriety and historical significance have survived largely, according to his count, in more than seventy-four literary anthologies. In the absence of carefully preserved records and drafts of poems, establishing the chronological development of Davis's writing is therefore problematic.

Like some other writers, such as Sterling A. Brown, Davis was not interested in leaving us a paper trail to follow, which would allow us to trace the growth and development of his work. In most cases, documenting the dates of composition for his work is nearly impossible. An explanation for this problem perhaps can be gleaned from a letter Davis wrote to fellow Kansan Irma Wassall about his reluctance to date his letters: "I don't date my letters because of caution. If you don't date a letter, there's no way of proving when it was written should it ever fall into the wrong hands. . . . This letter says 'Tuesday.' There are 52 of the blamed things every year. But there's only one December 20, 1940, in the whole history of time. Or am I being too smart? It's a habit of long standing" (letter in editor's possession). Despite a political vision some would deem subversive, Davis had little to fear from writing poetry. We can assume that his habit refers not to his being "too smart" but to his being cautious about personal matters. It is a habit that also figures prominently in his memoir, *Livin' the Blues*.

For the unpublished or uncollected poems, I have provided dates, if they are known, that might prove useful in determining a chronology of Davis's poetic development. If the date of *composition* is known, it appears in italic following the poem. If the date of first *publication* is known, I have listed it in roman following the poem. For a few poems that appear in Davis's published collections I have provided dates of their composition or first periodical publication. Because Davis's unpublished "You Are My Universe" differs only slightly from "You Are My All" and because the latter poem was published in *47th Street*, only "You Are My All" is included in this volume. In "To One Beloved" Davis employed many of the lines from "To Helen." Since "To Helen" is more polished, I take it to be his last and therefore best draft and include only it here. I have created titles for "Ike Mosby" and "In What Strange Place" and have designated those choices with brackets. To assist readers with Davis's references, I have glossed terms in notes gathered at the end of the collection. I have made no attempt to annotate every item Davis cites; the notes, however, do provide information on a wide range of names, dates, places, and other references that are crucial to understanding the poems or the context in which they were written. I have reproduced the introductory essays to *Black Man's Verse* and *47th Street* because they help contextualize the poems they precede. Although Davis modified "War Quiz for America" for publication in *47th Street* as "Peace Quiz for America," I include the original version in the appendix because it resonates with the superb blend of history, social consciousness, and poetic engagement that characterizes Davis's distinctive voice. Finally, minor editorial changes have been made to spelling, grammar, and punctuation, and stylistic changes in word treatment have been made for consistency.

Black Man's Verse

BY FRANK MARSHALL DAVIS

CHICAGO · THE BLACK CAT PRESS · ILLINOIS

1935

This book has been undertaken in a chance effort to eradicate the writer's bewilderment. I want to know whether to believe certain magazine editors who, in form letters, have thanked me "for the opportunity of looking over this material but regret it is unsuitable to our needs at the present time," or accept the enthusiastic praise of other editors who have done some plain and fancy raving over much of the stuff presented within these covers. Obviously somebody's wrong.

Blazing of the trail leading to this small volume was begun ten years ago while a sophomore at Kansas State College. My chief delight has been to experiment with free verse which I greatly prefer to the usual run of rhyme. It has been constructed mainly to please my own ego. Much of my material has been lost. I state this baldly even at the risk of having unsympathetic readers bemoan the perversity of fate in not causing the entire manuscript to vanish many moons ago.

In planning this volume, it was at first intended to have an introduction by one of the Big Names of the writing world. Of course, that would have certain theoretical advantages, but it seemed to me that unless the book could stand on its own merits, its production would not be worthwhile. To hitch a wagon to another's star is an indirect admission that the hitcher lacks something. Therefore, it is up to the reader to determine whether or not he likes this verse without being prejudiced for or against by the made-to-order opinion of a literary tailor hawked within these covers.

I shall be happy indeed if "Black Man's Verse" meets with the approval of the representative public and shall look forward to the future publication of another volume of later—and perhaps more mature—verse experiments. On the other hand, if this book is roundly condemned (or, what is worse, ignored) I have enough ego to blame it upon the innate stupidity of the human species, and shall go my way smiling in a superior fashion from my perch on Parnassus while I continue to conjure up verse for my private consumption. But of course the weakness of the latter position is that it won't help my publisher.

Perhaps I should thank in print those whose kindly criticism and cooperation have made "Black Man's Verse" a reality. But it would be no more fair to put them on the spot for their bad judgment should this book flop than to point the finger of scorn at any editor by name who rejected certain poems should the volume tickle the public's palate.

It is merely enough to say that I, Frank Marshall Davis, a Duskymerican born December 31, 1905, in Arkansas City, Kansas, and exposed to what is termed education at the public schools there, at Friends University in Wichita and at Kansas State College, have written this foreword in Chicago, Illinois, June 24, 1935.

Chicago's Congo

(Sonata for an Orchestra)

Chicago is an overgrown woman
    wearing her skyscrapers
    like a necklace . . .
Chicago's blood is kaleidoscopic
Chicago's heart has a hundred auricles

⌐⌐

> *From the Congo*
> *to Chicago*
> *is a long trek*
> *—as the crow flies*

Sing to me of a red warrior moon victorious in a Congo sky . . . show me a
    round dollar moon in the ragged blue purse of Chicago's heavens . . . tell
    me of a hundred spoil-laden blacks tramping home from the raid . . .
    point me out a hundred brown men riding the elevated home on pay-
    day . . . pick me the winners . . . in Chicago? . . . in the Congo?

Skyscraper pinnacles rip great holes in the rubber balloon bag of the sky . . .
    do spears kill quicker than printed words? . . . midnight lies and cobra
    fangs . . . ask me if civilization produces new forms of biting and tearing
    and killing . . . see three million whites and two hundred thousand blacks
    civilized in Chicago

> *From the Congo*
> *to Chicago*
> *is a long trek*
> *—as the crow flies*

⌐⌐

I'm a grown-up man today Chicago
My bones are thick and stout
    (when I moved to new districts bombings couldn't break them)
My flesh is smooth and firm
    (look—the wounds you give me heal quickly)

See how the muscles ripple under my night-black skin
My strength comes not from resting
You should be proud of me Chicago
I've got a lion's heart and a six-shooter
I've got a fighter's fist and five newspapers
I've got an eye for beauty and another for cash
Nothing you've got I can't have

A song dashes its rhythms in my face like April rain
My song is a song of steel and bamboo, of brick flats and reed huts, of
    steamboats and slim canoes, of murder trials and jackal packs, of con
    men and pythons
My tune I get from automobiles and lions roaring, from the rustle of bank-
    notes in a teller's window and the rustle of leaves in Transvaal trees
I ask you to find a better song; a louder song, a sweeter song—
Here's something Wagner couldn't do

State Street is a wide gray band across Chicago's forehead
At night a white-faced mother moon clothes skyscrapers in gray silk
At night when clocks yawn and hours get lazy
At night when the jungle's symphony in grays . . .
Oh mother moon, mother of earth, bringer of silver gifts
Bring a veil of stardust to wrap this Congo in
Bring a shawl of moon mist to clothe Chicago's body

⌐⌐

Between the covers of books lie the bones of yesterdays
Today is a new dollar
And
My city is money mad

⌐⌐

Across the street from the Ebenezer Baptist Church women with cast-iron
    faces peddle love
In the flat above William's Funeral Home
    six couples sway to the St. Louis Blues
Two doors away from the South Side Bank
    three penny-brown men scorch their guts with four-bit whiskey

Dr. Jackson buys a Lincoln
His neighbor buys second-hand shoes
    —the artist who paints this town must
    use a checkered canvas . . .

Tired-looking houses of brown stone
Ramshackle flats with sightless eyes
A surface car throws a handful of white sparks at cracked red bricks
An L train roars oaths at backyard clothes lines
Mornings on South Parkway flats sit like silent cats watching the little
    green mice of buses running up and down the boulevard
And only grass has heard the secrets of vacant lots

⌐⌐

This song has no tune. You cannot hum it.
This song has no words. You cannot sing it.
This song everybody knows, nobody knows.
It is in a pattern of brown faces at the Wabash Y.M.C.A., a 35th Street gam-
    bling place, a Parkway theatre—you get it or you don't
It is a melody of everything and nothing

I saw twelve stars sitting along the edge of a four story flat
I saw a moon held by leafless tree fingers
I heard a shot tear huge holes in the blanket of silence
Later—just a little later—the moon got away and the stars stepped back
    into the sky

There will always be new wordless songs, new humless tunes
Chicago sings these songs each day
Chicago who wears her skyscrapers like a necklace . . .

Only My Words

I will not build with stone and steel
For the rat teeth of decay are sharp from biting
And the legions of dust fight slow but sure

With words . . . naught else . . . only words . . . I shall build my castles, kiss-
ing the sky, hugging the stars . . . gruff, stout, big muscled words . . . bear-
ing the big and little thoughts of mankind on their broad, bent backs

Let my dreams flow from me in a torrent of words seeking form, begging
life . . . let them spatter into thoughts to be kissed by the eyes of lovers,
clutched by the eyes of drowning men, leaned on by the eyes of tired men

Let me take the little, pale, wan, penny apiece words, weave them into gay
tapestries for beauty's sake . . . let me rear young words into proud sen-
tences to step high and swiftly across a printed page

My mind reduced to black and white . . . served like strange wines for the
world to drink

Let my words tinkle like bells in the souls of men . . . let speakers fling them
at the ears of men

My words I want from the bowels of the earth . . . hard as granite, glittery as
diamonds, new as Tomorrow

Jumble them together . . . pale green words of an afternoon tea . . . red words
of passion, black words of long nights . . . gray words of loneliness, steel
blue words of courage . . . jumble them together into a crazy quilt to
please mad minds like mine . . .

Give me words . . . a pen . . . words . . . a pen
Words pregnant with life, strength
And let me build to cheat the iron jaws of rust and ruin

1927 ∎

What Do You Want America?

What do you want, America?
Young bearded nation of the thick muscles
that does not sleep
against the breasts of past greatness—
What do you want, America?

Sprawling across a continent
your feet washed in two oceans
and your goal above high heaven
Thousands of miles of steel veins
through which flows your life blood
hauled by bellowing freight engines
Your brain at work in Wall Street, Washington
telling the world to cut it out or keep it up
through a thousand mouths
at Geneva, London, Paris, Berlin, Rome, Tokyo

Your six-foot scientists smart enough to measure
stars billions of miles around or split unseen atoms
Swimming in a sea of gold
strong men going from rags to riches to rags to riches
Leading little nations by the hand
Your army and navy a Medusa's head
turning potential enemies to stone—
Why search the Sahara
for ME, one grain of black sand
to blast the heart of
to knife the soul of—
How can you answer this?

Black scars disfigure
the ruddy cheeks of new mornings in Dixie
(lynched black men hanging from green trees)
Blind justice kicked, beaten, taken for a ride
and left for dead
(have you ever heard of Scottsboro, Alabama?)
Your Constitution gone blah-blah, shattered into a
thousand pieces like a broken mirror
Lincoln a hoary myth
(How many black men vote in Georgia?)
Mobs, chaingangs down South
Tuberculosis up North
—so now I am civilized

What do you want, America?

If you ask for blood and bravery I show Crispus Attucks martyred in Boston . . . from his blood the first red dye for the Stars and Stripes . . . The mud-black skin of Peter Salem and his flinging of searing lead at Major Pitcairn on Bunker Hill . . . Three thousand brown men helping nurse suckling America when Britain fought to keep her new child . . . A red interlude when blood of black and white mingled to cement new and sturdier foundations with Perry on Lake Erie, at Gettysburg, on San Juan Hill, in the Argonne and at St. Michel

If you want blood and bravery search the pages of crimson yesterdays . . . see a history written by strong, laughing black men dying . . . today twelve million march singing against the foe of prejudice and leave the burned, the hanged, the shot, the raped, as casualties of war

Perhaps, America, you want beauty and art?

Then let me show you Phyllis Wheatley before this nation walked alone, Dunbar in adolescence, Johnson, Cullen, Hughes, McKay today . . . Tanner who dreams on canvas . . . Hayes and Robeson, their souls bathed in melody . . . and there are more for the asking

Did Bert Williams, Miller and Lyles teach you new laughs?

Where were new tunes for dancing before Handy bore the blues?

Let us turn to serious things, you ask, America

Let us turn to Carver, sold for a mare, at whose feet chemists sit . . . to Washington and DuBois, unlike, yet two Moseses leading the way in the wilderness of race hate with neither to view the promised land of interracial harmony . . . Benjamin Banneker, the Boston clockmaker . . . yet you know these and others

You teach white boxers to fight like Jack Johnson, sprinters to run like Eddie Tolan, jumpers to fly like Dehart Hubbard . . . you knew Bessie Coleman before Amelia Earhart . . . and how many Fritz Pollards, Duke Slaters can you boast?

I, too, know names, America

Kill me if you must, America
All at once or a little each day
It won't matter

Black eyes saw the Pharaohs rise, the Kaiser tumble into the dust, strong ox
    nations whimper and cry before stronger ox nations . . . where is the
    Rome of Caesar? . . . what lives but the dust which covers all?

Yet today is today
Today must be emptied like a bucket before it dries into history
Today is an eagle, lingering a while, ready to fly into eternity
Today I live
Today I tell of black folk who made America yesterday, who make America
    now
Today I see America clawing me like a tiger caged with a hare
Today I hear discords and crazy words in the song America sings to black folk
So today I ask—
What do you want, America?

I Sing No New Songs

Once I cried for new songs to sing . . . a black rose . . . a brown sky . . . the
    moon for my buttonhole . . . pink dreams for the table

Later I learned life is a servant girl . . . dusting the same pieces yesterday, to-
    day, tomorrow . . . a never-ending one two three one two three one two
    three

The dreams of Milton were the dreams of Lindsay . . . drinking corn liquor,
    wearing a derby, dancing a foxtrot . . . a saxophone for a harp

Ideas rise with new mornings but never die . . . only names, places, people
    change . . . you are born, love, fight, tire and stop being . . . Caesar died
    with a knife in his guts . . . Jim Colosimo from revolver bullets

So I shall take aged things . . . bearded dreams . . . a silver dollar moon worn
    thin from the spending . . . model a new dress for this one . . . get that one
    a new hat . . . teach the other to forget the minuet . . . then I shall send
    them into the street

And if passersby stop and say "Who is that? I never saw this pretty girl be-
fore" or if they say . . . "Is that old woman still alive? I thought she died
years ago" . . . if they speak these words, I shall neither smile nor swear . . .
those who walked before me, those who come after me, may make bet-
ter clothes, teach a more graceful step . . . but the dreams of Homer nei-
ther grow nor wilt . . .

Lynched

(Symphonic Interlude for Twenty-one Selected Instruments)

*The bass drum starts
slowly, gathers
speed each beat.
All other instruments
silent except two
bass viols,
three 'cellos, two
oboes, one baritone
saxophone.
Music low, slow,
increases steadily in
tempo, loudness.*

It is night
The lean fingers of an oak
paw at the moon.
It has worn no cloak
since fall stripped it clean.
In the light
it seems a huge hunchback
on the firm hard ground. Black
stones squat where the green
of Spring never comes.
No joy here.
This tree stands as one
left to die alone.
Its gnarled trunk
in the wind is like a drunk
who drowns fear
in wine and a sea of hate
for Life and Law. Its fate:
to be a sentinel of hell.

Here they come.
Thrice twenty on metal steeds.
They talk and laugh as if such deeds
were less than cotton sowing
There are some
who'll view this cursed night
as joy filled. The wretch's plight
when life from him goes flowing
will be the horseplay of a clown.

By the oak and the squat black stones
that will break his bones
they throw the victim down.
The wind's stroke on bleak tree limbs,
bass curses, the victim's
cries are the only sound.

One violin joins in
at augmented speed
of bass instruments,
runs the scale.

Clouds gather.
A lover's moon
should not hear the tune
of a man begging death or life
Much better
the moon stay dark
than see the stark
horror of the kill at its height.
So dark clouds leap across the sky.
They drape the moon in black.
And like an eerie cataract
they vomit blackness from on high.
Fitting shrouds
to hide the deed from Heaven's Eye.

Cruel rope!
It hungers for ebon meat.
Soon it will eat
—but slowly and not fast.
His black throat
it will seize and clutch
—but not too much
for the wretch's pain must last.
Still it lies
on the grassless ground
in a round thick mound
like an adder coiled to spring.
He who dies
in its hempen grasp
knows that its clasp
is a terrible, vicious thing.

A sextet of alto saxophones joins the instruments playing wildly. The tempo takes a sudden spurt.

"String him up!"
Sixty echo the manpack's shout
for blood. They mill about
like lean wolves for the feast.
Soon they'll sup
on the victim's cries
ere he dies
a gudgeon of the human beast.

He is down.

He falls like lead
his face is red
where they strike him with their fists
and around
they move and swear
they taint the air
with threats from hell's deep mists.

Enter three trumpets with wah wah mutes. The music now is wild, fast, held together by only the speedy monotony of the bass drum.

"You nigger!
You bastard son
from a harlot's womb
you'll rest in hell tonight!
You nigger!
We'll teach your race
to keep its place
and respect any man that's white!"

His dry lips make no reply
but in his eye
Now the look of a man unafraid—
He who sips
the cup of Death
with every breath
soon eludes Terror's Aide.

His thick neck
the thin rope grabs
it stabs
his throat with wiry strands.

Some inspect
the biting noose
others use
this time to tighten his bands.

They stand him up.
WHUP ! ! !
A bullet rends his flesh
a gash . . .

"You goddamned coon!"

Here a trombone is
heard above the
rhythmic bedlam
sliding its way from
lowest to highest
notes.
Finished,
it becomes silent.

The rope
tightens
The oak
branch bends
He's fighting
thin air
A prayer
his soul sends
"Give me power
to stand this hour . . ."

Stones rain.
Pain . . .
grips his body tight.

"Kill the bastard!"

They leap and prance
as at a dance
they watch his body swaying
swaying . . .

The bullets *thud*
against his frame
blood
drips to the ground
round
holes make a polka dot pattern . . .

A banjo joins at the
terrific tempo.
All other
instruments stop.
The banjo swiftly
and smoothly
reduces the time
to that of a dirge.

His face
a darkened space
in the lightless night
they cannot see.
There agony
lies
His eyes
slowly lose their sight

Numb
his body
Dumb
his tongue

Life slips quietly away.
Like night from day

Strings of the
banjo suddenly
break. There is silence.

Thus he dies.

For him no sobs
nor anguished cries
Naught but the mob's
insatiable hate
to speed him on
to be Death's mate.
And in this way . . .
and in this way
did White get its revenge.

The bass instruments,
led by drum, play
as they did at the
beginning.
But the tempo
does not increase.

It is day.
By the leafless tree
the sheriff stands
His hands
resemble the oak
"You see,"
he explains
while there swings
the ebony, lifeless mass
"Some niggers don't know
where they belong . . . So—"

As the six saxophones
join and play two
measures,
the music ends
suddenly in discord.

Back in town
a report
he sets down
"Died
at the hands of parties unknown"

What's a New Full Moon?

Through jail windows a new full moon is a round white door rendered use-
less by stout steel bars

Frogs see a new full moon as a luminous toadstool sprouting from the black
floor of a pond

To the thief and the murderer it is a busy stoolpigeon tipping off cops and
intended victims

To a young man in love the new full moon is a priceless pearl he would tear
from the sky . . . set in a ring woven from sparkling stars . . . place on the
finger of his sweetheart's hand

The new full moon is a beautiful woman . . . ageless . . . deathless . . . inac-
cessible . . . and infinitely, mysteriously sad . . . who gazes in my window
through a dark veil set with shimmering stars . . . the poet said

"A new full moon," the scientist stated, "is a periodical phenomenon occur-
ring when the lifeless half of our planetary satellite revolves to such a po-
sition that solar rays are reflected from the whole of its atmosphereless
surface to our own stellar body . . . "

Rain

Today the rain
is an aged man
a gray old man
a curious old man
in a music store

Today houses
are strings of a harp
soprano harp strings
bass harp strings
in a music store

The ancient man
strums the harp
with thin long fingers
attentively picking
a weary jingle
a soft jazzy jangle
then dodders away
before the boss comes 'round . . .

Gary, Indiana

In Gary
the mills
feast
on ore and men . . .

Like potbellied hoboes
the mills snore
lying face upward
on the north horizon
their breath
like winter exhalation
fogs redly
the night sky
capers madly
on a black stage
hoboes
yes
hoboes
their stomachs filled
with ore
and men
hoboes

yes
they'll hit the road tomorrow
if the food runs low

The mills are always hungry
what a beast
they make steel in their bellies
it's hard to tell
men from steel

To the south
the town
squats on sand—
a lanky woman
the steel mills'
concubine

A hundred thousand people
Europe in America
Africa in Indiana
an extension of Mexico
The Orient transplanted
another Babel
all different
all alike
steel-faced men
iron-featured women
and plenty of women
for the steel-faced men

A mayor
yes
and a city council
and officials
and graft
sure
and banks
and stores
and places
they eat the crumbs

the hoboes drop
and grow potbellies

Suffering
now and then
in the town
the hoboes
get indigestion
now and then
and don't feast
on ore and men

Well
anyway
old Judge Gary
knew his stuff . . .

1928 ∎

Jazz Band

Play that thing, you jazz-mad fools!
Boil a skyscraper with a jungle
Dish it to 'em sweet and hot—
Ahhhhhhhhh
Rip it open then sew it up, jazz band!

Thick bass notes from a moon-faced drum
Saxophones moan, banjo strings hum
High thin notes from the cornet's throat
Trombone snorting, bass horn snorting
Short tan notes from the piano
And the short tan notes from the piano

Plink plank plunk a plunk
Plink plank plunk a plunk
Chopin gone screwy, Wagner with the blues
Plink plank plunk a plunk
Got a date with Satan—ain't no time to lose

Plink plank plunk a plunk
Strut it in Harlem, let Fifth Avenue shake it slow
Plink plank plunk a plunk
Ain't goin' to heaven nohow—crowd up there's too slow . . .
Plink plank plunk a plunk
Plink plank plunk a plunk
Plunk

Do that thing, jazz band!

Whip it to a jelly

Sock it, rock it, heat it, beat it; then fling it at 'em

Let the jazz stuff fall like hail on king and truck driver, queen and laun-
  dress, lord and laborer, banker and bum

Let it fall in London, Moscow, Paris, Hong Kong, Cairo, Buenos Aires,
  Chicago, Sydney

Let it rub hard thighs, let it be molten fire in the veins of dancers

Make 'em shout a crazy jargon of hot hosannas to a fiddle-faced jazz god

Send Dios, Jehovah, Gott, Allah, Buddha past in a high-stepping cake walk

Do that thing, jazz band!

Your music's been drinking hard liquor
Got shanghaied and it's fightin' mad
Stripped to the waist feedin' ocean liner bellies
Big burly bibulous brute
Poet hands and bone crusher shoulders—
Black sheep or white?

Hey, Hey!
Pick it, papa!
Twee twa twee twa twa

Step on it, black boy
Do re mi fa so la ti do
Boomp boomp
Play that thing, you jazz mad fools!

Mojo Mike's Beer Garden

Four fat white spiders of throttled electric globes cling motionless to the
   ceiling spinning a misty web downward through the porous air

Soft runners of light finger the brown contours of a gambler's chin, a har-
   lot's face, a pimp's profile, then go floating on

The room is filled with the misty web, the white thin web four spiders spin

Two yellow gals take 'em their beer and wine and gin . . .

   This room is an unscored symphony
   of colors and sounds
   People sit like geometric angles
   awaiting measurement
   Their talk is countless bubbles
   breaking against the ceiling
   Sharp scissors of a radio
   snip fancy cutouts in the thick noise
   Gray pigeons of tobacco smoke
   fly lazily in the air above
   Like a leafy tree in high winds
   the room moves its heads and hands

Two slate-black men and two orange-brown women spill low stories into four
   steins of beer

From her youngly rouged face fifty year old eyes look out like unwashed
   windows in a newly painted house . . . this woman who sits alone tosses
   a promise through her gaze to all male youths

Words shoot from the lips of three race track losers like water from a hose at
   the Stockyards Fire

Before the long flat back of a brown-stained bar men and women laugh, talk, drink, sweat, swapping monotony for alcohol

From his stool by the cash register Mojo Mike sees nothing but faces and each face is a nickle beer or the price of a pint of whiskey to be put away and counted when his joint is emptied for the night

And . . . while the spiders spin . . . two yellow gals take 'em their beer and wine and gin . . .

Cabaret

O the big bassoon leads the members in prayer
The sax sings hymns, cornet hums the air
The banjo's conscientious, begs the viol to reform
The piano titters lightly, goo-goo eyes the trombone horn
And the solemn bass drum takes up collection
And the solemn bass drum takes up collection.

Before me sways a dirt-brown woman with one hundred dollars worth of fifty-cents-a-pound flesh
She has a voice the color of new straw steeped in molasses and vinegar . . . a voice for hymns or blues . . . her voice is a jacket buttoned 'round her soul . . . from one pocket she pulls a song:

> "*My mama told me*
> *My papa told me too*
> *I say my mama told me*
> *My papa told me too*
> *They said 'Don't let no yellow woman*
> *Take your man away from you.'*"

If she'd reach again in the pocket of the jacket buttoned 'round her soul she'd take out "All God's Chillens Got Wings"—where do blues leave off and hymns begin? Isn't there a church in hell and a cabaret in heaven?

Grotesque gyrations
Rhythmic contortions
Ambulatory mammals
Unconscious aesthetes
Irrefragably urged
(These the dancing dozens)
By importuning inhibitions
The jazz band conjures

I've never talked to a jazz band. But I'd like to
I'd like to say to the sax, "Will you be busy tonight? May I see you alone?"

I'd like to point my finger at the violin and shout, "You're no virgin. You're just a two dollar woman in thousand dollar clothes."

I'd like to yell at the grunting tuba, "Come on outside and I'll fight you any old time."

I'd like to shake hands with the cornet and say, "Sure, you can get my vote for alderman."

I'd like to whisper to the trombone, "Say, who makes the best highballs in town?"

But I don't think I'd talk to the banjo. We both suckled at Sorrow's breast and I have no more time for pain.

Weave for me a strange garment, O Maker Of All
Make me a jacket of silver stolen from the cornet's high C
Take the violin's tremolo and make a shimmering golden waistcoat
Of black, O Maker Of All, the piano has plenty to spare
Just a little of its bass would make a long thick cloak
I'll die some day I hope
Death must be a winsome hermaphrodite
    or men and women would leave those arms
I'd like, O Maker Of All, to wear these garments when I take my last dance
    with Death.

Returned

When I tire of life, when the wheels start to jam, let me die some red dawn . . .
poof . . . the brown flesh men called me back to thin sand again . . .
poof . . . dreams handed back to the stars

One spermatozoan which survived . . . a leopard, a lamb, a sage, a fool . . .
dipped in the paintpots of civilization, hung on the line to dry, put on
the counter to be bought . . . maybe . . . and rust . . . but I want to beat
the wagon to the city dump

I would use neither loud lead nor messy steel but the hot quick kiss of a
poison . . . and when Death opens the door I want to take him by the hand
and say "Come on, Old Boy, let's get goin' . . . "

He'll give the leopard his jungle, send the lamb to his flock . . . he'll give the
fool a book, the sage a dunce's cap

Let Death come to me at a cabaret while a jazz band prays to its god . . . let
the jazz heart miss a beat . . . then let a trumpet cry, a saxophone sob out
Handy's hymn of the St. Louis Blues . . . Life's a ragtime da-de-da, da-
de-da . . . you stay in tune or quit the band

In the cool soft loam I shall snore . . . the same six feet of damp sod hugging
banker and ragpicker, lyncher and lynched . . . the lover who always wins

I am but dirt and dreams, matter and sky dust, egotistic owner of nothing . . .
a tune frozen into flesh by the infinite . . . borrower among borrowers . . .
melodies end and lenders must be repaid

When a marcher quits the goose-step of life what's the difference? . . . they
call out another and keep going . . . who misses Hannibal and Michelan-
gelo?

I ask only this: let me quit and check in my time . . . let me go before the Boss
comes around and says . . . "Sorry but we can't use you any more . . . we
need your space for a smoother and better worker . . . "

The Slave
(For a Bass Viol)

Here was titanic sorrow
condensed
in the ebony splendor
of a black man's face

Here was a form
on which the mark
of a parasite civilization
had been branded
burning deeply
exposing a soul
contaminating it
with the purple of sadness

Should not a soul sing of joy?
Should not a soul sing of peace?

> *"Lord, deliver me*
> *You helped Daniel*
> *You helped David*
> *You helped Moses, too*
> *Lord, let my people go"*

Here was sadness . . .
carved on a black man's soul

1929 ∎

Five Portraits of Chicago at Night

I

Night clothes my city in black
My city is a strong-backed giant of a farm boy . . . my city stands with head
    thrown back . . . shouting . . . swearing . . . my city dares the weak sissy

cities to come out in the yard and fight . . . my city is thick-muscled and big-boned
Night is a loose black jacket my city wears

II

Lighted skyscrapers are diamond-studded fingers of my city
From Lake Michigan Chicago's Loop is many fingers plucking stars, beating a silent rat-tat on the white drumhead of the moon

Fingers crease the purple velvet of a smooth sky
When my city rests tall buildings hold high their jeweled hands in worship to the great skyscraper god, a Jehovah of steel and stone

From Lake Michigan my city is a geometric giant snoring in black as skyscrapers rise to sing and pray

III

Streets are gray veins on the thick body of a drowsy giant
Chinatown, The Congo, Maxwell Street, Little Italy, The Gold Coast huddle together like hoboes in a ten-cent flop house

Lighted buildings stare motionless at black faces of dark neighbors like pensive old women in church . . . as the toothless mouth of a door gapes open men and women passing out are phlegm coughed from a dwelling's throat

A sleek greyhound of a car sniffs its way to a slow stop . . . a mangy flivver growls along the avenue . . . surface cars like fat rats prowl cautiously over the floor of Chicago streets . . . overhead the green caterpillars of L trains crawl horizontally

The sharp dagger of a tugboat's whistle on the Chicago River explodes the toy balloon of silence . . . like haughty dowagers the iron network of city bridges lift the stiff lace of their petticoats to a patch of dark gray sky

By the hard glare of a street lamp the colorless stone of an old hag's face is chiseled into shaded curves and angles . . . light is dashed into the painted face of a street walker like buckets of clear cold water

The breath of my drowsy giant reeks of gin and ashcans, gasoline and hamburger stands . . . three million who love and hate and rest are troubled dreams as Chicago sprawls restlessly with its belly to the stars

IV

Chicago is a man-child suckling at the dark breasts of night
Lake Michigan is a young mother crooning lullabies

Gaunt trees in still parks have heard my city whimper and cry for the rubber ball of the moon

Even weary cobblestones know the star-embroidered sky is a blanket tucked around my city's crib

V

My city is a drunken ditchdigger on payday . . . my city swaggers . . . brags . . . roars coarse songs to the blaring tune of many freights hauling grain and cattle and steel, to the indigo jazz of mills and men and sweat

Night . . . a $2 prostitute . . . leads my city to the lustful comfort of her dark room . . .

Hands of a Brown Woman
(For a Quartet of Two Guitars, a Banjo and a Tom-Tom)

Your hands, Mandy Lou
(At night, under June trees
when the gray moonlight
spills through green leaves
and paints your hands a brown
the color of newly-plowed earth)
chant to me whole histories
of the sensuous African jungle
    before You were You
    and I was I.

Your hands
build brown jungle huts
    with the memories they hold.

Hands, (brown, even as yours)
    have loosed long straight arrows
    that struck suddenly,
    quick as the fangs of the African cobra,
    deep into the hearts
    of the lion, the leopard, the antelope.

Hands, (brown, even as yours)
    have held six-foot spears
    that plunged deep into the hearts
    of other men with brown hands—
    relentless
    like the paws of Great Cats
    have plunged deep
    into the quivering flesh
    of small jungle hares.

Hands, (brown, even as yours)
    have had ten fingers tighten
    to crush the soft dark neck
    of an enemy
    even as the giant python
    has felt his great coils tighten
    about the carcass
    of some luckless beast
    in the deep green forests of the Congo.

Yet . . .

Hands, (brown, even as yours)
    have caressed sensitive cheeks
    of lovers, husbands, sweethearts
    of hunters, warriors, fighters
    and have insinuated sweet things
    understood by them alone.

Hands, (brown, even as yours)
    have held small dark children
    and have reprimanded
    because of some childish prank.

Brown hands
    Were with the Pharaohs in Egypt
    Were with Cheops at the pyramids
    Went with Christ to Golgotha.

Brown hands
    And the white hands
    Of Columbus, Cortes
    Laid stones for the foundation
    Of a New World.

The sky is an inverted bowl of blue china
So—
Brown hands pluck white cotton
from a sea of plants
even as brown New England rocks
pluck white foam
from a gray December Atlantic.

The hands of you
    Mandy Lou
    have ten brown fingers
    and many tales to tell . . .

1930 ∎

Creation

I will build a universe
I will take a cloth of dark velvet
sprinkle a box of white diamonds upon it
sew them wherever they fall
and I will call it a sky.
A yellow candle flame
and a white silken cloth
correctly placed
will do for sun and moon.

I haven't decided about my world.
I would like to use a ball of gray mud

and paint my people every conceivable color
in order to give variety.
But then—
Why not a square of red flannel
with all the people black?
Black against red
red setting off black—
but would that be a symphony
or a jazz band?

One god will be enough.
We can let the people amuse themselves
in other ways.
I shouldn't give them any
but they would find one anyhow.
I shall call this god Beauty
yet some of my people
will liken it to the Beast of Mythology
but why shouldn't they?

If I were to build a universe
what good would it do?

Which One?

Benny Goldblatt kneels in a synagogue to chant solemn praises to a frown-
    ing Jehovah flanked by Isaac and Abraham

Ahmed Tagore lifts his hands at midday to a watchful Allah pointed out by
    Muhammed

Samuel Middlebrooks prattles of a Christ Jesus who washed away his sins . . .
    Samuel Middlebrooks sings loud hosannas to a Holy Trinity at the
    Wednesday night prayer meeting of the Second Baptist Church

Wun Chong burns incense to a frozen-faced Buddha who keeps his eye on
    the strength and weakness of all mankind

Four omnipotent, omnipresent gods
Which one made me? . . . Or was it any?

Lullaby

(Melody for a 'Cello)

Listen—
The moon is whispering
    baby
    my baby
    my black baby

The moon is whispering to you.
    "Come and take me, baby
    Fondle me with little fingers
    Kiss me with soft, dark lips
    I was made for such as you, baby."

Listen—
The wind is whispering
    baby
    my baby
    my black body's baby

The wind is whispering to you.
    "I will go through all the world, baby
    I will gather perfumes
    I will weave a garment of strange harmonies
    I will bring it all to you, baby."

Listen—
The whole night is whispering
    baby
    my baby
    my own baby

The whole night is whispering to you.
    "You are one of us, baby
    You, too, are dark and mysterious.
    We are brothers, baby."

The moon . . . The wind . . . The night
    Whisper . . . baby . . .
    Whisper your lullaby . . .

1928 ∎

death

(overture for an organ)

too few
those
who could
die graciously
escaping from life
only half regretting

death

my fearful people
is an art
which few learn
and yet we
are dead
longer
much longer
than we live

when death knocks
one should rise
cloaked
in a crimson robe
burning candles
candles
purple candles
at a platinum altar
no black
my fearful people
death brings joy
here is a chance
to think new thoughts

to drink new wines
without even asking

a grave
you know
should not be
of earth
rounded over
like a cupcake

bury me
on a stormy night
in a clump of pines
the wind
running through pine branches
will be dirge enough
the rain falling
will be weeping enough

mourners
mourners
i would
not have mourners
only dancers
naked
and no music
a funeral
my fearful people
with no sobbing
no tunes
not even the latest jazz
nor hymns
by all means no hymns
you understand
this is not a time
for religion
one hears enough
of a man-made god
on sundays
and six other days

death

should free one
and not bind
to useless convention

death

is a wedding
nothing more

the individual
and the universal
become one

man cannot struggle
and overcome
all that is

death ends the fight
satisfactorily

and who is there
to change this?

Georgia's Atlanta

From a billion billion spermatozoa
which might have produced a hundred geniuses
there evolved 270,000
    thieves preachers—pacifists killers
    merchants politicians—teachers ditchdiggers
    a dozen or so Smart Men
    and the Complexes
who combined themselves
into a sprawling town
    two-thirds white, one-third black
rooted in Georgia clay
and called Atlanta . . .

As omnipresent as air
are the Complexes
reminding white folk of superiority
keeping black folk subdued
God
it so happens
either sleeps in the barn
or washes dishes for the Complexes

Black Shirts—B.Y.P.U.'s
Ku Klux Klan—Methodist Conventions
Colleges—Chaingangs
Millionaires—Breadlines
and taxes for the poor
(—out of every dollar . . .
take twenty-five cents
to feed the Complexes
who keep white folk black folk separate)

The streets careen
like drunken lads
past tenements—mansion
banks—barbershops
then fade to highways
feeding small towns
    lying hungrily in the red clay
    which mothers Georgia—
    The streets careen
    because they're brain emanations
    of the Complexes

"Yas suh Yas suh"

"You niggers ain't got no business bein' out past midnight"

"I know it's so . . . a white man said it"

"That black gal you got there, boy, is good enough for any white man. Is
    she youah wife or youah woman?" . . .

"S'cuse me Boss"

"You niggers git in th' back of this streetcah or stand up"

"We's got seats reserved for you white folks at ouah church Sunday night"

"He's a good darky"

"I know'd mah white folks'd git me outa dis mess from killin' dat no good nigguh"

"I've known one or two of you Nigras who were highly intelligent"

These, in case you don't know, are extracts from the official book on race relations as published by the Complexes

Well
All but a few
of the one-third black
and two-thirds white
were at their zenith
when spermatozoa . . .

Portrait of an Old Woman

Leather skin of a tom-tom
stretched loosely
over dried marrowless bones
then painted a brown
the color of parched corn
old and bent
like the hands
of the town clock
at two minutes past six
eyes the color of
weather-beaten brown calico
and with just that much brilliance
born working
will go out the same way

she had a son
he is now doing time
at Leavenworth
for dope peddling
her tomorrow
will be like her today
yet she can sing
of a Savior Jesus
who washed away
the sins of the world
and left her white as snow
of a rest that will come
in the Great Beyond.

What a tragedy it would be
if she were mistaken . . .

1927 ■

South State Street Profile

A great oak-brown face, a strange face with inch-and-a-half eyes placed three
inches above two mustache-guarded lips has Joe, a seller of hotdogs on
State Street

A seventy year old voice has this man of fifty . . . his eyes seldom see what
they gaze upon . . . he appreciates words unspoken better—much bet-
ter—than those one says

Joe swims in a sea of yesterdays . . . memories of better times beat against his
mind like a lash . . . his lips tell tales while his hands make a living

"Way back down home," he says while brown hands paint red frankfurters
a thick yellow with French's mustard, "I used to didn't know no trou-
ble . . . but the Wah came and I lost two sons and my wife died and I came
up No'th . . ."

He sells another and still he sees dreamed-of things with his eyes while his
hands make a living . . .

FRAGMENTS

I. Finding

In the attic
in the bottom
of an old tin trunk
I found a woman's soul
tied with blue ribbon
just so
in neat packages
6 by 3 by 3
and covered with gray dust.

II. Christians?

A word about those people
'most everybody
who would buy righteousness
like groceries
once a week
Sundays
from a beggar-god
for two bits
or a dollar
a throw.

III. Query

Who knows?
Perhaps the cloudless night
is a veil of dull black silk
set with small white diamonds
and one yellow pearl
to cover the face
of the infinite
from the vulgar gaze of man.

IV. Dreams

are children
who come at night
to play make-believe

V. Kansas Winter

The moon
pours liquid beams
on hard white snow
that hit with a splash
then freeze
to nothingness
while the wind
laughs at pines
thoughtful
shivering
sighing for spring
leaning on hills
coldly defiant
guarding bodies
of dead streams
in hard coffins
of smoky gray
ice.

VI. Failure

I would sing a song
but I have no words
I would hum a tune
but I have no melody
success
like grains of brown sand
at the sea-shore
slips through my nerveless fingers
the world

has not time
even to laugh.

VII. Race

Four puppets
one white
one yellow
one red
one black
amuse the gods.

VIII. April Night

Fingers
Fingers
Hundreds of fingers
Black
Clutching—
Leafless branches of trees
Projected against
A blue-gray sky.

Fingers grasp
At the silver-spun dress
Of the moon-goddess
As she lazily passes
Leafless branches of April trees.

I. Tryst

(Melody for the Tenor Strings of a Harp)

Come to me in the baby hours of morning . . . when the moon is a full grown woman letting her platinum veil trail from heaven . . . before high hills toss a yellow sun into the sky like a boy with a rubber ball

Let us meet beside a cool tall pine with stars in her hair . . . only a pine . . . the thin green fingers of grass . . . and the small hushed voices of wood-folk

I must sense you as you come to me . . . the warmth of you like a rolling prairie fire . . . searing flame . . . eating into my mind with sharp hot teeth

Moon slivers, sun parings, a basket of ripened dreams . . . show me these lovely things again . . .

We shall not speak, you and I, nor let flesh touch flesh . . . the eagle of silence must not fly away . . . nor the pot of passion be set to boil

We shall watch the slow treading slave night carry a burden of a million stars on his black back and I shall know you, too . . . are a star . . . a pine seeking the moon . . . the green fingers of grass pointing the way

And when the gray slants of day scourge night from the sky I shall look around but you will be gone . . . the moon mother . . . and you . . . gone . . . how can a fighting man-day know dreams . . . peace . . . rest . . . the silence of night things?

Yet there will be other new baby mornings, moon kissed, star cradled . . . knowing this . . . I too shall go . . .

II. To You

(Aria for a Violin)

Gray haze of a summer afternoon
Green of the Pacific Ocean
Brown of oak leaves in November
and You—
These are lovely things

Your eyes—more beautiful than April rainbows
Your lips—sweeter than old wine from Bordeaux
Your touch—softer than the fall of snow upon a hillside

Yet it is not for these things that I remember You
I do not love You for just your body
for bodies become old . . . bent . . . condemned
But I do say your soul is a golden chalice
into which I have poured the rich red wine of my own

We are old
yet I do not measure our ages by calendars
Out of the haze that was Yesterday
Out of the womb of Civilization
Into the chaos that will be Tomorrow . . .
forever . . . a Tomorrow
there comes and goes one Shining White Thing . . .
Very—Love!

Nothing . . .
This world
empty
Nothing . . .
only Your form, Your soul
Nothing . . .
these words
Nothing . . .
save a song
To You . . .

III. Love Notes at Night
(Melody for a Zither)

> Stars are leaves, the night's a tree
> Clouds are birds that a-nesting'd be
> And the moon's a plucked blossom.

꒰꒱

Come, Mandy Lou, let us play make-believe . . . at dusk when the moon's a
   dancing girl smoothing her hair before the mirror of still pools . . . while
   the wind is an ancient sailor telling soft yarns of strange climes . . . while
   the earth is a tired child resting against the dark bosom of night

Into the woods we shall go beneath a round frosted cake moon on a blue and
   star painted platter . . . where three straight pines lift their leafy hands in
   prayer we shall build our house . . . moon silver for walls . . . a velvet sky
   for the ceiling . . . we shall sit on the green blankets of grass

Let us burn our clothes . . . may the snake tongues of fire lap fast . . . let the
   fingers of night wrap free flesh in soft air

There will be gifts for you, Mandy Lou . . . a song . . . rainbow words for a
   moon-white voice . . . a tune to ride broad shoulders of April nights

Take the sun for your necklace . . . the moon for a dinner ring . . . cut a tur-
   quoise gown from the sky . . . pinch a mountain into sand . . . these are
   simpler tasks than changing my love for you

When you speak your words are trusted slaves carrying priceless jewels from
   your mind to me

Your lips are softer than the petals of young roses . . . your smile more lovely
   than a golden orchid . . . your body more beautiful than an artist's dream
   of the Acropolis . . . your soul an alabaster temple amid the green chaos
   of a jungle waste

Let us dream a little longer, Mandy Lou . . . let us keep the night while the
   wolves of reality sleep

Tomorrow is unborn . . . Yesterday is a musty myth . . . Tonight is a wild,
   white stallion roaming the plains of time . . . saddle Tonight with a
   silver dream . . . weave moon slants into a lash

Dip your hands into a muddy pool or bathe them in the sparkling dust of
   a million stars . . . which matters most a thousand years from now?

The day must not spatter our dreams into spray like a stout rock battering
   an ocean's waves

Again we shall meet, Mandy Lou
When a maiden moon
lies in the arms
of her lover, Night,
wait . . . for me . . .

IV. The Story Ends

You are gone . . .

Through my mind there scampers a crazy jargon of words . . . ideas stum-
   ble about like a mob of mad blind men . . . beneath my feet are the jagged,
   dagger-sharp edges of broken skyscraper dreams now crashed to the
   ground . . . before my eyes . . . asleep . . . awake . . . there dances the lovely
   image of your face . . . my universe is a woman . . . that woman . . . you . . .

Our love is a mountain pressing its strong head against the ceiling of heav-
   en . . . clouds gather . . . only its earthly base remains for mortal eyes . . .
   a stranger passes . . . stops . . . looks . . . "another pile of dirt" he says and
   wanders on . . . yet the thing we created remains . . . misunderstanding
   is a mist . . . behind its dense nothingness lies strength as eternal as this
   earth . . . we speak, but it will not crumble into dust . . . we turn away . . .
   but it will not vanish . . .

Memories of your body are great scars on the flesh of my mind . . .

Flesh, soul, heart cry out in vain . . .

You are gone . . .

⌐⌐

In you is the one slim key unlocking the door to the garden of dew-embraced, sun-loved dreams which I . . . for such a little while . . . saw . . . touched . . . dared to pluck . . .

When we met I became a god to you although my flesh was but the earth of all other men . . . you prepared a place on highest Olympus then bade me sit . . . before me you put the nectar of your lips . . . the spiced wine of your body . . .

I became drunk with the gifts of you . . . I reeled against the banquet table . . . my feet became entangled in the silken cloth . . .

Because I was human and not a god you hurled me from the palace of Zeus to the dung heaps beneath the floor of Hell . . .

I knew my place was in the long crooked streets fighting and tarrying with mortals . . . all Olympus knew that their goddess who brought into their midst an earthling would eventually learn the truth . . .

Yet I have no regrets . . .
I tried because you wished it . . .
I failed because my body was keeper over my soul . . .
Now . . . with you gone . . . the story lags . . . ends . . .

Steel chests in the sanctuary of my mind bulge with treasures of my memories . . .

There are your old words to me . . . like priceless gems I shall take them out . . . gaze on their beauty . . . dream a little while . . . then I shall lock them sadly away . . .

I have ripened memories of the honey flowing freely from your lips into my mouth when first we kissed . . . of your body hot and soft against my own . . . of days and nights together over which Time himself was mute . . .

Your promise of eternal love is emblazoned in flaming and deathless words on the wall of my sanctuary . . .

Over all there is the perfume of Purple Hyacinths on Easter Morn . . .

I thank my Fates that these gifts are my own and beyond the pale of the cleverest thief . . .

While I live . . . they live . . . when I go, they cease to be

You have gone yet the great heart of the world beats on . . . the sun rises in the east and drowns itself in a sea of western sky.

On streets men and women curse and laugh, love and hate . . . I am a luckless spermatazoan which survived . . . my affair is merely my affair . . . and who am I but an atom Time-spaced against the eternal infiniteness of the universe? Hundreds of millions of people do not know that I exist . . . who on far off Betelguese would know that even this world exists?

To me only am I important . . . but in me lies the strength of a hundred cultures which have survived since man began . . . why should I cease to be because your leaving burned dreams into gray ashes?

You have gone . . .

I cannot forget . . .

Come back any time . . . tonight . . . two decades from today . . . my love is a beacon lighting the way . . .

Yet . . . if you stay away . . . if there is no returning . . .

I shall not die!

V. Realization

Your love
was a warm, yellow light
shining through white windows
of a green cabin
as I stood alone
at dusk
in the black forest
of my loneliness.

My body ached from weariness
my soul cried out for comfort
I entered
I thought that smiling mask . . .
that lovely smiling mask . . .
was you.

I asked for food
you gave me dried bones on a wooden platter.
I asked for drink
you gave me brine in a cracked glass.
Yet I was content
I had starved so long.
And the night was dark.

But you should never have let me see the day
then how could I know the hut was filled
with the rotting forms of other
fools like me?

EBONY UNDER GRANITE

I. Rev. Joseph Williams

Being a Man of God
and a child of flesh and blood
my soul thirsting for truth
and my body hungering for eat and drink
realizing that the satisfaction of one
depended upon the survival of the other
and this could best be done
by preserving the Second Baptist Church
and that on the sisters
depended such preservation
you can understand
why the congregation stuck together
and why, when I died
the sisters mourned
and why so many children
will likewise search for truth
and have moles on their necks
like the Rev. Joseph Williams.

II. Goldie Blackwell

My three sisters and I
traded virginity
for comfort
my three sisters
got rings and Mrs.
and respectability
I got two dollars
and independence
and kept respectability
to myself.

III. Acey White

Acey
being a gambler
always knew that some day
the Big Dealer
would win the pot.

IV. Robert Whitmore

Having attained success in business
possessing three cars
one wife and two mistresses
a home and furniture
talked of by the town
and thrice ruler
of the local Elks
Robert Whitmore
died of apoplexy
when a stranger from Georgia
mistook him
for a former Macon waiter.

V. Arthur Ridgewood, M.D.

He debated whether
as a poet
to have dreams and beans
or as a physician
have a long car and caviar.
Dividing his time between both
he died from a nervous breakdown
caused by worry
from rejection slips
and final notices from the finance company.

VI. George Brown

For forty years in Mississippi
Voteless he watched white men swept into office
by a tidal wave of race hate
Powerless he saw the crooked politicians
eat the money he paid for taxes
at the table of Public Service
Voiceless he saw bigots who demanded
respect for the Constitution
stand with gun drawn if he tried
to exercise his Constitutional right
of the ballot
I say for forty years
he saw the majority vote given a winner
was less than a fraction of those taken
from his disfranchised people.
So when he came North to Chicago
and a man blacker than he
sought a seat in Congress
was it so wrong of him to use
five of the votes
saved from Mississippi
even though it meant
the rest of his life
in the state penitentiary?

VII. Giles Johnson, Ph.D.

Giles Johnson
had four college degrees
knew the whyfore of this
the wherefore of that
could orate in Latin
or cuss in Greek
and, having learned such things
he died of starvation
because he wouldn't teach
and he couldn't porter.

VIII. Roosevelt Smith

You ask what happened to Roosevelt Smith

Well . . .

Conscience and the critics got him

Roosevelt Smith was the only dusky child born and bred in the village of Pine City, Nebraska

At college they worshipped the novelty of a black poet and predicted fame

At twenty-three he published his first book . . . the critics said he imitated Carl Sandburg, Edgar Lee Masters and Vachel Lindsay . . . they raved about a wealth of racial material and the charm of darky dialect

So for two years Roosevelt worked and observed in Dixie

At twenty-five a second book . . . Negroes complained about plantation scenes and said he dragged Aframerica's good name in the mire for gold . . . "Europe," they said, "honors Dunbar for his 'Ships That Pass In The Night' and not for his dialect which they don't understand"

For another two years Roosevelt strove for a different medium of expression

At twenty-seven a third book . . . the critics said the density of Gertrude Stein or T.S. Eliot hardly fitted the simple material to which a Negro had access

For another two years Roosevelt worked

At twenty-nine his fourth book . . . the critics said a Negro had no business imitating the classic forms of Keats, Browning and Shakespeare . . . "Roosevelt Smith," they announced, "has nothing original and is merely a blackface white. His African heritage is a rich source should he use it"

So for another two years Roosevelt went into the interior of Africa

At thirty-one his fifth book . . . interesting enough, the critics said, but since
    it followed nothing done by any white poet it was probably just a new kind
    of prose

Day after the reviews came out Roosevelt traded conscience and critics for
    the leather pouch and bunions of a mail carrier and read in the papers
    until his death how little the American Negro had contributed to his
    nation's literature . . .

I
AM
THE
MERICAN
NEGRO

FRANK MARSHALL DAVIS

THE BLACK CAT PRESS · CHICAG

I AM THE
AMERICAN
NEGRO

BY FRANK MARSHALL DAVIS

BLACK CAT PRESS · CHICAGO, ILLINOIS

1937

Forewarning

Fairy words . . . a Pollyanna mind
Do not roam these pages.
Inside
There are coarse victuals
A couch of rough boards
Companions who seldom smile
Yet
It is the soul's abode
Of a Negro dreamer
For being black
In my America
Is no rendezvous
With Venus . . .

I Am the American Negro

(A sequence to be imagined)

    A very small, dark lad dressed in a linen robe of dazzling whiteness stands speaking on a busy corner. Passersby gaze at him curiously. Some stop while others hurry on, but his voice carries his words evenly until he has finished.

"Amid the colossal cacophonies
the strident symphonies
of your sprawling steel mills
of your star-snatching skyscrapers
of your bellowing freights and expresses
of your rich-loamed farm lands
of your lusty cities and your crawling towns
amid your frenzied hallelujahs
to a mighty masquerader
to a robot of levers and wires
you call either God or Progress
I lift up my small voice . . .
I, a numerical non-entity
in your already forgotten
twelve million brown stepchildren . . .
Will you listen awhile?
There is much I could say."

The scene vanishes.

Now is shown the interior of a tall temple in semi-darkness. The dim figure of a giant of indeterminate brown, his arms and legs shackled, is faintly seen, kneeling before an altar. There is heard the low monotony of a prayer. White faces peer through the dark windows showing increased satisfaction at every word.

"Lord, have pity on me!
From my soul's depth I speak
It is truth You hear
Although my words have a strange sound—
For I am the American Negro!
I am a man apart . . . "

A mist falls over the faces at the windows. A strong white light plays on the kneeling giant's features. The jangle of the shackles on his arms beats a tom-tom rhythm to the words that come first slowly and deliberately, and then more quickly from his mouth.

"I, the American Negro, am a rainbow race, a kaleidoscopic breed found only in this land.

In my veins runs the blood of Caucasian Europe and of the Indians of America for my slave women were tempting to their white masters and my men came to the New World with Cortes.

In me is a monstrous union of many African tribes . . . tribes who were mortal enemies in the deep green jungles of the great dark continent.

Yet I do not value my savage ancestry for my white folk tell me black Africa has given nothing to civilization . . . my historians sing of the golden glories of the ancient empires . . . of Mandingo, Benin, Yoruba; of old Timbuktu, Kana, Zimbabwe, Zegzeg, of the great king Abuade Izchia but I will neither listen nor believe for no white lips have phrased these words, and therefore they cannot be true.

My dream is to be physically white . . . so I straighten my kinks, bleach my skin and look down on those darker than I . . . For myself I build pale gods to serve . . . whatever white folk do I imitate."

⌐⌐

The voice of the giant grows louder. The jangle of his chains almost drowns out his words. He stops kneeling and stands erect, his head thrown back, blood trickling from his legs where the shackles dig into his flesh. Great drops of sweat glisten on his forehead. The white faces at the window reappear and smiles play on their features.

"But most of all, dear Lord, I have no guts and I refuse to heed the law of
   self-preservation.
I cry . . . yet I will not heal those ills bringing tears to my eyes.
I will not support men and movements battling for my betterment.
I will not pool my dollars to fight in the courts atrocities committed
   against me or illegal laws denying rights guaranteed by the Constitu-
   tion of my country.
I will not unite my resources to found businesses giving jobs to my peo-
   ple nor will I lend wholehearted support to enterprises run by men
   and women of my race.
I send my young to college and then I let them go forth as graduates into
   hotels as waiters and bellhops, into railway stations as redcaps for I
   have no work they may do but teach or sell insurance.
If I am lynched or shot or my women raped I will complain in low whis-
   pers to my black brothers and sisters . . . more I dare not do.
I am afraid to protect myself against anything white."

⌐⌐

Great veins stand out in the giant's throat. His hands claw the air before him. His body rocks and sways. His hair mats against his forehead from the sweat that pours from his body and mixes with the small ooze of warm, red blood.

"I grin, I dance, I sing. I am the minstrel man for white America!
I am a hodge-podge of paradox, a crazy collection of inconsistencies.
Seldom to myself and before no whites dare I confess these traits.
Pity me, Lord, for there is none other like me . . .
I am the American Negro!"

Suddenly the temple is brilliantly lighted. The giant—still chained, still erect—raises his arms above his head. His face changes constantly, chameleon-like, from milky white to inky black. Then the light fades and the giant stands still. As he speaks, the white listeners cease their smiles and, one by one, leave the windows. Only one or two remain. His voice is low, deliberate . . . the tone firm and even . . . he drops wearily to the floor with his hands in an attitude of prayer before him.

"And yet, Lord, with my weakness there is strength, for who but I could carry these bonds and still exist?

I have given America loyalty unequalled in man's history.

From the loins of my brown women, sons have come forth to fight and die for a democracy that may lynch the survivors.

I have planted seed deep in the womb of the good earth and reaped only cotton . . . and mobs . . . and peonage.

I am the public martyr for America's arena . . . I gave Crispus Attucks at the Boston Tea Party and today I am handed Scottsboro, in Alabama.

My country's papers give me front page headlines for my murderers and one paragraph beside the want ad section for my men of letters and science.

"God the Father" and "Love thy Neighbor" shout my white brothers in Christ from behind the doors of their gaudy churches slammed shut and locked when I seek to enter.

Writers sling buckets of ink to show the skin You gave me proves inferiority . . . purses bulge with cash exchanged for the mass privilege of systematic hate.

In courts down South I am fodder for chain gang and electric chair since any white convict has more say-so than my Doctors of Philosophy.

Only my dollars know no color line . . . and sometimes even they are banned!"

The forehead of the giant wrinkles in a frown. His eyes open, stare before him . . . his face looks puzzled . . . wonderment . . . incomprehension . . . hesitancy . . . amazement . . . all these expressions pass across his countenance. His voice goes on . . . slowly . . . carefully.

"Yet I cannot hate America for this land sprouts out of my bleached
    bones from Bunker Hill to St. Michel and in my veins flows the
    blood of these my brother races.
But I cannot love America for my back is sore from the welts of preju-
    dice rubbed with the salt of segregation.
Lord, what shall I do?"

*Beside the giant there suddenly appears a form neither male nor female,
neither black nor white. It wears tattered clothing and holds its body with stately
majesty. The newcomer speaks. The giant turns his head to listen. Fear passes
first across his face . . . then as the newcomer goes on in a satin-soft voice the
low hum of a mighty choir is heard in the distance . . . the sound gains momen-
tum . . . the music can now be heard quite distinctly . . . yet the satin-soft voice
of the speaker is heard above it all . . .*

Choir: "Come on
         Black man
         Grab your hat
         Let's get goin'
         MMMMmmmmmmmmmm
                            mmmmmmMMMMM"

Voice: "Fathered by Lincoln
         Mothered by a Civil War
         Born in the smoke and blood
             of Spottsylvania Courthouse,
             Bull Run, Gettysburg.
         Given the sharp daggers
         Of three Constitutional Amendments.
         Clothed in the greatest
         Civilization known to modern man
         Then set on the road to town . . .
         But today
         You lie sleeping
         Far, far outside the City Gates."

Choir: "Come on
         Black man

Grab your hat
Let's get goin'
MMMMmmmmmmmmm
                            mmmmmmMMMMM"

Voice: "Singer of hymns, warbler of the blues, picker of cotton, layer of
          railroad ties . . . poet and bone-crusher . . . big muscles and
          Ph.D.'s.
          America has seen you go to school at Howard, Atlanta, Tuskegee; at
          Harvard, Oxford, Berlin and come out prattling of Plato and Ein-
          stein in sixty different jargons.
          Poppies in France grow from your blood and flesh . . . San Juan Hill
          knows the victorious tread of black feet . . . but here the story
          ends.
          String 'em up in Alabama . . . burn 'em in the hot-seat in Georgia . . .
          give a cop a bonus for every one he kills . . . kick 'em till they're
          down, mister, then kick 'em again for fallin' . . . they're black and
          they won't fight back."

Choir: "Come on
          Black man
          Grab your hat
          Let's get goin'
          MMMMmmmmmmmmm
                            mmmmmmMMMMM"

Voice: "Arm your Christ with a shotgun . . . hire six attorneys to work with
          Jehovah . . . teach your priests how to uppercut . . . if David had
          slung a prayer and a hymn Goliath would have chalked up an-
          other win.
          Sure, we all know there's one of you to nine of them so try to win
          sitting down . . . but if that won't work let 'em have it, buddy . . .
          you can't live forever anyhow!"

Choir: "Come on
          Black man
          Grab your hat
          Let's get goin'

You can't live forever
Anyhow!
MMMMmmmmmmmmmm
                            mmmmmmMMMMM"

⌐⌐

*The giant trembles from head to foot . . . his voice rumbles . . . roars . . . as
he stands before this stranger . . .*

Giant: "Who are you? Who are you? I never saw you before . . ."

*The stranger fades into the deepening shadows . . . and as the figure disap-
pears only a satin-smooth voice is heard.*

*The giant, strengthened by the stranger's words, tears the shackles from his
arms. He takes a step forward, forgetting his legs are shackled too . . . He falls
crouching on the floor . . . He beats the floor with each heavy, bleeding fist.*

Giant: "Who are you? Who are you?"

Voice: "I am experience!"

*The giant crawls to the edge of a window. With great agony he draws his body
up closer . . . closer . . . closer to the sill . . . Finally he stands erect . . . weak . . .
tottering . . . he peers through the window into the coming darkness . . . the low
humming sound of the choir can still be heard.*

There are no faces left at the windows.

*The giant turns . . . looks at the emptiness around him . . . frowns in dis-
gust . . . opens his mouth to speak when the temple falls in a crash . . . and the
voice of the giant is stilled.*

*The low, satin-soft voice he heard is drowned out by the rolling tumble of
loose, crashing stones . . . these stones that formed the temple of America's So-
cial System end the life and problems of the Negro giant as they collapse.*

Barely audible above the din there sounds the laughter of the gods . . .

Dancing Gal

Black and tan—yeah, black and tan
Spewing the moans of a jigtime band
What does your belly crave?

   A brown-sugar brown
   Slim gal sways
   Pretzel twisting
   Beneath a yellow thumb
   Of steel-stiff light
   Amid a striped rain
   Of red note, blue note

   Jazz—hot jazz
   Gazelle graceful
   Lovely as a lover's dream
   Silken-skinned, still-water soft
   Young girl breasts in gold encased
   Scant gold around her lower waist
   Red lips parted
   Dark eyes flashing
   She dances
   Dips, whirls, undulates
   Her body a living chord
   Set loud and sweet
   Against the bitter quiet
   Of drab and muted human shapes

   I see a long lean god
   Standing in painted splendor
   Motionless in the scented air
   Of Tanganyika
   I see a frozen idol
   Set free from a single stone
   Shielding with seven arms
   His world in Hindustan . . .
   Africa's madness, India's sadness
   Wedded in Chicago

By a Midwest gal
In a Jew's cafe . . .

Black and tan—yeah, black and tan
Drenched in the jazz of a swingtime band
Is this what your belly craves?

Flowers of Darkness

Slowly the night blooms, unfurling
Flowers of darkness, covering
The trellised sky, becoming
A bouquet of blackness
Unending
Touched with springs
Of pale and budding stars

Soft the night smell
Among April trees
Soft and richly rare
Yet commonplace
Perfume on a cosmic scale

I turn to you Mandy Lou
I see the flowering night
Cameo condensed
Into the lone black rose
Of your face
The young woman—smell
Of your poppy body
Rises to my brain as opium
Yet silently motionless
I sit with twitching fingers
Yea, even reverently
Sit I
With you and the blossoming night
For what flower, plucked,
Lingers long?

They All Had Grand Ideas

Alexander cried for new worlds to conquer and he was hustled into the stout
tombs without learning millions stood ready to split his skull in unknown
China, Africa, America, Australia and the South Sea Islands
Christ went hoarse telling them to toss in their swords, give away their cash
and put on a perpetual brother act . . . Judas sold him down the river for
forty pieces of silver and they lynched him with nails sharp as any spear
or dagger
Columbus located new real estate for the Big Dogs of Spain . . . France and
England muscled in . . . today the United States holds up the Monroe
Doctrine and dares any of the elderly mother nations to come over after
more than what little they have left
Lenin and Trotsky fought for a Russia without czars and aristocracy . . . to-
day both are in the city dump as Stalin and his crew strong-arm the lib-
erated peasants into accepting state control and ownership
Napoleon licked 'em all until Waterloo . . . an actor slipped Lincoln the last
curtain call—
They all had grand ideas.

⌐⌐

Men dream and die to give way to other men with a different slant on
the same idea
Muhammed for Christ, Kaiser Wilhelm for Hannibal, Einstein for
Newton, Shaw for Shakespeare
Each caught the deathless butterfly of a grand idea in the silken mesh
of his mind . . . held it for such a little while . . . then had to let it go
I pick no winner
There isn't any

The world slushes on
The world where men struggle for victuals and shelter and safety today as
when Adam strode Eden and Ab hid from the sabre-toothed tiger
The world where women want their men and babies and bank accounts or
soft skins and trinkets hidden deep in a cave
What has it mattered? . . . what has anything mattered?
What has the world done but smash its dreamers?

These men with the grand ideas—
Do they dream in the sod of success?
Do their hopes spill over into the cool silent earth?
Or do they laugh at the new dreamers and say "Boy, you'll learn . . . I
    got that way once and see what happened?"

Tomorrow more dreamers
Yet nothing wins but the hungry waiting graves
Chisel these words on the tall tombstones and you get the whole story yes-
    terday, today and forever—
"I had a grand idea—but it wouldn't keep . . . "

Christ Is a Dixie Nigger

You tell me Christ was born nearly twenty centuries ago in a little one-horse
    town called Bethlehem . . . your artists paint a man as fair as another New
    White Hope.
Well, you got it all wrong . . . facts twisted as hell . . . see?

Let me tell you wise guys something
I've got my own ideas . . . I've got a better Christ and a bigger Christ . . . one
    you can put your hands on today or tomorrow.

My Christ is a Dixie nigger black as midnight, black as the roof of a cave's
    mouth
My Christ is a black bastard . . . maybe Joe did tell the neighbors God bigged
    Mary . . . but he fooled nobody . . . they all knew Christ's father was Mr.
    Jim who owns the big plantation . . . and when Christ started bawling out
    back in the cabins Mr. Jim made all three git
You see, I know
Christ studied medicine up North in Chicago then came back to Mississip-
    pi a good physician with ideas for gettin' the races together . . . he lectured
    in the little rundown schoolhouses awaiting Rosenwald money . . . he
    talked of the brotherhood and equality of man and of a Constitution
    giving everybody a right to vote and some of the nigger listeners told their
    white folks . . . then they found how Christ healed a white woman other
    doctors gave up for lost . . . the two things together got him in the cala-
    boose

They called him a Communist and a menace to the Existing Relationship
    Between Black and White in the South
Sheriff and judge debated whether to open the hoosegow and tell reporters
    the mob stormed the jail or let the state lynch him on the gallows
Anyhow they got him
Maybe the rope was weak or Christ was too strong to die . . . I don't know
They cut him down and they patched him up . . . he hid in the swamps until
    he got well enough to get around again . . . then he lectured a little
    more . . . and faded out
Whether he went to heaven or Harlem or the white folks broke his neck and
    hid the corpse somewhere is a question they still ask—
See what I mean?

I don't want any of your stories about somebody running around too long
    ago to be anything but a highly publicized memory
Your pink priests who whine about Pilate and Judas and Gethsemane I'd like
    to hog-tie and dump into the stinking cells to write a New Testament
    around the Scottsboro Boys
Subdivide your million dollar temples into liquor taverns and high class
    whore-houses . . . my nigger Christ can't get past the door anyway

Remember this, you wise guys
Your tales about Jesus of Nazareth are no-go with me
    I've got a dozen Christs in Dixie all bloody and black . . .

Washington Park, Chicago

The heat roars
Like a tidal wave
Over Chicago's Congo
Inundating
A rusty raft of a house
On Dearborn Street
A sleek schooner
Of a brownstone mansion
On South Parkway.
Long foam fingers
Of wet heat
Clutch ebon throats

Paw bronze thighs
Tear into shreds
Thin white sheets of coolness.
High breakers of heat
Split into dry mist—
A harmless spray—
As the tidal wave
Dashes against strong rocks
Of tall trees
In Washington Park.

Upon the wrinkled green skin
Of growing grass,
Amid fat shrubs
Squatting in lazy content,
Beneath willow and oak
Watching like anxious mothers,
Along the tangled yarn
Of gray paths,
Beside still pools
The color of old ice
In Washington Park
The people go—
When the heat
Is an African python
Crushing amid its coils
The black carcass
Of Chicago's Congo . . .

II

Sun by day
Moon and mazda by night
Rinse kaleidoscopic faces
Twirling slowly against the light;
Faces of infants and con men
Of turnip breasted virgins
And worn out prostitutes
Their bodies piled along the grass
Or poured into wooden benches.
Others walk up and down

Up and down
Then back,
Men call to girls
And to other men.
Voices swing like monkeys
Through a thick forest
Of continuous sound.
Here one may be
Surrounded and alone.

Along pretzel crooked roads
Race horse autos gallop
In great herds
Or stand in insolent silence
Rubber feet among green blades of grass
Sniffing in mechanical disdain
At those who walk
And barely dodge
A mile a minute hoof.

The park shoulders
Its people and cars
On a verdant back
And marches on
To the steady boom
Of the taut heat drum.

III

In the wide pocket
Of an aged bench
Sleeps ragged Sam
Covered with old newspaper.
Above his face smiles Dolly Smythe
Queen of the Burlesque Houses
In her printed magnificence.
Martha, the Love Murderess,
Is an unconscious pillow
For his head.
But Sam, remembering many,
Has forgotten women;

He dreams these nights
Of steaks and chops three times a day
Of a soft bed in a quiet room
Then stirs his homeless bones
And Dolly Smythe,
Queen of the Burlesque Houses,
Falls face down into the litter
From Sam's nickel dinner
Bummed off a peanut vendor . . .

Until anyway eleven
By a park policeman's watch
They will sit
This boy and gal,
On the soft sweet sod
Or a silent bench
His head against
Her warm thighs
The brown full moon
Of her face above.
The heat that sniffs
Like a curious cur
About walled flats
Is left behind—
For them the fire
Of two dry sticks
Rubbed together:
And only they know
Which is harder to bear . . .

A lanky Communist
Tosses baited words
To faces beneath him,
Faces fish-mouthed
In a sitting sea
Of human forms.
"Proletariat" . . . "Bourbon"
"Workers" . . . "Starvation"
"Equality" . . . "Comrades"
Are flung at 'em

By the glib fisherman
On the angler's stand.
And if now and then
A fish lands the Red
Will Stalin sniffle in his vodka?

⌐⌐

Does the Rev. Moses Wagner,
Pastor of Golgotha Church,
Come here to pick up chippies?
When Inky White strolls here,
Inky the broken down pug,
Is it to hunt out pansies?
Does Montell Duke,
Poet and Ph. D.,
Stride the winding paths
Gnawing an ice cream cone?

I don't know—
Lord, I don't know—
Ask me some other time . . .

IV

Impatient tomorrow
Jerks at the chains of Time;
The tiger heat
Crouches low and tense;
People leave
Or they remain;
Dried pea faces
A-rattle in a pod
And tender sprouts
For next season's harvesting . . .

I saw the night
Tuck Washington Park
Into her star-torn apron

And dodder on
As an aged woman
Gathers wood for the stove
From a fallen-in house.

I saw the sun
Sputter and mew—
A great yellow cat
Walking the backyard fence
Of a gray new day . . .

V

A white cloud hand
Writes on the blue sky wall:
"Men build skyscrapers
Cleaving the air;
Men boast of Progress
Of steel-thewed Science
Of a million Inventions
Advancing the human race;
Of Edison, Marconi, Einstein, Darwin,
Yet if the thin green grass
The humble waving grass
That crawls on its belly
Should not return
With its cool soft kiss
Which one could make
A duplicate?"

None reads but the park
Inarticulate, strong;
Holding Chicago's Congo
To its soothing breast
While the heat roars
Like a tidal wave
Dashed to harmless spray
Against strong rocks
Of tall trees . . .

Note Left by a Suicide

Tomorrow I shall die
Suicide, the coroner will say
Electric light of a heart switched off
Yet to me only another death . . . nothing new . . . nothing new
I have seen my dreams yanked from me, tossed to the earth, ground into thin
   dust
I loved . . . the woman who bore my name passed into infinity bearing a son
   for another
I offered the world my soul in words . . . rejection slips from editors buried
   my gift in the Potter's Field
What have I left but flesh? . . . of what use are walls of a building when fire
   eats all else?
Tomorrow I shall die . . .

Today I rose to the fortieth story of a skyscraper
Through a window I gazed at two-legged ants of men crawling about streets,
   busying themselves in anthills of steel and stone
As a boy, I crushed anthills with one shoe . . . what did it matter but to the
   ants themselves? . . . did this universe stop? . . . if a greater shoe should
   stamp out Chicago what would it matter except to ants in other hills? . . .
   then what of the life and death of one ant?
I looked again . . . yet I could not leap
You say it takes strength to live
I have seen Masks of Fear worn in hospitals, sickrooms, death cells of stout
   jails
I know man flees from the unknown mystery of Death
I know from Terror comes strength to run
I did not leap
I lacked the greater strength to die
For that I am ashamed

But tomorrow . . . surely, surely
I shall dwell with billions who have swung on . . . today the poorest idiot
   among them wiser than Socrates, Espinoza, Kant, Einstein
I shall not linger dreading the certain step of Death
A year or a century . . . then curtains

Food by day, sleep by night . . . will-o'-the-wisp dreams . . . if caught, a quest
    for more . . . it has always been
They all wait tossed by chance into existence . . . for what? to be tossed again
    into oblivion?

You think Life . . . egotistic, hairy-chested, strong-armed . . . has conquered
    me?
Go ahead, you . . . bare your back to his slave whip
But not I
I seek freedom . . . I go before Life cuts me, worn and useless, from his chains
Now or later . . . for fifty years more what could I gain but new scars?
So I go
I am too brave to live!

To One Who Would Leave Me

Not yet . . . not yet
Unended is the Opera of Us
This curtain . . . only a pause
Time has new tunes
Life is a husky scene-shifter
Arranging new backdrops
Soon the show goes on . . .

   ⌐⌐

With a ballet of smooth dancing words
Amid a jargon of sharply silken sounds
Behind steel strong lights
Hoofing a crazy razzle-dazzle of mental jigs
Before the sixty gods of Happiness
We sang
Sang a year and a day
I played a stumbling Romeo
To your dulcet Juliet
Soon the show swings on
The Great Author cannot
Hustle in another cast . . .

⌐⌐

Sure, I understand
Ask Bernhardt, ask Duse
They both got that way
Sure
Life's not always sprayed with attar of roses
Sometimes Trouble comes around with a dun
Or grief camps on the back stairs
It's not easy then
To smile like a Christ-kissed angel
For the stuffed shirts
In the orchestra seats
Out front

⌐⌐

You won't really go, will you?
I look into your brown eyes deep as high lakes clasped to the breast of un-
     known African hills
I have reeled and rocked in shameful drunkenness from the scented wine
     of your red lips
Circe's wand is less potent than the feel of your velvet flesh against me
I am Midas with the wealth of your love
Yet you are a woman
And I cannot tell—
You won't really go, will you?

⌐⌐

The orchestra clears its throat for speech
Time beckons
Life steps into the wings
All unended is the Opera of Us
Not yet . . . not yet
Shall we take our places
Or must we tell the sixty gods of Happiness
"That's all there is . . . that's all there is
Go out and get your money back . . . "?

'Mancipation Day

Hallowed be the memory of Abraham Lincoln!
He was a great man, he gave us our freedom!

In Chicago, Atlanta, Louisville, Memphis, Kansas City, Los Angeles, Miami,
    Boston a million kaleidoscopic people gather and lift high hosannas in
    memory of a misty Emancipation Day

(In hobo camps from Maine to California sprawl a thousand bums recall-
    ing the hour gates closed behind them at Sing Sing, Joliet, Leavenworth,
    San Quentin)

In Birmingham they ride Jim Crow cars to a nigger park guarded by white
    cops ready to shoot to kill if the black bastards annex the idea they're hu-
    man and Citizens of Alabama . . . listening brown folk balloon with pride
    as sweet-speeched speakers canonize Lincoln—the air reeks with the
    stench of burned brothers lynched in courthouse yards

In Gary, Indiana, from the hot bellies of steel mills come celebrants . . . to-
    morrow some will starve as their jobs are snatched and given to Jan Pi-
    darski direct from Ellis Island . . . tomorrow others sweat gold for the gods
    of the steel corporation in whose shrines none may walk

Words splash like water over ebony skulls . . . see a people proud because
    white men died, another freed them when impotent ancestors worked the
    plantation while Ole Massa fought their liberators

(In the hobo jungles let there be barbecues and long-winded programs . . .
    let Convict 67895 and his comrades burst with pride . . . are they not the
    ones set free by the whims of the prison commission?

Praise ye Warden Laws of Sing Sing
And the New York Board of Pardons and Paroles:
They gave us our freedom!)

Notes on a Summer Night

Past wood and water, over steel and stone
Through the forty-room mansion of a millionaire
Into the one-room cabin of a cotton picker
Dark purple runners of darkness run—
Today is another grain of sand
And the shore is long and smooth . . .

Twenty brownskin babies suckle the wet teats of gin bottles at Mojo Mike's
    in Chicago
Twenty gin guzzling gals gone to the dogs with a grin at two bucks a throw
The hot air staggers under the heavy smell of beer and bourbon, dead tobacco
    and dripping sweat
A five cent phonograph flings vermillion streamers of jazz through the at-
    mosphere
Outside a mazda-bandaged night limps slowly along 47th Street in Chica-
    go's Congo.
(Do you remember, Mandy Lou,
When shadows of oak leaves danced a slow mazurka
Plucked by clouds from a banjo moon
Near Kankakee?)

"Not now, anyhow" says the barbershop porter
In a forty dollar suit ogling sheer frocked gals
"Gimme a skinny chick
When it's too hot to cover up nights
They don't cut off no breeze
It ain't like sleepin' wit' a furnace
An' yuh don' need brakes to keep from slidin'
Yuh wants a fat broad in wintah
But kiss 'em goodbye in June
I don't want no heavy mama—
Not now, anyhow . . . "

I have seen nights like this piled bargain counter high with lust
I have seen paunchy pimps loll in darkened doors while their painted wom-
    en pulled in poor suckers
I have heard the man-pack tear down a county jail and burn black Mose
    beside the Baptist Church

I have watched a ghetto father fix it for his daughter who bedded without a
    license
I saw them bring back Nicky Pottello . . . Nicky crammed dead into a cul-
    vert for crossing the Malorto Gang
I have heard a hundred wives lying naked with their lovers as their husbands
    sought out other women
And . . . Yes . . . Indeed
I have heard America at the breakfast table froth for the blood of uncivilized
    Chinese bastards who dared kidnap the daughter of a Wall Street broker

Anxiously the moon clucks to a new brood of white moonbeams hatched in
    the Missouri River at Kansas City
On Lake Michigan boats move like phosphorescent water spiders
The tall tree of the Empire State Building holds ripe clusters of white lights
    above the groping fingers of New York's skyline
Butterfly cars flit along the gossamer highway between Denver and Colorado
    Springs
A bluefire diamond night glitters through all the land
"Christ" mutter ten thousand cops in a thousand snoring towns between
    Miami and Seattle "Five more hours t' daybreak" . . .

In the director's chamber of the First National Bank in Cincinnati
All is quiet
In the shuttered room of one just passed
There is silence
Dollars and death have spilled their small talk—
Only the star-white stars
Whisper in lazy circles above Ohio . . .

Ninety thousand Negroes sleep in Atlanta
Ninety thousand dreams spin in black heads
Atlanta now is a bearded myth
Of Jim Crow laws and hair trigger cops
The Coast Line Railway to Jacksonville
Is a lie in steel
Maybe such never was—
A Pollyanna moon croons a soft lullaby
"Everything's all right, honey
Tomorrow will be different, don't you know . . . "

Awakening

Born in the pages of letters
Nursed by strong sweet words
Reared in the vast expanse of two wild minds
Is Our Love . . .

Vigorous—Big Muscled
Tender as a mother caring for her first born
Soft as the fall of night
Massive as the universe
Eternal as life and death
Blinding as the midday sun
Is Our Love
Now
In his steel arms he has taken us
Welding two souls, two bodies
Into a boundless one
Inhabiting a sky world built for us
By us
Vigorous, big muscled Love wraps our world in a blanket
Only if vigorous, big muscled Love goes shall we leave . . .

Yet flesh has not touched flesh
Our words . . . our only caresses
Just our minds have kissed
For Love has saved hot blood for the last
For another beginning . . .

I know your lips have the honey from dreamed-of wildflowers
I know your fragrance surpasses Purple Hyacinths
I know your eyes have the deep beauty of clear dark pools on mountaintops
I know your hair is more radiant than a rainbow
I know your body is more beautiful than an alabaster vase . . .
Why wonder then, that my heart falters, breath leaves me when I think of
    you?

When we meet
How shall we ever part?
Can lip leave lip, breast quit breast, or thigh be torn from thigh?
How can I take away the Me you own . . . which is a part of you?

I want the warm loveliness of you branded into my flesh . . . your kisses a song
   in my soul . . . hands-full of soft words . . . your breath on me like a spring
   zephyr . . . your hair a fountain bathing my face . . . let me lose myself in
   the ageless beauty of you . . . let our passion be incense burning on the
   altar to Very-Love . . .

We shall never quite part . . . the scars left by hot flesh on hot flesh will hurl
   us together at night with their throbbing even though we are separated
   by a million miles . . . our world will always be . . . for Our Love belongs
   to the Infinite . . .

Come to Me

Ah, beloved,
Come to me—
My throat is leather dry
The flesh of my parted lips
Lies taut and burning
My heart pounds
Like a thousand lashes

The kiss of your small hand
Has soothed my brow
Your warm breasts
Girl-firm, woman-soft,
Have pressed hard against me
The fragrance of your body
Has been incense to my soul
Your wet mouth—
A rose with burning dew—
Has lain trembling
Against my own

While I drank
Until
No honey remained

I have had so very much of you
But never enough . . .
Never enough
Always
The feast of your love
Increases my hunger
And I cannot end
Either feast or hunger

Come to me
Kiss me . . . hold me . . . kiss me
Ah, sweet,
You of the midnight hair
Cascading
About your face
Like a blackened waterfall,
Let me place my mouth
In the smooth valley
Between twin hills
Of your barren bosom
Let my lips clothe
The flesh of you
In a warm robe of kisses
All unashamed
You will lie
Against my racing heart
Eager life
Careening joyously, madly,
Through taut veins
As we drink
The perfumed wine
Of our love

I know of you,
Broken melodies of living;
Human harps strung, tuned, played

Then snapped into silence
All strings forever useless
With so much music waiting
With so few chords rendered
And the never knowing
When melodies will crash
Into infinite nothingness.
Soon we too will hush
Stop
Be stilled
You, beloved,
And I, your lover,
But today
You are very much you
I am still I
Worshipping
At the temple
Of your soul and body
Today we live—
Come to me,
Beloved!

Modern Man—the Superman

(A Song of Praise for Hearst, Hitler, Mussolini and the Munitions Makers)

Eight airplane motors, each keyed to a different pitch, are turned on and off to furnish musical accompaniment within the range of an octave.

Let us have war
A pedigreed, civilized war
With gas for the women
Dumdums for the kiddies
Shrapnel and bombs
For Red Cross Hospitals
And gold for the munitions makers

Heigh-ho!
We have come a long way, don't you know;
Only savages
Savages and heathens
Would use sharpened spears
Flint-tipped arrows flung from a bow

Or cool silent knives
Killing one at a time
With a personal touch.
In a day of big business
Mass production
Sanitary methods
And "untouched by human hands"
With millions of acres
To seed the dead
Tons of lead and steel
For guns and bullets
A billion two-legged mammals
To shoot and be shot
(They'd die someday anyway)
Politicians and moneyed men
For masterly direction—
In such a day
War takes on
A respectable dignity

Alexander was a neighborhood bully
Caesar was a piker
Only Napoleon
had some pale glimmer
Of the right idea
And thank you Kaiser

*Music of an organ supplants the
airplane motors only to be
drowned out after a few bars by
the whir of a dynamo, an occa-
sional shriek from a factory whis-
tle, and the approaching and
receding gong of an ambulance.*

Don't you think—
Mister Hearst
Signor Mussolini
Herr Hitler—
It's time to change
This Bible and God
To a civilized
Misconception?

Let us revere the machine which gives to us
   our life, our joy, our well-being, our
   progress
In St. Judas hospital . . . machine construct-
   ed, machine equipped . . . is born a child
   who may soon return the victim of oth-
   er machines
Up and down in streets outside machines
   run . . . they carry men and women to
   work at different machines for food and
   clothing more machines have made . . .
   they use their rubber legs and metal
   backs hauling men to murder with other
   machines called guns . . . they crush
   blood and life in scornful vengeance
   from those not moving by steel and oil
Nearby a small boy hawks the daily press
   displaying smooth lies machine-printed
   to tighten the grip of those controlling
   machines at work
Come let us sing mechanical hallelujahs to a
   pile of levers and pulleys high as the
   Chrysler Tower
By such a God do we live and die
Through orders of His priests do we kill in
   battle
And civilization marches onward
For Jehovah is always just

ᒡᒢ

*The accompaniment again
changes. A uniformed marks-
man fires a loaded pistol at
eight differently pitched bells,
each giving a strong metallic
sound when hit. They are la-
belled "Jews," "Negroes," "So-
cialism," "Communism," "Tol-
erance," "Independence," "Free
Speech," and "Individuality."*

Give us another war
Shaming antiquity
Belittling the puny efforts
Of ignorant ancestors
Let us slaughter the unfit
For science knows
The fit will always survive

Have we sufficient rifles and howitzers?
Will our poison gas
Make death horrible enough?
Can our dumdum bullets
Shred the target's vital organs?
Have big guns the range
Of the largest hospitals?
Do our bombing planes know
Where the women and children will flee?
Then let's go!
Let Modern Man, the Superman
Make civilization safe

The bells break and fall to the   For Hearst and Hitler
ground as the song ends.   Mussolini and the Munitions Makers!

Two Women

As maid for Mrs. Harold Billingsworth
Dahlia Green
supplemented the Petite Beauty Salon
by curling her mistress' straight hair
several times weekly.
Paydays
Dahlia went straightway
to the Afro Beauty College
to have her own moss unkinked.
At sixty both women
from efforts to imitate
the natural appearance of each
above the ears
were forced to buy wigs
from the salons.
Yet this was a triumph for civilization
and American progress—
Think how they aided
the entire hair industry!

For Any Unborn Negro

Brush his
Lips lightly, Life!
Though this is home he's black.
Too soon he'll know that none loves him
But Death . . .

"Onward Christian Soldiers!"

The religion of Sweet Jesus
The spirit of Our Saviour
March on
With missionaries
And civilization
Into darkest Africa

Day by Day
Black folk learn
Rather than with
A heathen spear
'Tis holier to die
By a Christian gun . . .

Midsummer Morn

A tom-tom sun awakens day's jungle with heat beats
The moon was a white war canoe moored to the night
Morning stars scurry to cover like shaking hares fearful of the Great Yellow
    Hunter
Last night's tall hunchback fishing in a pool of raven's breasts is a green
    elm tree
Thin wings of grass pound helplessly against hard ground
And the robins are no longer afraid . . .

I. Moses Mitchell

It was in 1917
That Moses Mitchell
Left Natchez, Mississippi
To help make the world
Safe for democracy
Thereby gaining
A distinguished service cross
For conspicuous bravery
In the Argonne Forest

Eighteen years later
Back home in cotton country
Moses' life was saved
When the metal decoration
Pinned inside his shirt pocket
Stopped a leaden bullet
Sheriff Pete Jones fired at the Negro
Blonde Victoria Bates
Swore assaulted her
As she hoboed through to New Orleans
From Scottsboro, Alabama,
And in so doing kept herself
From being picked up for vagrancy

How fortunate!
Because he served his nation bravely
Moses now was able
To die upon the gallows . . .

II. Sam Jackson

The moon was a thick slab of yellow cheese between thin slices of toasted
   clouds

The night air spilled steak and coffee smells from a sack of odors hauled from
the Elite Cafe

Beneath penniless Sam Jackson's window two dogs argued like nations over
a morsel found in a garbage can

Strong Hunger slashed Sam's belly with eagle talons until he staggered
wounded and sore to the street

Daily papers itemed: "An unidentified Negro was shot and instantly killed
late last night by Officer Patrick Riley while trying to break into the rear
of the Dew Drop Inn . . . "

III. Jonathan Wood

Editors said
Jonathan Wood
Never found the path of words
To his star high dreams
At twenty-five
Even Life
Sent him
A rejection slip . . .

IV. Cleo and Sarah Greeley

At the age of sixteen
Cleo Greeley
More female than feminine
Had learned to walk
With a suggestive slither
To her unhampered hams
Firing the lusty lads
Of both races
In Charleston.
At thirty
Tired of peddling love
At bargain prices

Cleo went to Los Angeles
Under another name
And wed the woman-hungry pastor
Of Big Bethel A.M.E. Church.
Being thoroughly trained
She kept him content at home
Thus avoiding
The forked tongue of scandal
Which added respectability
To their marriage
And indirectly prosperity
To the House of Worship.

Sarah was twenty-five
A voluptuous Madonna
Nursing the crimson child
Of her virginity
When she mated
With Oscar Simmons
Who had just inherited
The Excelsior Cafe.
It was scarce six months
For all her eyesome charms
Before her husband
Sick of inexperienced flesh
Turned to the brazen buttocks
Of the moral-less ladies
Who patronized his restaurant
Thus signaling the slinging
Of sharp darts of pity
By the town
At Mrs. Oscar Simmons.

Cleo and Sarah
Are both dead
These five years—
Who remembers either?

V. Benjamin Blakey

Benjamin Blakey
Did quite well for himself
And the people of his town
It isn't everybody
Who leaves behind
The showplace of his state—
A six-story Odd Fellows Temple
He built and managed—
As well as control of the affairs
Of big Sinai A.M.E. Church
A son who finished Harvard
A daughter with a Vassar degree
A wife so well satisfied outwardly
She never showed jealousy
Of the six women
The town whispered
Her husband kept

Still
Benjamin Blakey
Would have died more content
Had he ever learned
From which of his mistresses
He contracted
That fatal social disease . . .

VI. Nicodemus Perry

Walking pensively along
looking at the narrow sidewalk
Saturday afternoon in Reelton, Alabama,
thinking how his mother
while a young girl
working for Judge Stinson
bore a child that died
how his oldest sister
was known to be intimate

with the mayor's son
and how only last night
his youngest sister
coming home alone
was raped by three white men
and the sheriff
merely asked how much she got
Nicodemus Perry
was shot and fatally wounded
by several corner loiterers
who said something about "assault"
as he bumped smack into
a white woman.

VII. Mrs. Clifton Townsend

High yellow and snobbish
Proud of her family and color
Was Mrs. Clifton Townsend
Of Nashville, Tennessee,
For in her veins
Flowed the blood of Senator Withers
(Her maternal grandmother
Was productively seduced)
Thus this lady's marriage
To Dr. Townsend
Equally yellow and ancestored
Had satisfied the families of both
As did the birth
Of their near-white daughter, Angeline,
Who was trained to follow tradition
And eventually mated legally
With young Anthony Monroe
(A secret descendant
Of Governor Windsor)
Who could pass for Nordic any evening.

It was not childbirth
In her forty-second year

That took the life
Of Mrs. Clifton Townsend
But shame at bearing
Through inconsiderate Nature
A penny-brown son ...

VIII. Editor Ralph Williamson

For twenty racing years
As editor of
The weekly *News-Protest*
Ralph Williamson
Had been a verbal swashbuckler
Waging unending battle
Against discrimination
In courts and public places
Jim Crow both North and South
Racial designations in
Columns of white papers
Fighting for an end
To the color question
And the treatment of black folk
As Americans instead of Negroes
Thereby building himself
A national reputation
As a great leader
And a respectable bankroll.

Given a testimonial banquet
Starting his twenty-first year
For "service to the race"
Ralph Williamson
Died of shock that same night
From the horrible dream
Of a perfect nation
Without prejudice or segregation
Racial complaint or color line
Thus causing the weekly *News-Protest*
Now with no excuse for being

To pass into nothingness
Hand in hand
With the editor's
Checking account and income . . .

IX. Frank Marshall Davis: Writer

> "He is bitter
> A bitter bitter
> Cynic"
> They said
> "And his wine
> He brews from wormwood"

I was black and black I always was

From the ebony house of me I watched days swing into weeks to months to
years

I hunted golden orchids where "All Men are Created Free and Equal"—and
my skin lay raw and sore from the poison ivy of discrimination and the
hidden brambles of Jim Crow

I say no sensitive Negro can spend his life in America without finding his cup
holds vinegar and his meat is seasoned with gall

A Mississippi manpack, mobbing bent, beat a tinpan bedlam when I would
pluck sweet airs from a Muse's harp

I aimed my eyes at the holy doors of a white man's church and I heard God's
Servant say "Niggers must be saved elsewhere"

While thousands cheered as the Governor of Georgia thundered "Stand pat
on the Constitution" I saw the hungry mouths of six-guns daring his
black folk to come to the polls and vote

I turned to what was called my own race . . . and I looked at a white man's
drama acted by inky performers

I was a weaver of jagged words
A warbler of garbled tunes
A singer of savage songs
I was bitter
Yes
Bitter and sorely sad
For when I wrote
I dipped my pen
In the crazy heart
Of mad America

Wormwood wine?
Vinegar?
Gall?
A daily diet—
But
I did not die
Of diabetes . . .

+7TH STREET

FRANK MARSHALL DAVI

47TH STREET

POEMS BY
FRANK MARSHALL DAVIS

The Decker Press
Prairie City, Illinois

I am a Negro writer.

A Negro is an individual who has been shunted aside for discriminatory treatment as an inferior because an ancestor is known to have been a dark African native. That is the only possible definition of Negro on the basis of science and actuality.

You see, Negroes do not belong to a distinct race because there is no such thing as a Negro or black race, just as there is no Caucasian or white race, and no Mongolian or yellow race. The so-called black race has blue eyed blonds who are lighter than the swarthy brunettes classed as members of the alleged white race. To call a blue eyed blonde a member of the black race is a monstrous absurdity to be expected only of the United States which boasts it has bigger and better everything, which automatically includes absurdities.

So when somebody points to a person of light complexion and asks, "Is that person Negro or white?" I reply, "If you can't tell, what's the difference?" Without giving an inch on race, I concede that a person classed as white gets certain considerations from our society that are vastly superior to the treatment accorded those people called Negroes. It's all right with me if he is so consti-tuted ethnologically to be able to choose between the two kinds of treatment.

Frankly, I should like to see the term, race, cast out of our language. The word itself, because of its implications, is a barrier to smooth relationships between individuals and groups. Tradition has grown so strong that when race is used, one automatically thinks in terms of people set apart from each other by ironclad, insurmountable barriers of physical differences, culture, and geography. Whether they know it or not, even the most militant orga- nizations weaken their cause when they call themselves "interracial" com- mittees or seek to battle "race" prejudice, for they call to mind the creature they would destroy and base their own existence upon the presence of some- thing that does not exist: race.

Science is, of course, pretty far ahead of the general public. But those seeking to combat racism and its attendant evils have got to keep abreast of science and use the ammunition furnished by science. It's rather silly to use slingshots when there are atom bombs available.

Our widespread belief in race goes back rather far and must be blamed on men who posed as scientists without having facts to back their theories. In the 1700's, the German, Karl von Linne, sought to divide people into such races as the Caucasian, Mongolian, Negro, etc., on the basis of skin color. The concept of race was created from his distorted imagination, strength- ened by others posing as scholars, and became the basis for what we call race prejudice.

Since then others have been destroying the Linnaeus misconceptions. In 1885 Unna discovered that variations in skin color were useful in adapting the individual to his environment. Wedding, in 1888, discovered and Char- cot confirmed that pigmentation is a protection against excessive radiation. Finsen in 1896 concluded that skin color was possibly originally induced by the sun. Evidence gathered by Sambson and Bailey supported the theory that pigmentation affords an efficient natural protection against the ultra-violet rays of the sun. Robert G. Stone pointed out in 1939 that pigment protects the body from overheating. Griffith Taylor maintained in 1937 that the logi- cal explanation of dark skin color seems to be that it is the result of expo- sure to the sun's heat. It is also common knowledge among scientists that an individual's color is determined by the amount of carotene and melanin present in his skin.

More recently Dr. Herbert L. Fleure, distinguished anthropologist and geographer of the University of Manchester, England, has offered to the world revolutionary concepts of color. He is convinced that climate, solar radiation, geographical location and prehistoric migration explain the shades of skin color among the peoples of the world.

With science throwing out color as a basis for classifying mankind accord- ing to race, what have we left? Surely not physical structure, for in the last half century research has shown that people with dark skin and kinky hair no more form a distinct group than do those with light colored eyes, hair or skin. Important differences have been discovered in the bony frame of body, limbs and head among the dark-skinned peoples as well as among the blonde peoples of northwest Europe. The pygmy of Africa has little in common except color with the six-foot Senegalese of the same continent.

Said Dr. Fleure in a lecture before the American Geographical Society delivered in April, 1945: "It may thus happen that successive drifts of mankind into an area, despite their diversities of inheritance, come to resemble one another to some extent in one or more characteristics. Groups with diverse origins as regards skull and skeleton may be dark skinned and kinky-haired, and people with light coloring may share the same inheritance of skull or skeleton with people of dark skin and kinky hair."

In other words, neither facts nor logic support the popular conceptions of race. The concept is basically political, the false barriers of race being utilized to justify the domination of an "inferior" by a "superior" group and discouraging an alliance between the exploited members of both. So long as the white mill worker can be led to believe in a racial superiority over the black sharecropper, or the Welsh coal miner over the Hindu, just so long will the imperialists and monopolists wallow in wealth while the millions of common people fight for pennies.

Although there is not one iota of evidence to substantiate beliefs in race, there are cultural differences between peoples, even those resembling each other physically. Norway, for example, differs from Germany in many of its customs, language, etc. While the French are not considered a "race," there has developed in the popular mind a definite conception of the "typical" Frenchman.

At the same time, it should be obvious that a black Negro and a blonde Caucasian of middle class homes reared in Seattle would have more in common in all ways, other than that of color, than would a white boy reared in Phoenix, Arizona, and a white youth brought up in Antwerp, Belgium, even though both belong to the same "race."

And yet knowing these things does not prevent my being a Negro writer. Living in the special circumscribed world set aside by the rest of America for those known to have had dark African forebears produces certain distinct ways of thinking. I am not an escapist running to an ivory tower to blot out life. I am not an embittered black nationalist. I am a realist, and so I write primarily of the impact of discrimination upon me and the others singled out for this specialized treatment. But since I am also one of the common people, and realize that this specialized treatment is a way of keeping us divided for continued domination by the economic rulers of the world, I write of all the common people, even though I know that many of another color and culture in their confusion consider me foe instead of friend.

There are, of course, writers of dark African ancestry who are not Negro writers, for they were not victims of the treatment meted out in America. But had Pushkin of Russia, Dumas of France or Browning of England lived in America with Senator Bilbo and the Jim Crow system, they, too, would have been primarily Negro writers.

America will have Negro writers until the whole concept of race is erased.

47th Street

From hollow backs
Of uneasy packhorse buses
Whinnying nervously
At 47th Street intersections
In Chicago's Congo
Caucasian faces peer momentarily
In curious contempt
Then turn back to "Orphan Annie," "Popeye"
News of the juiciest murders
Or bargain basement sales
Unconsciously sure of superiority
Within furnished apartment minds
As the green buses snort
From gasoline spurs
Then gallop on.

But a new moon
Lingering longer
Sees the spotted soul
Of this straining street.

I have watched a new moon crawl
Like a pale and eager child
To a lean building
And rest its white face
On the creased dark edge
Then look in platinum wonder
Upon the restless canal
Of 47th Street below
Flowing in mathematically precise channels
Between cement walks.

⌐⌐

A human kaleidoscope
Spins dizzily
From soot black to cotton light—
A rainbow race is this
Flung bold and sure
Against dusk-kissed fronts
Of glass eyed stores;

There is gladness here
And suffering
In these revolving faces—
Faces of easy lovin' gals with public bodies
Of giggling fearful virgins
Of ancient angled women whose passion died unused
Of two timin' wives creeping back from their lovers
Of the contented mate who locked her sex at home;
Faces of gambling men and preachers
Of pigfaced pimps and hogpursed physicians
Of beaten men hauling dead minds in two-legged tombs
And of pale and paunchy merchants;
Faces, waves of faces
In them the bold black pride of Africa
The restless upward surge of Europe
The moody mystery of America's Indians
Now wedded
By the constant catalyst of copulation . . .
These faces float
Like assorted berries
Agitated
In the white milk
Of mazda light.

By the calendar
This girl is young;
By life itself
She is older than the crippled crone
Who now for yearning years
Has grieved her sweetheart's death on San Juan Hill.

Where the rays of the nearest light
Feebly fumble like an old man's hands
This girl stands
Waiting, beckoning,
Every move an invitation
For love at bargain prices;
The crimson gates of her lips
Swing open
Gaily gowned words dance out
"Daddy, let's me 'n' you
Get together now
It ain't gonna cost
More'n a coupla bucks
An' I could do you
So much good . . ."
Her pounding eyes
Drive deep into yours
Her body strains
At the frail bonds of clothes
As she would become
To you
Reincarnation in brown
Of Helen, Venus, Cleopatra—
But to this girl
You are merely cash in hand
An impersonal two dollars
To be collected
Then forgotten . . .

Mojo Mike's Beer Garden
Sits motionless on its haunches
Like a hazy hound
While the frisky fleas of frivolous folk
Hop back and forth.
In the open nest
Geometric eggs of bottles lie
Under the mother hen
Of watchful electric bulbs
Hatching broods of new dreams
Young strength for weary souls

At two bits a shot;
Inside
Garrulous gin gobblers
Fling tireless tubs of laughter
Through the open door—
Laughter red and ready
Laughter drenching dried faces
Of heedless passersby . . .

A barrister turned editor in the late 1920's
Breaking dotted monotony of ward politics
Parties, murders and other social notes
Flashed a slogan in his weekly sheet—
"Don't Spend Your Money Where You Can't Work"
Picket lines sprouted
And the concrete fist of the boycott
Walloped white business in the pocketbook plexus;
After awhile
They hired black clerks in 47th Street stores
And the pickets melted away
And the white proprietors grinned as cash returned
But they didn't forget this editor;
Already they'd snatched their ads away
Now they had downtown friends to do likewise.
Meanwhile
When people got their new jobs
They quit buying that paper
Because they didn't need it now;
Thus when all available jobs were gone
So were circulation and advertising
And the paper died
The editor changing back to law.
That was near two score years ago.
"Yeah, I remember that sheet,"
Said the black assistant chainstore manager yesterday
(He was hired in 1930)
"Too bad it had to close up
But I guess the fellow that ran it
Jus' didn't have no eye for business . . ."

Sam Roberts
Friend of any man
At five percent per month
Takes one last look around
Then locks in place
Defiant gates of blackened iron
Before bulging windows
Of his Imperial Loan Shop.
He leaves now
The store is empty—
If a morgue is empty—
For at night
Ghosts gather.
Diamonds, watches, cameras, guitars
Lonely clothes
Huddle dejectedly
Like friendless souls
Shadow blackened
In the crowded concentration camp
Of the pawnbroker's window
Silently dreaming of happier times.
This white gold ring
Recalls the hour it met
Trembling flesh of a bride's hand;
For twelve years it proudly spoke
The owner's wedded joy
And lived as a part of her body
But one day
Hard times broke in
The husband died, insurance money melted
Jobs she couldn't catch laughed at the widow
So one by one her possessions left
Until at last
Nothing remained but the ring;
For three days the woman lay
Chained to the spear-tipped rack of hunger
Then went to Sam's
And the ring clung to her finger
As would a sorrowing friend
At eternal parting—

Four dollars the widow got
To buy an option again on living.
That was five years ago
But this white gold ring remembers;
And each lonesome companion thing
Likewise lives again
Its better days
Calling forth old ghosts
To linger in the nightbound morgue
Of the Imperial Loan Shop . . .

"Five cents'll git you five dollars
A dime brings ten iron men
So gimme your gigs
An hope t' God you hits."
This man
Long and brown as an earthworm
Crawling familiarly
Into barbershops, poolhalls,
With pencil, pad, printed slips, jingling coins
Is a policy writer.
With him he carries
Hopes and analyzed dreams
Backed by pennies
Of the trusting many.
Of course
They placed bets on three numbers this afternoon, morning,
Yesterday, the day before, last year
With only a few winning more than experience
Yet still they play
Fearfully, cynically, eagerly—
        "You know
I'm in such hard luck
If I didn' take a gamble
After playin' this number so doggone long
It'd come out sho
Jus' t' spite me
Then where'd I be?"
        "I knows my gig
Ain't comin' out

But I figgers I may's well play
'Cause I'd throw this nickel away anyhow."
        "Lawd, I knows
I'm gonna hit
That gig I got's plenty hot
I done dreamed it las' night
An' it's sho comin' out today!"
The owners fatten
As players tighten notched belts
Cut down on children's milk
Dodge haunting landlords
And measure time by
Three sets of daily results;
But the writers
Swear their job's the last thin door
Between crime or the dole—
Be that as it may
There is nothing bigger
Along this straining street
Unless it be
Life and death itself . . .

Hawking sales, shows, dances
Or pointing out in over-developed letters
Special business services available
The sound truck
Injects shots of hottest jazz,
In the straight black arm
Of 47th Street.
(Louis Armstrong is a genius
Whoever heard of Leopold Stokowski?
A dozen Paderewskis
Are less than one Count Basie.
Give 'em the St. Louis Blues
And keep Le Miserere—
It's just another arrangement
Of the same eight notes
Anyway.)
Brown feet pound
To the razzy dazzy jazz

Torrid tunes
Fall like roarin' rain
After a quiet drought
Ruby rhythms
Form scarlet pools of notes;
Then the truck plods on
Music dwindles to a misty mist
And there comes again
An unconscious symphony
In the modern manner
Brass calls of taxicabs
Grinding bass of surface cars
Monotonous percussion of private autos
And the furry woodwind
Of talking, laughing,
Walking thousands . . .

╓╜

From the elevated railway platform
People are all head and waving arms with toes weaving back and forth be-
    neath hat brims
A human from a gutter level is big feet and grasshopper legs ending in a tiny
    twist of head
Bob Mitchell, Inc., sees each one as a ten dollar dress or a thirty dollar suit
    of clothes
Place a Hollywood director here and this street has ten thousand bit players
    of Liza the maid and Rastus the dancing singing clown
To a strange Gold Coast matron each male is a potential rapist disrobing her
    with his eyes, to the wandering Caucasian man each gal is an exciting hour
    in bed
And the hurrying Duskymerican sees only a lane with shifting obstructions
Yet these are the same people
All carrying the usual inventory of limbs, body, head, brain, big and little
    dreams duplicated in the Blackstone Hotel, Park Avenue, Piccadilly Cir-
    cus, Hong Kong
You choose your own perspective . . .

Remember in 1942 the dark waving wings of war
Remember a barrage of talk on corner, in barbershop, saloon

"I ain't mad at nobody I ain't seen. If I gotta shoot somebody, make it Ol' Man Cunningham down in Mississippi an' I's ready. Wuhked on his plantation ten long yeahs with no payday an' when I left I owes him money"

"Hitler? I knows a dozen white men's worser'n Hitler just in Oglethorpe County, Georgia. Hitler ain't done nothin' to me"

"Well, I been cut off WPA, relief ain't nothing an' I ain't smaht enough t'land a defense job. If I can eat regluh an' don't hafta dodge no landlawd, I'd take a chance on fightin' Mistuh Christ"

"Th' white folks started it, so let the white folks end it. If Uncle Sam don't know me in peace, I don't know him in war"

"Sure, I'll go over an' fight. These white folks here's bad enough without takin' a chance on some more I ain't never seen lickin' America an' moving in"

"Don't know much 'bout them Japs, but they did kill some black boys at Pearl Harbor. If this country's fightin' 'em I'm fightin' 'em too"

"They oughta get a switchblade brigade so's I c'n be captain"

"You c'n tell 'em two peoples ain't goin' to no wah. That's me an' whoevah they sends aftah me"

"They got me in 1917. Said somethin' 'bout making the world safe fo' democracy. I knows that's bull, but if they still got the same kind of gals ovah theah now, damn if I won't go again"

"I ain't fightin' until I find something to fight for. I ain't doing nothing until they moves the wah over heah and starts droppin' bombs on 47th Street and South Parkway"

⌐⌐

Do you want to know
Why Joe Adams, Negro
Sat this one out
Under government orders
With the notation—
"Draft Dodger"?
It's like this:
After Pearl Harbor
He boiled for battle
But they wouldn't enlist him
"Go home and wait on your draft board"
The recruiting officer said;
Same day he got his call
He saw a morning paper cartoon

An article in the evening paper
And heard two radio commentators
Proclaim
"This war with Japan—
"It's white against the yellow race."
Then Joe Adams remembered
For twenty-seven years
America never let him forget
The cocoa brown of his skin,
And that he knew no ancestors
Traceable to Nippon;
The flame of fight therefore died out
Doused by waves of logic
And he remained
At home.

The Jew and the Negro should know each other
Since most of the stores are in Hebrew hands
Thus forcing a black observance of Yom Kippur;
Even the business of saving souls
The process of salvation selling
Of peddling passes to heaven
In the storefront church
Beside the Kosher delicatessen
Revolves about a Jew named Jesus . . .

Attorney J. Tyler Brooks sits at midnight weighing his bank balance against
    unpaid bills
When Attorney J. Tyler Brooks began practice twenty summers ago he end-
    ed his first year with a $900 income and many small debts
Today Attorney J. Tyler Brooks counts his annual collections in five figures
    and keeps many large debts
Attorney J. Tyler Brooks and his society mate could keep up with the Jones-
    es if the Joneses didn't try to keep up with the Williamses . . .

⌐⌐

Where the street like a straight gray vine
Grows across the busy trellis
Of South Parkway

Young men stand on warm nights
At the four corners
Like bunches of dark grapes
The wine press of conversation
Forcing a ready juice of words
From ripened lips.
Sidewalks stagger
Under the load of shifting feet
Lighted stores call like prostitutes
Soliciting the sailor trade;
Sleek as proud cats
The gals slink by
Hurling fashionable hips
Into male consciousness.
Eyes take quick inventory
And the little groups of men
Return each to its vocal world
Discussing newest styles from *Esquire*
Reigning kings of the baseball field
And whether it really pays
To trust a woman.
"Man she sho was a killer . . ."
"You coulda fooled me . . . "
"Ain't none of you cats got a bottle? . . . "
"Then I looks around and sees her old man . . ."
"Tip it, Chick, you's too fat to fly . . . "
"That ain't no chick, that's a full grown hen . . ."
"That broad's got a form outta this world . . ."
"Form? That ain't no form, that's a plantation . . ."
"She may be mellow but you c'n have her, Jack. I ain't dealin' in no mo'
    coal. It ain't mellow unless it's yellow, and when it's white it's right . . ."
"Boy, d'you call that thing a drape? Wait 'till I get my new double breasted
    front out Sat'day . . ."
"An' I says, 'Baby you c'n stay, but that noise has got t' go' . . ."
"Man, did I pitch a drunk las' night . . ."
"Lemme hold a buck a coupla days? . . ."
"Not unless you got ruffles on yo drawers. Or gimme yo right eye . . ."
"I tol' her I wasn't puttin' out nothin' but the light . . . "
"I'm gonna quit shootin' craps . . ."
Until well past midnight

Unless moved by cussing cops
The young men stand
On motionless parade
One face coming, another going
Laughing, talking, ogling, joking
Each a part of the whirling scene
Each eating life like an apple
Each ruled by only three desires
Money . . . women
And stacks of mellow nights
Along this dusty Nile
Of Chicago's Congo . . .

Dr. Richard Martin
Keeps an office suite of four large rooms
And a properly fumigated mind
Stored with ready made ideas
From bargain counters of Sunday paper supplements
On matters nonmedical
And moves about
As success animated.
He is conveniently Republican or Democrat
But definitely anti-Communist
Since, among other things,
He believes Communists cannot pay for his services.
He has prepared learned papers
For medical societies, journals
And demonstrated new clinical methods
Wildly applauded by both races;
Dr. Martin has banked
Plenty of What it Takes
And has watched his Position in Life
Rise in direct proportion
To his evidence of wealth
And Caucasian acceptance
When he personally drove a Model T Ford
None noticed him;
Today he has a chauffeur
Handling a long yellow dragon of a car
And the street knows him a block away

The street waves his name as a banner
Shouting to the rest of Chicago
"He's got money, reputation, ability;
This shows all we need is a chance
And we'll equal anything
The white man does . . ."

Maybe this is the promised land
Elsewhere they say Opportunity knocks but once. In Chicago Opportunity
    bangs loud enough to rouse the family in the flat below, leaves a calling
    card, then telephones next day to learn whether you got it
There is that one who could not vote at home in Alabama. From his law office
    on 47th Street he went to Washington as a congressman from Illinois
Or consider this one from Iowa who served 60 days in the county jail for
    stealing a ten cent loaf of bread. He is now in Joliet for 20 years after a
    thousand dollar robbery of a 47th Street currency exchange
This is a street of bigger and better things . . .

⌐⌐

This street is a woman of bulging bust and ready hips
Many scars cover her body, for the Depression was a cruel lover
Her breath shouts of gin, for she and the taverns live as man and wife
Speak to her softly, and she will tell of her dark children who have grown
    hard and strong as any others in this broad city from the thin milk of
    her brown breasts
Roar at her, and she will answer with a thousand curses
I have seen her with ragged apron and torn underskirt reeling crazily
    along on Sunday morning
And . . . also
I have seen her walk with cultured pride shaming the little pale debutante
    streets into slovenly slatterns
Whatever you ask of her, she will give.

Snapshots of the Cotton South

Listen, you drawing men
I want a picture of a starving black
I want a picture of a starving white

Show them bitterly fighting down on the dark soil
Let their faces be lit by hate
Above there will stand
The rich plantation owner, holder of the land
A whip in his red fist
Show his pockets bulging with dollars spilled
From the ragged trousers of the fighting men
And I shall call it
"Portrait of the Cotton South"

⌐⌐

Co'n pone, collard greens, side meat
Sluggish sorghum and fat yams
Don't care who eats them
The popping bolls of cotton
Whiter than the snobbish face
Of the plantation owner's wife
Never shrink in horror
At the touch of black cropper's hands.
And when the weevils march
They send no advance guard
Spying at doors, windows
Reporting back
"This is a privileged place
We shall pass it by
We want only nigger cotton."

Death
Speeding in a streamlined racing car
Or hobbling on ancient crutches
Sniffs at the color line;
Starvation, privation, disease, disaster
Likewise embarrass Social Tradition
By indiscriminately picking victims
Instead of arranging
To visit white people first
Black folk later—
But otherwise

Life officially flows
In separate channels.

⌐⌐

Chisel your own statue of God.
Have him blonde as a Viking king
A celestial czar of race separation
Roping off a Jim Crow section
In the low lying outskirts of heaven
Hard by the platinum railroad tracks
Where there will dwell for eternity
Good darkies inferiority-conscious
Of their brothers and sisters
In the Methodist Episcopal Church
Or
Have him a dealer of vengeance
Punishing in hell's hot fires
Lynchers, quick trigger sheriffs,
Conniving land owners, slave driving overseers
While today's black Christians
Look down at their endless torture
Then travel the golden streets of paradise
To the biggest mansions
In the best districts
And there feast themselves
On milk and honey
As say the preachers
In the little colored churches.

⌐⌐

Of course
There is no intermingling socially
Between the races
Such is absolutely unthinkable
Oh my yes
Still
At regular intervals

The wife of Mobtown's mayor
Sees an Atlanta specialist
For syphilis contracted from her husband
Who got it from their young mulatto cook
Who was infected by the chief of police
Who received it from his washerwoman
Who was made diseased by the shiftless son
Of the section's richest planter
One night before
He led the pack that hanged
The black bastard who broke into
A farm woman's bedroom—
But
As was mentioned before
There is no intermingling socially . . .

Neither Socialist nor Communist lingers here.
The Southern Tenant Farmers Union
Is a Grave Menace
Here we have Democracy at its best
Amid "native Americans"
"Bedrock of the nation"
Untouched by "The Foreign Element"
They have "Rugged Individualism"
"Any man may be President"
"Equality of Opportunity"
Which, translated means
The rich men grow richer
Big planters get bigger
Controlling the land and the towns
Ruling their puppet officials
Feeding white croppers and tenant farmers
Banquets of race hate for the soul
Sparse crumbs for their thin bodies
Realizing
The feast of animosity
Will dull their minds
To their own plight.

So the starving po' whites
Contemptuous of neighboring blacks
Filled with their pale superiority
Living in rotting cabins
Dirt-floored and dirty
Happy hunting ground of hookworm and vermin
Overrun with scrawny children
Poverty sleeping on the front stoop
Enslaved on islands of rundown clay
And to the planter-owned commissaries;
Dying, then dumped into the grinning graves
Their worm-picked bones resting silently
In a white burial ground
Separated even in death
As were their fathers before them.

No matter what the cost in taxes
Sacrificed by penniless croppers
Unmissed by money grabbing land owners
There must be separate accommodations
And public institutions
For each race.
Impoverished white schools
Loosing tidewaters
Of anti-Negro propaganda
While the fallen-in buildings
For black children
Have courses in Manual Arts,
Writing, and a little figuring
In between cotton picking and sowing
And of course
Care must be taken
By public officials
Not to make jails too strong
And thus inconvenience
The hungry lynchers.

Now
There are some who say
Voteless blacks never get

A proportionate return of taxes paid
But since so many
Land in the hoosegow
On copyrighted charges
And the county pays their keep
In stockade, on chaingang
They really use their share
Of public funds—
The arithmetic and logic
Are indisputable.

⌐⌐

At sunrise
Into the broad fields they go—
Cropper, tenant, day laborer
Black and white—
Leaving behind
Shacks of logs and rough planks.
Arching their crooked backs
Slowly, like long mistreated cats,
They throttle the living cotton
Hustle it, dead and grayish white,
Into the gaping sacks
Portable tombs
For the soft body
Of the South's Greatest Industry—
While, nearby,
Overseers stand
Throttling the living souls
Of the broken workers
Choking their spirit
Until
Worn out and useless
They are crammed into
The waiting earth—
Another industry
Of the Cotton South . . .

Well, you remakers of America
You apostles of Social Change
Here is pregnant soil
Here are grassroots of a nation.
But the crop they grow is Hate and Poverty.
By themselves they will make no change
Black men lack the strength
Po' whites have not the vision
And the big landowners want Things As They Are.
You Disciples of Progress
Of the Advancing Onward
Communist, Socialist, Democrat, Republican
See today's picture—
It is not beautiful to look upon.
Meanwhile paint pots drip over
There is fresh canvas for the asking.
Will you say,
"But that is not my affair"
Or will you mold this section
So its portrait will fit
In the sunlit hall
Of Ideal America?

Pattern for Conquest

Across arched backs of tawny mountains
Crouching in leonine lethargy,
Into the buxom valleys beyond
Holding unknown black broods in their lush laps
Went the missionaries
Hawking yarns of a strange and peaceful religion.
Soon there followed the traders
Hungry for a hand in the rare riches,
Giving baubles for bullion
Alcohol for amethysts
Constructing new desires
Among the naive natives.

And then the people, awakening,
Saw their land was no longer theirs
And, rebelling,
Sought to sever tightening tentacles
Of the reaching corporations.
It was then the soldiers came
From the outraged motherland
To save white missionaries and traders
From unappreciative savages.
They beat bows with bullets
And handed the women a new freedom
Thus completing the gamut
Of God to gin to gonorrhea
Gaining another victory
For civilization and culture.
Glory be to empire!

Black Weariness

I am tired this night
I shall go alone to Mojo Mike's Cafe and bathe my body in high breakers of
    hot jazz flung tableward . . . molten notes falling in a crimson spray
I shall sink my soul in warm whiskey while the light-scarred night roosts
    nervously on the quivering limb of 47th Street in Chicago's Congo
For these hours I can forget that I am black

At school I honed my mind against sleek sides of white ideas
Mine was a leather covered silence in a room of chintz and red plush sound
    as I packed my bag with silver bits of knowledge
Later I learned these sparkling morsels gave little strength as I fought across
    burning sands of a Nordic land
Some I have thrown away
Others I shall guard as priceless treasure until the rattlesnake bite of death
    for some day yet I may have need of them
Although I move as one disgraced, outlawed by this my land for being black,
    I shall lift proud feet and walk by day past sneering townspeople return-
    ing blow for blow until my strength flees and I collapse in utter exhaus-
    tion

I would joyously use these silver bits of knowledge helping my white broth-
ers build America into America
But when gifts are flung back hard into the face of the giver and the hand
extended is seized and crushed between mailed fists what is there left but
fighting?

I am tired this night
My arms hang weary from battle
For these few hours
At Mojo Mike's Cafe
I shall forget civilization
I shall forget color, caste
I shall move in a fantastic world of raceless men and women
So that tomorrow
Refreshed by this wild dream
Goaded by this vision of America as America
I may go forth again
Fighting, fighting
Ever fighting
Until I am no longer one apart
Until they call to me as I tread our streets:
"Hello, Brother
"Hello, American!"

Egotistic Runt

Busy streets are a shifting pattern of assorted faces like a crazy juggler's
balls
There are old faces and new faces and tired faces and happy faces and
white faces and black faces and faces blank as a frosted mazda lamp
Each face tags a body
Each body tags—what?
Buy his clay from a chemist for several cents
Hire any one of a billion billion spermatazoa for nine months
Put 'em together
Take away a Lincoln, a Shakespeare, a Caesar, a sewer cleaner
Another copy of man, the egotistic runt
Flesh, bones, blood and thought

Struggling dancer
To a cosmic jazz.

One face strung to one body
Each steps proudly about
Not caring that he is
Condensation of matter about him
Atoms into elements into compounds
Born of yesterday's decay, disintegration
Fed, kept alive by grabbing other atoms
Moving, being for a day . . . several years . . . maybe a century
Then back to soil
Himself disintegrated, to atoms returning
His borrowed dust a fragment of Earth's bulk

His seconds of birth, growth, aging and death but a moment in man's history
Man almost a stranger to this sphere
Our planet new beside the bearded sun and barely a millionth part thereof
Nearby stars shaming our sun in size and antiquity
They together merely another solar system
Our constellation a foundling midget beside the hoary Goliaths of the universe
This universe holding its nebulae and stars like a dried leaf in the wide green palm of the ocean
Yet man, the egotistic runt, swaggers on
No known counterpart elsewhere in creation
Perhaps an undiscovered freak
Hiding, like an unseen bacillus,
In the body of All There Is
Fought by nature
Marooned at an atom called Earth
Beloved of disease
Wooed by flood, tornado, fire
Sweetheart of death and destruction
From dust arisen—to dust returning
But
Proud of his microscopic accomplishments
Glad for his fleeting kiss of life
Fighting for bread and air

Hating his brother runts
Slaughtering in games called war
Terming himself straw-boss of the universe
Too puffed to believe he can ever die—really
Thereby building heaven and hell for eternal use
Changing his fears and pleasures
Painting the process with a phrase named Progress of
    Civilization
Shrinking from death by his own contraptions of motor cars,
    airplanes, revolvers, while contemptuous of ancestors
    fearing brontosauri, dragons, flint tipped arrows
Talking, strutting, bragging
Living, dying
On a speck of mud
Invisible from the closest star.

Faces of today, tomorrow, yesterday
Uncounted, forever shifting
Tired, fresh, young, old, yellow, brown
Each face tagging a body
Each body that of man, the egotistic runt
Struggling dancer
To a cosmic jazz . . .

Chicago Skyscrapers

Here in this fat city
Men seventy-two inches short
Have frozen their dreams
Into steel and concrete
Six hundred feet high

Thin fingers
On the hard hand
Of Chicago's Loop
Are these skyscrapers
Rubbing bright sides
Of rainbow stars
Tearing the gray gauze

Of low clouds
Dipping in the sizzling pot
Of a summer sun
Passing the jeweled moon
From tower to tower
Like a sapphire ring

While below

The masters move
Dreaming greater dreams
Of taller buildings
Turning today's longest fingers
Into dwarf-like thumbs
Constantly pushing
Evolution in stone
Until some day
Heaven will be
Merely another high floor
Barked by a uniformed boy
On an express elevator
Then
A cranky god
Jealous of his privacy
May bend the fingers downward
Toppling tall dreams frozen
In steel and concrete
Upon the puny dreamers
Grinding all into
A chaos of blood and stone

But
Remembering the Tower of Babel
Even that would not
Discourage other builders
The tireless breed who dream
In iron and granite . . .

Tenement Room

Bruised and battered
By the dark silent hammers of night
The day creeps
Slowly
From the tired room.

Dirt and destitution
Lounge here in gaudy tatters
Through the bright hours
Forever shouting
Its bony nakedness—
A crippled table, gray from greasy water;
Two drooping chairs, spiritless as wounded soldiers shoved into a prison
    hole;
A cringing bed, age-weary;
Corseted with wire squats a flabby stove;
In the corner slumps a punished trunk rescued from Jake's Second Hand
    Store;
Through the lone window, broken-paned, spills light and weather on the
    dust-defeated and splintering floor—
Only night muffles
Those visual cries
Of the despairing room

The dusk
Lays a soothing hand
On its whimpering poverty
Even the solitary gas jet
Eases its quivering runners
Of chromium light
Along quiet surfaces
As
Exhausted
The room sleeps dreamlessly . . .

Four Glimpses of Night

I

Eagerly
Like a woman hurrying to her lover
Night comes to the room of the world
And lies, yielding and content
Against the cool round face
Of the moon.

II

Night is a curious child, wandering
Between earth and sky, creeping
In windows and doors, daubing
The entire neighborhood
With purple paint.
Day
Is an apologetic mother
Cloth in hand
Following after.

III

Peddling
From door to door
Night sells
Black bags of peppermint stars
Heaping cones of vanilla moon
Until
His wares are gone
Then shuffles homeward
Jingling the gray coins
Of daybreak.

IV

Night's brittle song, sliver-thin
Shatters into a billion fragments
Of quiet shadows
At the blaring jazz
Of a morning sun.

To Those Who Sing America

Well, gentlemen
You flag wavers
You rabble rousers
You who ask that I sing America
On patriotic occasions—
Here is one question:
What do you know of the song you chant?
You begin
"My country! 'tis of thee"
But here the patter ends.
Gentleman,
Haven't you forgotten
Something?

⌐⌐

"My country! 'tis of thee . . ."
(On the shores of this, my country, dwell Plenty in a forty-room mansion
and Poverty in a one-room hovel . . . a nation turned prostitute for the
fat pimps of Politicians and Captains of Industry . . . Sundays all rise to
serve a crippled Nordic God . . . His torn-out eyes replaced by dollar
signs . . . His belly bloated with the greasy gravy of the Profit System . . .
His spindly shanks molded from the spavined bones of the hungry work-
ers . . . His doddering frame supported by the props of Federal Dole and
Government Subsidy . . . this is my country with the star spangled robe
snatched away)
"Sweet land of liberty . . ."
(Do you remember Sacco and Vanzetti in Boston, Tom Mooney in Califor-
nia, nine Scottsboro boys in Alabama?)
"Of thee I sing; . . ."
(Yes—with words approved by the Daughters of the American Revolution,
Ku Klux Klan, American Legion and Boards of Censors of forty-eight
states)
"Land where my fathers died! . . ."
(While strong-arming the Indian owners . . . starving to fill money sacks of
Mistermorgan, Misterdupont, Mistermellon . . . human guinea pigs test-
ing crazy social systems)
"Land of the Pilgrims' pride! . . ."

(The Pilgrims, gentlemen, had not seen my country as a land of peons down
  South, wage-slaves up North . . . her wooded hills stripped to stony na-
  kedness by lumber corporations . . . signboards selling beer and bunion
  cures blocking her native scenery . . . lynched black bodies swaying from
  trees in a morning breeze)
"From ev'ry mountain side . . . "
(Including airy skyscraper and penthouse for the few, disease cradling tene-
  ment for the many)
"Let freedom ring!"
(Although the rich are counting dividends and dodging income taxes while
  the poor are scrambling for crumbs dropped from the Table of Capital-
  ism, let us hush . . . the Politicians and Professional Americans wish to
  lift their voices in song)

 ⌐⌐

We shall stop here
My flag waving friends
You don't remember
The other verses
Anyway . . .

Peace Quiz for America

(To Be Read Aloud by Eight Voices)

Leader: Who am I?

1st Voice: I am Crispus Attucks in Boston dying to give birth to America

I am Peter Salem stopping Major Pitcairn at Bunker Hill

I am John Johnson at Lake Erie, my lower limbs shot away, shouting "Fire away, my boys, no haul a color down!" I am 109 black sailors on whom Commodore Perry staked full trust

2nd Voice: I am Robert Smalls delivering my boat from the vest pocket of the Confederacy to the Union and freedom

I am the Tenth Cavalry rescuing Teddy Roosevelt at San Juan Hill in Crimson Cuba

I am Needham Roberts and Henry Johnson, first of the battling Yanks decorated by France for bravery under fire

3rd Voice: I am Dorie Miller at Pearl Harbor shooting down four Jap planes with a machine gun you never let me fire before

I am that one American in ten you have always depended on when trouble batters down the front door

Leader: Surely, you remember me

I am Roland Hayes slugged by police on the streets of Rome, Georgia

I am one of nine Scottsboro boys still rotting in Kilby prison in Alabama

I am Cleo Wright lynched at Sikeston, Missouri, while you cried for national unity in the face of Jap savagery

I am men and women murdered by police in Detroit, chased from my shipyard jobs in Mobile, creeping back by morn to my burned and looted homes in Beaumont

I am soldiers wearing your uniform beaten and killed down South without a chance to leave the fatherland and fight for continuation of this same American way of life

1st Voice: I am Paul Robeson singing "Ballad for Americans" through loudspeakers of radios all over the nation

A Woman: I am Marian Anderson, denied the use of Constitution Hall, thrilling Washington with "The Star Spangled Banner" in the open air at the Lincoln Memorial

Leader:	You have seen me barred from the polls in ten thousand towns and have given me nothing but tissue paper words
	You have seen me crowded six to a room in the covenant-fenced ghettoes of Chicago and denied the right to live in homes my taxes built in Detroit.
1st Voice:	When you cried aloud for more workers I rushed to your factory doors armed with Executive Order 8802 and escorted by the Fair Employment Practices Committee but still I was turned back by those who would rather fight me than whip the Axis
Chorus:	I am the American Negro
	I sent my soldier sons proudly into a Jim Crow army for America is the only home I know
	My young died to restore freedom to oppressed peoples of the world for who understands better than I the hurt of the aggressor's heel ground into the face
	I am he who traditionally gives you hundred percent support from fifty percent citizenship

⌐⌐

Leader:	Are these the Four Freedoms for which we fought?
	Freedom from want
Voice:	("So sorry but we don't hire Negroes. Our white employees won't work with you. The union, you know")
Leader:	Freedom from fear
Voice:	("Nigger, take off yo' hat and say 'sir' when you speak to a white man in Arkansas. A smart darky down here's a curiosity—and sometimes we embalm curiosities")
Leader:	Freedom of religion
Voice:	("Of course you can't come in here! This is a white church")
Leader:	Freedom of speech
Voice:	("We gits along with ouah niggers, so unless you want to leave here feet first don't be putting none of them Red social equality ideas in their minds")

Leader: Did you hear about regimentation in Washington?
            Ten men to run World War II
            A hundred to ration black participation

⌐⌐

1st Voice: Uncle Sam, Uncle Sam
               Why did you send me against Axis foes
               In the death-kissed foxholes
               Of New Guinea and Europe
               Without shielding my back
               From the sniping Dixie lynchers
               In the jungles of Texas and Florida?

⌐⌐

Leader: During World War II
               Down in Georgia a soldier said:
2nd Voice: "Me? I'm from Paine County, Alabama
               "Born black and I'm gonna die the same way
               "Went t'school three yeahs befo' it rotted down. By the time th'
                  w'ite folks got around t'fixing it my first wife had done died
               "But you oughta see my brothah. Finished State Teachuh's Col-
                  lege an' now he's making forty dollah uh month back home.
                  That's ovah half uh what they pays white teachuhs
               "Been helpin' Pappy work the same fifty acres fo' Mistuh Jim his
                  own pappy had. Pappy bought a single barrel shotgun from
                  Mistuh Jim five yeahs ago. Paid ten dollahs down an' a dol-
                  lah a week an' he still owes twenty mo'
               "Sheriff came 'roun' and tol' me they wanted me in the army.
                  Came heah to Fort Benning an' they give me a gun and a
                  uniform an' three good meals a day. Fust time I evah knowed
                  a white man to give me anything
               "This mawnin' I heard somebody on a radio say we was all fight-
                  in' fo' democracy
               "Democracy? What's democracy?"

■   133

┌┛

Leader:	Nothing is so final as a bullet through heart or head
	And a correctly thrust bayonet is an unanswerable argument
	For democracy against fascism
	For Four Freedoms against oppression
	This you taught me in camps from Miami to Seattle
	To use against Nazi, Jap
	And it worked;
	It worked in the Pacific Islands
	In Africa, in Europe
	Everywhere it worked
	You have convinced me completely
	Even as I have become expert
	In killing the mad dogs
	Leaping high to tear
	Democracy's soft throat—
	And if that's the technique
	If it worked in lands I never saw before
	Against strangers with faces new to me
	Then it must be the right thing to use
	Against all foes of freedom
	Against all apostles of fascism
	Against some people I know
	Right here in America
Voice:	I know more about Bilbo than I do about Tojo
	I've read about Hitler but I have also lived in Georgia when Talmadge was governor
Voice:	Talk about Mussolini if you want to, but did you ever hear Rankin rave in Congress?
Voice:	To me the Black Dragon is just a foreign nightmare but I have been beaten and murdered by the Ku Klux Klan
Leader:	So since I went over to clean up the Rhine
	I might as well include the Mississippi—
	With the understanding
	Of course
	That it will be only
	For democracy against fascism
	For Four Freedoms against oppression—

Say, Uncle Sam,
Are you sure you wanted me to have a gun?

┌┘

Chorus: Do you get it America?
If you take my brown sons to fight abroad for democracy then I
   have a right to expect it here
If you're going to carry the Four Freedoms all over the world you
   may as well start at home
If you want me to help crush fascism and oppression I want no
   distinction between foreign and home-grown brands

Leader: I know the glib guys were selling slogans
I know some top Britishers said this was a war to keep their em-
   pire intact
I know some people wanted to whip the Japanese for ever dar-
   ing to think they were as good as whites
I know some heavy investors sided with China because they'd like
   to keep 'em handy to exploit
I know some big shots were fighting to restore a 1930s world
I know some loudmouths rattled off sweet talk about human
   rights and world brotherhood and intended it as hogwash and
   I know there were some who saw me working and sweating
   and bleeding and dying and they said "You'd better you black
   bastard if you know what's good for you"
And it's up to the rest of us to set 'em right

Chorus: Do you get it, America?
Do you get it, Congress?

┌┘

Voice: Say, Mister, you with the white face, are you an American?
Where did you come from and when? France, Poland, England,
   Russia, Spain, Italy? Oh yeah? And how do you know some-
   body from Senegal never got mixed up in your family?

Leader: I know there are white Americans who want to be Americans,
   disciples of the square deal, lovers of the Constitution, believ-
   ers in raceless justice, equality
I've praised all 57 varieties of gods for Wendell Willkie, Eleanor
   and Franklin D. Give us enough guys like Henry Wallace and

we'll disintegrate Father Coughlin and Gerald L. K. Smith into friendless atoms

Voice: I know also that I have my dark Dillingers, my tinsel Tojos, my hybrid Hitlers for I've seen them loot stores in Detroit and Harlem, heard them hymn hate in Chicago's Congo, watched as they lynched opportunity in new jobs and public places, and I love them no more than you love your own pale troublemakers

Chorus: But what of the others, the worthy ones, millions of whites, millions of blacks, the common people, the workers, the doers, born under the same flag, dreaming the same dream of liberty and security, marrying and bearing children swaddled in similar dreams

Leader: These common people, the strugglers, why do they duel each other?

Why do they fight among themselves when there are bigger enemies? Why did the Detroit casualty list yield none but the names of the common people?

Voice: When white sharecropper rips the flesh of black sharecropper, who laughs and steals the shirts of both?

Who gains when white laborers bolt their union doors in the faces of their black brothers in toil?

Who loosed poison arrows at the Congress of Industrial Organizations for daring to recruit all workers in a raceless fraternity?

Does anybody clip bigger dividends in Wall Street when workers walk their separate ways?

Chorus: In a democracy the people run the country!

2nd Voice: What millionaire newspapers paint an idea Red because it would help the common people?

How much taxes go for costly sacrifices to the graven god of race prejudice?

Who walks to Congress across bowed backs of the quarreling masses?

3rd Voice: Who sold scrap iron to Italy to dump on Ethiopia, oil to the Japs to wing war planes over China?

How did "U.S. Steel Corporation" get on shrapnel extracted from Corporal Berowitz at Guadalcanal?

Chorus:	In a democracy the people run the country!
Leader:	Ideas slip together and a pattern forms.
	Hitler wrote:
Voice:	"America is a pushover. Get the races fighting among themselves and I can step in any old time."
Leader:	And Standard Oil in Texas gave pamphlets to white workers saying to join the CIO would mean social equality
	And Hirohito sent word to black men:
2nd Voice:	"Japan is the champion of all colored people. Stand ready to rebel."
Leader:	And a vice president at Packard got white labor to strike when Negroes were upgraded on assembly lines
	Who snipped this pattern? The common people?
Chorus:	In a democracy the people run the country?
Leader:	That's it!
	In a democracy the people run the country!
	Say, Mister, you with the white face, you toiler
	Come over here and let's talk.
	Maybe we both got the same disease
	But different symptoms;
	Mine pops out in humiliating race discrimination
	Yours is a rash of class distinction and poverty
	Coming from the same infection;
	Fascism and profit grabbing
	And we're both tired steppers to a dollar jazz.
Chorus:	In a democracy the people run the country!
	Who says we can't get along!
	We are the black workers and the white workers and all the workers
	We are the marching sweating fighting people
	We are the builders of America
	We are the keepers of America
	We are the breathing facts of democracy
	We are the people
	And in a democracy the people run the country
	Together we have whipped fascism in war
	Together we shall whip fascism in peace
	How about it, America?

For All Common People

Come here, you builders!
Gather these poor bones from the driven dead
Bring them from Sicily, Salamua, Stalingrad
Pile them as impersonal equals—
Jap, Chinese, Nazi, Communist, Negro, Nordic—
Crush these remaining selfless cells
Into gray brick;
Now take the robbed red blood
The red blood stolen by sudden bombs
In the martyred cities
And mix a pliant plaster
So that we may shape a tall tower
To mark the minds of those yet living;
A tower flying this flaming phrase:
"We who died never found our dream."

In what calm graves do the warlords snore?
Did any Russian sniper ever draw a bead on Hitler?
Has a mortar shell borne Tojo's name?
The Kaiser went in Holland, Napoleon on an island
And the munitions makers die of gout.

Soldiers kill one another without a formal introduction;
Maybe this farmer from Kansas could have liked the guy from Naples,
Who knows?
Each had identical inventories of heart, hands and head,
Maybe both liked ribald tales in a smoke-stuffed room,
Perhaps both had twin dreams for five rooms and a brood when peace
    fluttered home—
Who knows?
Your death was nothing personal, I assure you
But somehow you became part of a wrong idea which had to go.

Do common people beg for war?
Left alone would the people fight?
Who whams the drums of battle?
The people? Or the grafting global gangsters?
Sift each war and you claim this fact—

Plain John Smith who never thought harm to anyone got killed again in
    battle;
Plain John Smith, one of the people;
Plain John Smith, worker, toiler;
Plain John Smith from Chicago, London, Rome, Hamburg, Moscow, To-
    kyo, Hong Kong;
Plain John Smith, sucker for bullets and big talk;
Who will extend life for plain John Smith?
The people? Or the warmakers?
"This is the century of the common man" said Henry J. Wallace, his feet
    rooted in the strong soil of Iowa, his dreams rubbing the stars
So let it be
Let us the common people reclaim this earth;
We who are yellow in Asia, black in Africa, white in Europe, kaleidoscopic
    in the Americas;
We who have worked and fought and died to transfuse more power to the
    already powerful;
We who have been fed the burned bread of race hate to keep us apart;
We who have bloated our bellies on the brackish broth of superiority to
    others such as we;
We who are rival divers for pennies in a wide pool rich with handfuls of
    gold for everybody;
We who are the workers, the doers, the builders—
We the common people!

Let the common people smash all foes of the common people;
Let the people fade fascism to a sour memory,
Let the people snort goodbye to empire;
Prepare soundproof cells for the hating rabble rousers,
Plant the greedy in the earth they covet,
Chase the munitions makers to the poor house,
Spade soft soil over the warlords,
Sterilize the minds of all Hitlers from Berlin to Birmingham;
Then let us the people who never made this war mold a bomb-proof peace.
Let us build anew as brothers;
Let us walk as kinsmen;
Let us freeze a common dream;
Let us extend life for plain John Smith!
Are you ready, brothers?

War Zone

Must each junior generation be boiled in war?
In what mental foxholes do the elders hide?

Bullets hum your lullaby, baby,
Bullets and the shouting bombs
Sleep, dear child—
None may now awaken you.

Young woman, you have found a new lover;
For you the sharp caress of the bayonet
Searing kisses from sudden incendiaries
And in your yearning ears
Hear only the wild whispers
Of hunting machine gun slugs.

This is not nearly so sweet, soldier,
Walking with Death's right arm around you
As strolling with Eva or Troisha or Mu Lin
And knowing that none of the restless stars
Is a tracer bullet rushing your name.

The tired old women
And the tired old men
Have a rendezvous with the grave anyway;
Life is a fraying thread
And War wields sharp scissors
But few petition for the cutting.

This was not the first time
War has taken your guest room
And neither five-day notice
Nor the sheriff's men
Could put him out.
Each time War brings
New kinds of raiment:
Remember when War wore
A lion's skin and a stone axe?
Or when he came clothed

In bright armor and a bow and arrows?
Recall him dressed
In leather leggings and a musket
Straight as a sergeant's command;
You have not forgotten
How he came back in 1914
With new ideas for a wholesale trade
And when they did oust him
There was a hammered promise
To keep War away forever;
But he returned again
Thundering in on a dive bomber
Rumbling to the door in a tank
And he is bigger, smarter—
War has learned exactly how
To hurt everybody at once.

You men of the village council
Is there still no way
To bar our gates to his coming?

Nothing Can Stop the People

Across the tall tight trail to brotherhood
The hot red fog of war
Crouched hydra-headed, many-handed,
Pressing sudden thumbs to straining eyes
Of the climbing people;
Hiding dangerous stones on this strange path
In wide fog pockets;
Shoving stumbling stragglers
Into the hungry crevices;
But still the climbing people climb!

"Go back, go back!"
Shouted three sadistic voices
Not long ago,
"This is our private path.
What right have you

To walk this way?"
They were Mussolini in Ethiopia, Spain;
Hitler in Austria, Czechoslovakia;
Hirohito in China, the Philippines;
And confusion danced among the climbers.
A raised umbrella
And Chamberlain hypnotized at Munich;
Savage echoes hurled hard and loud
At Detroit, Beaumont, Mobile, Los Angeles
"Go back, go back—"
The angry spray of crashing words
"What! Me be friends with a lousy Red?"
"Trade unions? To hell with organized labor!"
"Let 'em fight and do business with the winners.
Our oceans will keep 'em away."
Hear again the helpless cries of black soldiers
Shot by confident cops in the Southland
Crescendo prayers of beaten Jews in Boston, Chicago—
But still the climbing people climb!

In this wide space
The Smart Boys have dumped their dollars
To build a beckoning brothel
(Cartel Castle, the trade calls it)
With suave barkers
Supplied by the National Association of Manufacturers.
"Stop here and have your fun—
There's nothing up the mountain anyway . . ."
And the painted women lounge unclothed
Luring the poor suckers—
But still the climbing people climb!

Do you know the climbers?
They are ditch digger, truck driver, bank clerk, farmer
Waitress, schoolma'am, stenographer, scrub woman
The crowd at a Legion parade, the population swellers
The customer who is always right
Dear reader of your daily paper
They are who Senator Puffington represents at Washington

That sea of faces the speaker sees
They are Jane Doe, Joe Dokes
They are all the ordinary guys
From all the big nations
And all the little nations.
Some don't know where they're going
Some have heard there's a good fight at the next corner
So they shove along
Like when it's quitting time at the big mill.
Up front was somebody named Stalin
Another called Churchill
One known as Roosevelt
And a fourth called Chiang Kai-shek.
They all had pretty good helpers
But Churchill often turned to walk backward
A pack of dogs nipped at Roosevelt's heels
And Kai-shek stooped under a heavy and ancient sack.
It was hard to keep to the tall trail
With the hot red fog of war crouching there
So maybe it was a good thing
Stalin knew this familiar path.

Queer, how three sadistic voices
Believe they could stop a march
Curving the people back down the high mountain
By condensing the hot red fog of war
About the steep tight trail.
Yes, the people died
They fell at Stalingrad, Pearl Harbor,
London, Warsaw, Guadalcanal, Hong Kong
And more will tumble to numbered nothingness
Before the air clears.
But they keep pushing on
They keep tramping on
They keep climbing on
They keep driving on
Thunder-footed, shouting new songs
Drowning petulant chirps
Of Nationalist, Isolationist, Fascist

Buying newly packaged confidence
From the cosmic counters
Of the democratic dreamers.
There is nothing—
Fog nor rain nor flogging wind—
That can stop these climbing people!

I Bring Proven Gifts

The gifts I bring you
Beloved
Are not wrapped in cellophane
Factory-fresh and newly white;
Rather
They are old things
Gloss-departed, tinsel-tarnished
But still surviving hammering years—
By this you know
They cannot be fragile.

My lips have followed rainbow kisses and now have stopped content at the
     searing red gold of your own
My body sought then left the flesh of others but to reach the haven of your
     loveliness
The burning rose of your mouth consumes the whole of my desire
And I have built a new and final world
With my love for you.

Slimly straight
Untouched by calendar years
You are a bright new beacon
Shining above the huddled maze
Of discarded dreams;
You are the blinding sun
Shaming the penny candles
Of your sisters.

I think that I have prepared these years
For the day I should find you—
Living, loving, breathing, being
Ground between hard sides
Of experience
With but one aim—
Meeting you.

Now that I have found you
The trail ends
And I can never go;
I pile these proven gifts
At the feet of you—
A poet's heart trained strong
A lover's love grown to maturity
And the tested steel of living;
In your slim hands
I pile barren bones of past yearnings
For in your young eyes
Lies the soul of all women—
I cannot give you more
These are all I have.

Take them inside the scented room of you
Or toss them into the alley—
They are yours
And I shall no longer need them.

Lines to a Summer Love

So little time ago—
The nests of flown hours are still warm—
You were a gay stream flowing
Laughing with the satin sun
Playing make believe with a maiden moon
As I sat beside your beckoning banks
Tossing bright pebbles of words
Soothing tired man hands
Among your ready ripples.

Those were the soft days
The long languorous lilting days.

In May the pebbles spelled
"I love you, my darling."
In June, July, August,
September, October

And now November
They spelled
"I love you, my darling."

Two days ago I went again to you
Pebbles in my pockets
Tired man hands twitching;
But your banks were hard, unfriendly
The sun frowned and turned his face
And the moon was a drunken hag;
Not believing
I tossed the pebbles of words—
"I love you, my darling—"
And they bounded back
To the unyielding banks
And my fingers blanched
At just the nearness.

Yes, beloved
I know this is November
Month of the dying
Time of the entombed;
But my bright pebbles
Tossed into your gay waters
Were all I had of gold
All my wealth to me
And still you have them
Inside your frigid home.

Today I ask
Must I edge the steel of me
To split the frozen ice now you?

To One Forever Gone

For you I have built a shrine of scented memories—
Turquoise, ruby and moon yellow;
A gay bright jewel of a shrine
Raised radiantly

Above rain-gray ruins
Of aged crumbled dreams . . .

Within these rainbow walls is all that I have left of you.
I go there silently and alone
And kneel, my head bared,
Burning ten brown candles
For each day we had together;
Touching each treasure softly
With the thin fingers of my mind;
And suddenly you are with me
Violets in your hair, jasmine in your breath
'Though my eyes cannot find you
I know that I no longer kneel alone . . .

Ah, beloved!
Do you remember?
I think again of when first I heard you speak—
"Your voice is liquid platinum shimmering beneath a May moon,"
I said—
But was that yesterday
Or in some garden in old Babylon?

There is that moment when first you came close to me—
Head bending shyly back,
Opening your eyes very wide
(Stars playing at midnight in a mountain pool);
Your hair brushed across your cheek
Slowly, as if each strand were alive
And wanted lingeringly to caress the flesh of you;
Your lips flowered into a smile
(Rose petals parting for a morning sun);
Your face was velvet and bright gold;
Suddenly the dam within me broke
And you were swept before wild waters—
It was then that I first kissed you.
I kissed you as if the world had never known a kiss before
Your mouth was flaming honey and wine
Your fragrant body . . . close to me . . . trembled and burned
Burned the brand of you inside my naked soul;

Yielding no ashes, needing no fuel—
It shall blaze brightly
Until my last breath . . .

In this chest of sandalwood
I hoard my gleaming gems
Of your words to me—
I know each precious stone intimately.
This diamond glowing as the Northern Lights
Is when first you whispered "I love you."
Behold this sapphire—
"I shall be forever yours," you said;
This long rope of throbbing pearls—
Somebody's poem about somebody's hands
You read to me on a wind-whipped night
As we sat inside a darkened room
Watching a dowager moon
Chaperone flirtatious stars;
There are whole handfuls more
When I pour them back into this box
Reflections of their polished brightness
Dart like fireflies
Over my temple walls . . .

There are many icons
In the niches of my shrine.
There is the silver memory
Of Tchaikovsky's Pathetique Symphony
Trickling softly from the radio,
Thin floating gossamer veils
Spun from our cigarettes,
And tiny frosted glasses of vodka;
You lay curled
Between hungry but paralyzed jaws
Of the big armchair,
I sat on the floor near your feet.
We knew this was our last day together
Yet we lobbed the tennis ball of conversation
Back and forth
In tall lazy arches

As if this were the dawn of creation
And we had time to watch
The death of the universe—
It must have been
That our hearts were too hurt to dance . . .

I knew you long before I ever saw you,
I have known you through long dead broods of man.
Our names now and on torn pages of the past
Do not really matter—
I played Romeo to your Juliet
Lancelot to your Guinevere
Always minor changes in the plot
Even as now
But the basic story stands.
You and I have ended our roles in this revival
And have left the darkened stage
To go our separate ways—
When shall we meet again?
Ah, my darling!
Does not each fresh generation
Produce new audiences and actors?
I shall wear another tag
Perhaps "Paul," "John," or "Frederick"
You will be "Elaine" or "Martha" maybe
Yet still we shall know each other
We shall meet as old lovers
Scornful of calendars;
For such a little while
We will again re-live our love—
Then part—
Even as you and I this life
And I shall build anew
Under another name
Within some other year
A shrine of scented memories
As I have always done
For you.

To Lorelei

Your lips have turned to frozen flame
Fire to my eye but ice to the mouth of me;
Since the shimmering satin gown of your love
Has turned to frowsy tatters
Throw it aside for the old clothes man—
I do not want you dressed in passion's rags.

Yes, I remember
It was a lazy night in August;
A spendthrift moon tossed silver coins
Among waiting urchin trees above us
Some fell to where we sat and caught in your hair;
I meant to brush them away
But your eyes . . . so close to mine . . . reached inside my heart and freed
    my soul

Your parted lips were fire . . . myself a maudlin moth
I have burned, died, arisen from ashes a thousand times
Even as I watched the flame grow cold.

Not since that night have you been completely mine
And I think today it was not nearness but the newness of me;
I was an uncharted sea for your body's sailing
A new sacrifice for your altar of vanity—
That was all.

Then you became curious—
Was this really my heart you carried naked in your hand?
You gave it every test but it remained unchanged
At last, satisfied, you shoved it carelessly
Into an unused bureau drawer
And there it now reposes.

I shall not ask it back
It is of no further use to me;
Perhaps never again
Not for even one brittle moment
Will you carry it into the light

Turn it this way and that, examine the jagged scars;
Yet I shall not care.
For, no longer having my heart to give
I may now move
Stripped of vulnerability
Unmindful of injury
Treading with bold contempt
Among your sensuous sisters . . .

Life Is a Woman

Life is an ebony and ivory dreamer's dream of a woman and I am her help-
     less lover-slave
Today she holds me to her naked breast . . . bids me kiss her parted lips of
     honey'd flame . . . her perfumed breath becomes my own . . . her warm
     body trembles and clings to the brown flesh of me . . . she leaves me dazed
     and spent from the rainbow joy of utter-love
But this is for only a little while . . . a diamond fragment of time found in
     the wide valley of years
Short moments ago Life was a cruel mistress . . . laughing as I stumbled and
     fell over sudden stones in the strange black pathway she bade me tread . . .
     herself lashing my bleeding back as I faltered beneath the camel's load
     of a brown skin in a white world
This is the price of loving her . . . forty days of torturous wandering for one
     hour of worship within the ebony and ivory temple of her loveliness
Yet I know some day she will call me to her side . . . thrust the sharp dagger
     of death through my heart . . . silent and useless I shall fall at her feet . . .
     never-very-much returned to nothing-at-all . . . she will turn away in
     complete forgetfulness
Life is the almighty tyrant-queen
Life is a quarrelsome shrew
Life is a cruel mistress
Life is a beautiful dreamer's dream of a woman
And I . . . her helpless lover-slave . . .

Alone

Without you
The slow night stumbles
Under a pack of heavy hours;
From the fulsome emptiness beside me
Memories rise to dance
And then dissolve;
I have no shield to stay
The thin dark dagger
Of loneliness.

You Are All

With you
Time spaced in these four walls
Is my universe.
Stars sparkle in your voice
Seasons come and go as your moods change
Moonrise, sunset stems from the eyes of you
And I am content with the world you give me.
I knew no life before I met you
When you have gone I shall no longer exist.
Tonight
My darling
We shall love again
Alone in my universe;

Look!
The impersonally waiting white sheet
Yields attentively
To the soft command of your body,
And the warm velvet of you
Is the Sahara sun
Projected against the ever ever snow
Of Baffin Land.
First I shall kiss you with only my eyes—
For I am still unconvinced
That you are not the flesh of fantasy

Waiting to fly into formless vapor
Should I dare breathe upon you.
Now I shall sit beside you
And lose exploring fingers
In the thick forest of your hair;
The clear fringed lakes of your eyes
Are closer now,
And I can no longer resist
The flaming flower of your parted lips.
You have never been more beautiful than you now are—
I said that yesterday and I shall say it again tomorrow—
You have never been more beautiful than you now are;
And still I do not know
What I love most about you—
Pointed breasts like peaks of twin hills
Electric softness of your freed flesh
Or the fragrant orchard where your thighs begin?

Kiss me, my darling!
Let our eager bodies melt, fuse into oneness;
Let us crush the wet rose of passion between us
Through the lightning flash of sweet night hours,
Until
Exhaustion steals us.

Tomorrow at nine you shall awaken.
Fringed lakes of your eyes
Cool in the morning sun;
Calmly our lips shall meet
Calmly as moon-silver spilling on cherry blossoms;
Attentive white sheets reluctantly yielding
The warm velvet of you.
Then you shall clothe yourself
And go—
I'll quickly close the door
So these four walls may keep
Their fragrant fragile memories.

Knowing you,
Beloved,
I have come to understand
How God created mankind
In His own image.

Coincidence

While the mother of Donald Woods, white,
Attended by leading specialists
Was giving him to the world
Her colored maid yielded Booker Scott
Observed by young interns
In the little Jim Crow section
Of the same hospital
In Birmingham.
The white boy grew in all nine rooms
Booker in the kitchen
And Donald's cast-off clothing;
The hour one took the measles
The other caught the mumps;
Donald shot his first deer
The day Booker first killed a rabbit;
Donald went to Princeton
Backed by his parents' wealth
White people's tips
Shoved in a bellhop's pockets
Put Booker through a colored college;
After graduation
Donald became general manager
Of his family's department store
Booker, refusing to teach,
Was made head janitor.
It should have surprised nobody
Therefore
That the very moment
Donald died in an airplane crash
Booker likewise fell to his death
As he slipped near a sixth floor window.

Would it be better understood
Why the lives of both

Traveled parallel
Yet in accordance
With leading Dixie tradition
Were it generally known
That the father of Donald
Under cover the same day
Had likewise sired Booker?

Man of Science

Professor Henri Paseau
Not satisfied
With existing conceptions
Of all that is
Built a bigger telescope
Delved more deeply into mathematics
Discovered new physical laws
And finally revealed
Six strange constellations of stars

Meanwhile
Atoms spun away
From his toiling body
As he spent day and night
Possessed by his obsession;
Each addition to the universe
Wore him thinner
So that when he had expanded the cosmos
To the limit of his ability
And far beyond the greatest previous borders
Of humanity
Professor Paseau
Himself
Was shrunken to
A wizened runt, whisper thin

This I hold
Exceeding strange—
How an entire universe

May lie
In the mind of one man
And he such a minute fragment
Of it.

Adam Smothers

Since the white people
Of Independence, Mississippi,
Believed a nigger shouldn't
Have that much money,
Ten hours after the account
Of Adam Smothers
Reached fifty thousand dollars
The Cotton Farmers State Bank
Went busted.
Going to New Orleans
He recuperated his fortune
By becoming founder and president
Of the Ethiopian Mutual Life Insurance Company
And at fifty-five was worth
Three hundred thousands
Which means he was a wizard
In the world of men and money.
One day
A blonde secondhand store clerk
Drunk in an ancient flivver
Zig-zagging down Rampart Street
Sent him to the cemetery
And escaped with a fine
For driving while intoxicated.

"All coons look alike to me"
Runs a Southern song
And if there is a moral
This is it.

Mental Man

Only the number of those believing
In His existence
Equals the different ideas of God.
Each atheist erects
His own temple of reason
To disprove a Supreme Being.
This indicates nothing
Unless it be
The mistake of creating
Man with a mind.

Spinster: Old

Phonograph brained
Repeatedly playing cracked records
Of turkey trot thoughts;
Her body a battered
Untuned gin mill piano
On which she discordantly plucks
Wagnerian compositions in clothing:
Now half-heartedly seeking
A male Stradivarius
Yielding yellow silken sound
At touch of the violin bow
Of her love;

Warping
Splintering
From years of use
Is her voice
Bridging the private chasm
Between self and world
Becoming
A path for stumbling
Undernourished words;

All else
Is no bigger than a pea;
The universe lies
In her goldfish bowl;
There
She sleeps, wakes, eats
Swims aimlessly
Marking time
Until one day
She floats
Belly upward
Dead . . .

I Have Talked with Death

I talked with Death last night
Talked with Death and shook his hand;
He came among the newborn nursing hours
(The sky was a gray-black parasol
Opened against white rain of light
Through small holes in the ageless cloth
Starbeams dripped in a platinum spray)
I looked around and there Death sat
Sat on the side of my bed
He was an elderly cheery man
And his clothes were faded and old
"You are Death?" I asked.
     "Yes. Death I certainly am."
"Then we are friends," I said,
"I have known of you since the day I was born
And I am not surprised at your coming."
     "You are not afraid?"
"No," I said, "for I expect to return
Every loan. And since I did not arrange
To buy these atoms and dreams
Nor possess any bill of sale
For teeth, heart, hands, brain
I know that I must give them up
When the owner sends his man around—

That is the law.
So take this sand that men call me
Scatter this restless dust
To wind, sea, earth, from which it came
That it may be lent again and again
To those who may have need of it;
Now help me from this home of flesh
And let us take our leave."

   "But I did not come for you,"
Death said, "I don't know when
I'll replevin your bones
So keep your borrowed body on
And wait awhile."
"Then why are you here?" I asked.
   "To chat," Death said,
"To chat of those who tremble at my coming
I, who never did harm to anyone."
"It is true the minds of men
Are swollen with fear," I said,
"And you are known as a terrible thing.
But to me you seem a patriarch
Kindly faced as a grandfather
Thinking lavender thoughts of a life well spent."
   "Terrible I seem," Death said,
"To those who think me so. But I am friend
To you who have no fear of me.
They say I ride a ghost-white steed
That I am dried bones with the gift of motion
A hollow skull seeking new companions;
That I carry a scythe in my skeleton's hands
To harvest bodies of men;
That I cut them down in the fields of the living
Tie them together, like bundles of wheat,
Toss them across the bony rump of my pale horse
Then gallop on," Death said.
"Some say I am a thief
Master criminal, committer of the perfect crime;
Though they bar their doors against me,
Seal windows, set men down to watch

Yet do I silently creep inside
Steal the precious gleaming life
Drop it inside my jewel bag
Before wide eyes of powerless guards
And go swiftly away," Death said.
"They tell one another my hands are cold
Colder than a million mountains of blue ice
That if ever my hands caress
Brow or breast, or my fingers touch the heart,
Life, in terror, flees forever," Death said.

"But there are those who call me mother
Woman with the never empty breast
Where tired and hungry may suckle eternally.
To some I am the perfect lover
Waiting, biding my time,
Until they sicken of the gilded gifts
And painted promises
Of my glamorous rival, Life;
Until they learn that Life's rich clothes
Hide a body diseased, deformed
Then they turn away
Turn and call for me
And I go to them
Go to their yearning couch
And they embrace me with impatient arms
And whisper, 'Lover, I am ready,'
Then I kiss their lips
And they lie with me, content, forever," Death said.
"I am whatever people think I am
I take the form their thoughts command
But remember this:
I never did harm to anyone," Death said.
He was silent then
And I aimed my hand at his wrinkled one.
"I think of you only as a friend of man," I said,
"It's a privilege to meet you
We'll get better acquainted some day
Meanwhile
Let's shake."

Death's palm met mine.
The moon bounced against my window pane
Like a tossed white ball;
Stars rattled
Like popping corn in a covered pan;
The sky exploded
Like a pricked balloon
As I shook his ancient hand.
Then Death left
Left without leaving at all;
His old man's body faded like tobacco smoke
But Death himself remained near me
As he always has.
I shall shake his hand and talk with him again
When next he appears before me—
When he makes a business call—
Maybe tonight, maybe years from now . . .

Self Portrait

I would be
A painter with words
Creating sharp portraits
On the wide canvas of your mind
Images of those things
Shaped through my eyes
That interest me;
But being a Tenth American
In this democracy
I sometimes sketch a miniature
Though I contract for a mural.

Of course
You understand this democracy;
One man as good as another,
From log cabin to White House,
Poor boy to corporation president,
Hoover and Browder with one vote each,
A free country,

Complete equality—
Yeah—
And the rich get tax refunds,
The poor get relief checks.

As for myself
I pay five cents for a daily synopsis of current history,
Two bits and the late lowdown on Hollywood,
Twist a dial for Stardust or Shostakovich,
And with each bleacher stub I reserve the right to shout "kill the bum" at
    the umpire
Wherefore am I different
From nine other Americans?

But listen, you
Don't worry about me
I rate!
I'm Convert 4711 at Beulah Baptist Church,
I'm Social Security No. 337–16–3458 in Washington,
Thank you Mister God and Mister Roosevelt!
And another thing:
No matter what happens
I too can always call in a policeman!

Peace Is a Fragile Cup

I sing for the silent slain
Speak for the dogtagged dead;
Soldiers shorn of expendable lives
Civilians cold among shattered stones;
I am their voice shouting for a living peace.

We have come a long way, historians say
Cave to skyscraper, oxcart to airplane;
But what does it profit a man
Penicillin saved from pneumonia yesterday
Only to die tonight by an atom bomb?

Pithecanthropus erectus to homo mechanicus
Runs the saga of science;
Maker of stone tools to smasher of atoms
(Flint-tipped arrows to block-busters)
Master of mass production
(Recall Nazi gas chambers at Lublin)
Enslaver of the sky
(Lunch in London, afternoon flights over Belgrade)
Who kicked civilization into the streets
Changing her
To a quarter prostitute?

The silent slain speak a common tongue
The dogtagged dead hymn a similar song;
This man's peace is signed with a wooden cross
One war ends each time a soldier dies;
Fighting there has always been
The lonesome warrior fighting the lonely fight
The centipede army smashing the multi-armed foe
Blood and brains splattered on impersonal soil
The hounds of hate baying and biting
Thermopylae, Gettysburg, Bataan
Repeating
Like a continuous performance
At the cinema citadels—
Because this ever was
Must it always be?

⌐⌐

You have to hand it to the experts
They've got it all figured out
Safe in their Home Offices;
It costs exactly this to kill a man;
To equip an army such a size
Means so many billion dollars in contracts;
And the profits are good—
No fighting for markets
No high powered advertising campaigns—
Deliver and get paid.

(Buddy, how much folding stuff
Have you left from your war plant job?
Soldier, which was closer:
The long green or the green earth?)
And after it's all over
Look at the pile you've made!
And you're left with a bigger factory
To make more, sell more.
Move in where the armies fought yesterday
And clean up—
They've got it all figured out
Safe in their Home Offices—
If they forget Hiroshima . . .

⌐⌐

I say
We have not been left among the living
To become a new generation of dying;
They who survived at Stalingrad
Do not covet the breath
Of the untouched millions in Chicago.

Peace was a fragile set of chinaware
But in this day of the atom bomb
Only one thin cup remains;
Take it then
From the careless fists
Of the money-drunk;
Place it in the reaching hands
The safe, wishing, anxious hands
Of the little people
So that we may set it,
Gently,
Behind glass doors in the cupboard
And point proudly to visitors
On an endless chain of calm tomorrows,
Saying,
"Look, there it is.
It's been in the family
For years!"

UNCOLLECTED AND UNPUBLISHED POEMS

1948-84

To the Red Army

Smash on, victory-eating Red warriors!
    Drive on, oh mighty people's juggernaut!
Grind into spreading dust the Nazi killers!
Since your soil is the land they wanted
Assure their murdering millions
Of remaining here forever;
Stake a permanent claim for each
To hold his blood and bones and ruptured dreams
Beneath your dark and dripping dirt.

Look into the closed face of this fallen foe—
It was 1941 that he came overrunning your home
Raping the young girls, enslaving, killing
Your mother, father, sister, too young brother;
"We are supermen," the invaders cried,
"None may stand against us!"
"This is a holy war against Communism,"
Shouted Hitler, beckoning to Britain, America,
As he turned toward the East
To the heavy breasts of the Ukraine;
And in Washington, London,
The experts shook their heads:
"He'll make Moscow in six months
Too weak, the Russians are
Stalin has purged his best generals
Poor transportation for men, material;
Not being capitalistic
Their industry lacks incentive
To produce instruments of war;
Being socialistic
The people have neither strength nor unity—
Maybe six months is really too long to hope!"
And the rich industrialists
Smiled in their private conferences:

"Let Hitler smash the Russians
And wipe Communism from the globe
Removing all threats
To continued ten to fifty percent on investments;
But let it not be too sudden like
Let 'em bleed each other white and weak
So that we may step in
And do thriving business with the survivors."
The plain people read their *Daily News,*
Thought of the church crushed by the Kremlin
Thought of millions starved in famine
Of free love, loose wedlock
Of Finland, Poland
Of no chance of dreaming to become
The Soviet equivalent
Of president of the U. S. Steel Corporation
And they knew the Bolsheviks were bad
For it said so in black and white
And they turned the page to Dick Tracy.
Move over, German dead!
Make room for these piled and decaying lies
The lies exploded like blockbusters
At Moscow, Stalingrad.

The Russian casualty list
Numbers more than ten million names
Toilers, sons and daughters of toilers
Dying to keep life
For the fighting free;
This was their home
Each had a personal stake
In every bullet, every clod;
None yielded his breath
For Standard Oil and a corporation investment;
The people owned all they died for
The living people own all they fight for!

Smash on, victory-eating Red warriors!
Show the marveling multitudes

Americans, British, all your allied brothers
How strong you are
How great you are
How your young tree of new unity
Planted twenty-five years ago
Bears today the golden fruit of victory!

Drive on, oh mighty people's juggernaut!
Hear in your winning ears
Shadow songs of your departed comrades
Telling you, "Be avengers, and kill our killers
And when you have struck the last foe to the ground
Then drop their fascist dreams below hell!"

I Have Faith

I have faith in the people
The people soil-born
Reaching hungry hands
To the white harvest
Of tall star-dreams;
I have faith
I know that some day
They shall gather these ripened dreams
The white stars
Of peace and brotherhood
And store them safely
Against the hard winter.

Creed for Hedonists

Yesterday is a bucket of bones
Picked clean by the tireless teeth of Time
Tomorrow stirs in the womb of Now
Felt and formed, but not yet being
Only today is real!
Today is a roasted pig
Soft, succulent, savory

Come, my starving friends
Let us brighten our bellies now
Let us feast our fill—
For who can surely say
He will be around
To dine tomorrow?

Ours Is a Modern God

Man creates his deities
Each age builds its God anew—
The primitive Father of All
His breathing the rambling wind;
The household God
Protecting family fortunes;
The powerful sky dwellers
Guiding Greeks, Romans, Vikings;
Neurotic Jehovah
Bossing, punishing Israelites;
That jealous Being
Loosing Christians to convert or kill the heathen
Each all-powerful God has died
Pulverized by progress—
Now we have taken
Electronics and computers
To construct a Mechanized Wonder
A modern Deity for moderns
Mindless as man himself.

Praise Be to Thee
Oh Deadly Deity
Thy miracle drugs
Extend life of the old
Another two decades;
Insure the young
Of becoming aged
Thus assuring

Overpopulation of the planet;
Thou has revealed
Innermost secrets
Of mass production
And
Most of all
Built-in obsolescence;
Thy spieling priests
Through Thine sacred commandments
Revealed
In press, movies, radio, video
Have taught us to want
Cars, appliances, carpets
All those Good Things
For the Abundant Life
Produced in plenty
For the drooling millions—
Sold today
Obsolete tomorrow
As time payments go marching on.

Thy highest apostles
(Chairmen of the boards of corpulent corporations)
Have taken holy vows
To save the world;
Salvation is
At least one car, one color T-V
Per believer
And woe betide
The unsaved sinners!

Undoubtedly
Our God is a just God—
Now that we
May overpopulate the earth
As we provide
Mechanical goodies for all
Our Deity

Has given us
Means for destruction
In kind—
For every person alive
Already has his fair share
Of a hydrogen bomb.
We have equated
Population explosion
With nuclear destruction,
Overpopulation walks
With overkill—
Our deadly Deity
Has provided for our nonbeing.

⌐⌐

Let us therefore tape mechanical praise
In stereo
To our great new God
Of the 20th Century
Science
Mad as man himself!

Little and Big

Little people often make big heroes;
From the unknown ranks
Of the population swellers
From the Joes and Janes distinguished
Only by Social Security numbers
Giants spring—
Giants whose names
Soon become a familiar taste
In the mental mouths of the world.

Sometimes those born big
Go with a slim sputter
And all the hymns money can buy
Praises hymned in printers' ink
Cannot magnify
Fizz into boom.

Summer 1984 ∎

Public Servant

Give this man
Who works for Uncle Sam
A medal for economy and efficiency;
Most patiently
He erased smudges from envelopes
To mail
Five checks
Each for over ten million bucks
In payment for aircraft
That rusted and rotted
In the South Pacific.

Give Us Our Freedom Now!

(100 Years after the Signing of the Emancipation Proclamation)

We have heard enough
Of the glib gab
Of two-timing politicians
Who for a hundred years
Have peddled putrid promises
Of teasing tomorrows—
We demand our freedom now!

Our dark dead
And our many maimed
Have fallen for a hundred years
On foreign battlefields
All around our globe;
We have watched peace exhumed
Revised, restored and move among us
As America walked in friendship
With old enemies of democracy
Everywhere—
Everywhere save our own battlegrounds
The magnolia marshes
Of Alabama, Mississippi
The crowded wildernesses
Of Chicago, New York.

A hundred years—
That's a long time brown buddy
That's thirty-six thousand five hundred
Long dark days
Of crawling in the gutter;
It's over fifty million minutes
Of staggering beneath
A cross of color
And it's too damned long—
We want our freedom now!

You
White-America-you
You showed us the tree of freedom
Filled with proud ripe plums
Of the Emancipation Proclamation
And three Constitutional Amendments
But when we stretched our hands
To pluck the sweet fruit
You fired the shotgun of Jim Crow laws
Loosed mad dogs of the Ku Klux Klan
And drove us back

But we would not leave the yard;
In a hundred years
Those first denied
Have died
Stilled faces forever frozen
With disillusioned disappointment,
But we their sons and daughters
Have pushed closer
Burying victims of your mad dogs
Hauling our hurt from your shotgun blasts
Forging armor
From Supreme Court Decisions
And the strong alloy
Of your need
For our sweat and swinging strength;
Today
That sweet fruit
Is less than an arm's length away:
Do you really think
You can stop us now?

You pale peddlers
Of sick democracy—
Along what swarming street
Will you find buyers?
Not in the new homes of Africa, Asia
Nor the old houses of Latin America
Not among the colored peoples
Anywhere in the world
Still fighting
The disease of prejudice.

You
White-America-you
Your color is no longer
A license for privilege
That day a hundred years long
Has passed;
Prepare yourself

For the integrated dawn
Of a salt-and-pepper-time
Equality of condiments
To season our common land.
March with us!
Together
We shall heal democracy;
But fight against us
And that grand invalid
Dies
With our own dark dead.

Even though we stand alone
We shall not turn back;
If we must climb
Over our fallen brave
We shall not stop.
We're marching on
We're swarming on
We have one song
Loud, strong
Roar it through the day
Shout it through the night—
Give us
Our freedom now!

18 May 1963 ■

Finality

In the beginning
Man created God
In his own image
Complete with anger, revenge and sword
(Read the Bible lately?)
As eternal retribution
Man invented hell
Final, catch-all punishment
For nonbelieving

Today
We await the supreme achievement
The all-devastating super bomb
Eventual product of nuclear fission
Entirely ridding the world of sin
And himself
In one final blast

I know not
How many uninhabitable planets
Once peopled by rational beings
Builders of civilizations
Far surpassing all we may ever know—
(People too intelligent for their own good)
Now spin lifelessly around other suns
In unseen solar systems
Victims of themselves
And their love affair with the splitting atom

Why must this be?

Hey, you guys in Washington
Let us begin at home
How about a Secretary of Peace
To snip a pattern for the world?
For years we lived with
Survival of the whitest
Murder by the malignantly militant;
Let there enter now
A new day of gauze and gold
With equality for ethnics
And love for the lowly,
Surely
A Secretary of Peace
Might pulverize power
And transfer tranquility
To troubled waters of the globe

Instead of millions for munitions
Presto
Plenty for the poor of all colors,
Send the whoring generals and admirals
Along with their fat pimps
In plush corporate offices
Battered and begging to the breadlines
Then let the men of science
Who dreamed bigger and better mass destruction
Now shackle their genius
To blueprint bountiful lives
For all humanity.

To Those Seeking Fame

Go, set your wings and sail for the sun
No time to stop
On mountain tops
The journey there for you's just begun.
Where others stopped and called the flight done
On high hills—
Folly to stay!

On peaks not long can eagle-men rest.
Earth-men climb
In black night time
With pock-marked hands tear eagle-men's nests,
Clip birdmen's wings, crawl back to ground. Best
Stop not
But fly on!

Who gives caught eagles carrion food
Bones to eat
Stones for meat
Chain souls for soaring? (Cowardly Brood!
They rivet steel to worm-eaten wood!)
The worm hates
All flying things!

What matters if you reach not the sun?
Better to try
And, failing, die
Than fold your wings, on hills sinking down.
Fear not to fly. Remember: None
But bird-men
Scale star sides!

1929 ■

Black American

I am a Black American
Me: woman, man, child
Ancestry?
Mainly African in blood, background, behavior
Centuries ago I knew no other home
But that was long before
I became a Black American
Biologically mixed but ideologically Black
Now I am blonde to ebony
Europe, Asia and the Indians of America
Contribute to my ethnic hash—
How can I physically deny them
Without denying part of myself?

But no longer am I the good nigger
Bowing, grinning "yassuh boss"
To Whitey
Of thee I do not sing
Having reached the now of today
I have jumped that old reservoir
Of Uncle Toms
No more will I inhabit a hut
Amid those ashes of the putrid past

When I look back now
It is to the shining glory of Timbuktu
The bright days of Zegzeg, Benin
And to Nat Turner, Harriet Tubman, Frederick Douglass
Guerrilla fighters for Freedom

The steel rope of blood
Ties me to brothers and sisters
In Africa
But now I am also bound
To America

My sweat and blood made mortar
To build this land
And I, too, own it
If need be
I shall sweat again
And bleed
To make America yield my equity

This nation has tried to force feed me
Monotonous meals of bullshit *à la carte*
And I will eat this no more
The time has come
To quit barn and kitchen
And move into the parlor

Naturally
I love my African kin
But I was not born there
My home is America
And nothing shall drive me away
Accept it, Whitey
And stand aside

Burn your tired trash of racism
Mixed with the moldy manure
Of unlimited dollar profits
Burn your racism
Or watch our America burn
I am your equal in every good way
I will settle for nothing less
And if I must die for what I own
So be it.
Today at last
I am a proud Black American.

May 1975 ∎

Three Average Americans

1

His life was a darkened cave
Where he had been shoved by Birth;
For countless carbon copy days
He groped aimlessly
Until one night
Quite by accident
He stumbled into the exit
Of Death

2

He found life
Was a rented apartment
In a restricted sub-division

With certain utilities
Provided by the building's owners;
Of course
He supplied his own furniture
Of personal beliefs
But even they must conform
To community standards
Else what would the neighbors think?
In the recent days of World War II
When the fashion was anti-fascist
He dutifully bought
A modern living room suite
And put pink curtains at the windows;
Today
With the experts decreeing
Return to American period style
He has traded it in
And sits smugly with his friends
In the over-stuffed creations
Mass produced in the tireless factories
Of press and radio.

3

He intended to keep an open mind
Even if it killed him;
At college he passionately consorted
With Negroes and Jews
And nearly got a blackball
From his father's fraternity;
Starting at the age of twenty-three
He ate breakfast
With the *Chicago Tribune*
And dined with the *Daily Worker;*
He died in a crash
Racing from a meeting of the Ku Klux Klan
To a memorial service
For Leon Trotsky.

Winter 1950 ■

[Ike Mosby]

Ike Mosby paid taxes
In Blythe County, Texas,
On a 200-acre farm
He had enough profits deposited
To make the bank president
Seriously ponder Failure
Ike Mosby was the first man
In Blythe County
To buy an automobile
Whereupon his jealous neighbors
Sent him a delegation
Telling Ike it was all right
So long as he didn't use the
Highways
So every Sunday
Ike and his family of 10
Spent the day joyriding
Just inside the barbed wire fences

Miss Samantha Wilson

In her sixtieth year
Miss Samantha Wilson
Recluse and religious
Suddenly as a dictator making new laws
Turned from the wilted loneliness
Of her dejected-brown cottage
Companionship of two pious cats
Mothership of a mannerly brood of potted plants
And moved among the ailing townspeople
Hovering all night

Beside the beds of the deathly sick
Like an agéd angel
Bathing souls with purple prayers
Refusing to leave before life left
And the town that had known her
Only as a name and a gray-haired virgin
Now praised her unselfishness
Shared its most fragile secrets
And erected its new hospital in her honor

But it was not for these things
That Samantha Wilson labored.

Knowing death eyed her closely
Dreading eternity friendless
She was arranging for companions
Among the fatally sick she'd tended
To be watchfully waiting
In that misty place
Beyond the grave.

Winter 1950 ∎

To a Young Man

When I was your age
Fifty years ago
I knew everything,
The old man said
Pointing with his cane
Of memory;
When I was twenty

I saw a scarlet sky
And a blue balloon sun
And I had
An explanation;
Since then I have drunk
Half a hundred liquid years
Distilled
Through restless coils of wisdom
And if you asked me now
Do one plus one
Make two or three or four
I would have to say
I do not know.

Then the old man turned
His hammered face
To the pounding stars
Smiled
Like the ring of a gong
And walked until
On the slate horizon
He erased himself.

1975   ■

Billie Holiday

I think I'll be going now,
So long.
And the transparent lizard
with the blue blue gizzard
and the candy striped
bones
wailed and went
mourning
her opaque scent

By the presto of electronics
I reincarnate Lady Day
Listen as her rum-brown rope of a voice
Fastens flannel strands
Around stiff sides of staid notes
Sitting properly
On their oh so proper scale
She pulls
Notes fall
Into her molten mold
Of flaming sound
Burning
Bright as a hungry sun

She sings
And her words taste
Of lavender butter
Spread with a unicorn's horn

How easy it is
A switch turns
And the dead breathes again
How easy
And no mosquito swarm
Of biting responsibilities

No pushers now
Peddling a promise
Of pilfered peace
In return
For a dawn-kissed soul

Arrogant amphibians
Proper in their prim dull scales
Sinned and sunned
    "My man he don't love me
    He treats me awful mean ..."
        And the transparent lizard
        with the blue blue gizzard
        moaned
                and went.

February 1974 ■

Duke Ellington

Comes now
Taste of firecrackers
in my mouth
Sound of honey
In my ear—
Gentlemen
I dig you!

Hum a hymn for the happy hip
Every hipster completely happy
Send 'em on a banana balloon
Riding toward a grapefruit moon.

Conjure man of music
Magician of sharps and flats
Inventor of forty-nine new ways to bend a chord, shape a note
Crazy painter brushing kaleidoscopic sounds on aural canvas
Mad sculptor melting metronomes into liquid mobiles
Pardon me; wasn't that a black-maned lion pawing party piano in a Park
    Avenue penthouse?
Who gathers the gold-red orchids raining on the jukebox sea?

Someday someone should give a dance for the band
Let the instruments dress and have a ball
I'd like to ease around slow, you know with the alto sax in a tight silk
    gown and no bra
You take her tenor sister
But keep an eye on baritone brother he can be mighty mean

If somebody gave a dance for the band who'd make music?
A fine fat quail with rhythm in her tail and hungry hips for the long
    trombone?

Music cascades from brass and reeds in rhythmic rainbow waterfall
Coiled snakes of biting notes spring from bass and drums
Through it all the piano darts like a boisterous bumblebee
And a cool cat falls to his knees shouting hot hosannas in a jingling
    jangling jiving jargon to a Jazz Jehovah.

Light the cannon crackers
I have a taste for the exploding hot
Turn on the cool
Give me the sound of honey in my ear—
Gentlemen
I am gassed!

February 1974 ■

Charlie Parker

Who named him Yard Bird?
He was a homing pigeon
With no home to fly to

Sky unlimited
Route uncharted
Eagle strong
He scorched his wings
Haunting the heavens
Buzzing the sun

As the feebler fowl
Looked up in awe
But played it safe

In the rambling sky
He lived!
Here he rendezvoused
With freedom
Flashing feathers
Of burning blue
Dipping, darting
In strange and wild
Ecstatic arcs
Dazzling with his daring
Flying
As none before had ever flown

Even an eagle tires
And returns to his airy crag
A homing pigeon
Cannot soar forever
But this majestic bird
Had no home
To go to;
Helpless
On the ground
He wandered aimlessly
Pecking in garbage
Like a common sparrow
With a weary wing
And he was trapped
And hooked
And cooked—
That's the simple story
Of the heaven-haunting pigeon
Who flew his way to glory.

February 1974 ■

Louis Armstrong

Any day at court
Before the Zulu King
You'll find twenty-six
Of the wildest chicks
Shakin' that thing.

King of the Zulus
Wears a swingin' crown
Made from a silver trumpet
Set with fiery blue diamonds.

He was a young 'un
When he blew himself
Smack dab on the throne
An' ain't nobody yet
Been able to blast him off;
They've tried many times
These challengers
Their lips tough as elephant hide
Lungs like blacksmith bellows
The King grabs an earful
Then reaches for a horn,
Any old horn
Dips it in,
His barrel of blues
Loosens his chops,
Mugs lightly
Slightly
And politely
And blows—

Notes swing out
Shining like sun-stroked gold
Lithe as contortionists
Or maybe
He stomps it off
And the music darts

Like stunting jets
Burns like boiling lava
Then the ambitious Cats
Shake their heads
And slink away—
Later you hear
Sound of gravel
Fallin' in a tin bucket
With a melodic beat:
It's the King
Callin' the Cats
To a victory feast
Of red beans and rice.

Visit if you like
With other tribes
The new cool people
Of the jazz jungle
Then bring it on back
Back to the court
Of the Zulu King
Where you see twenty-six
Of the craziest chicks
Shaking that thing!

February 1974   ■

Lady Day

Her rum-brown rope of a voice
Fastens flannel strands
Around soft sides of staid notes
Sitting properly
On their oh so proper scale
She pulls
And the notes fall
Into her molten mold
Of flaming sound

Ella

Swing your hot hammer
Gal
Beat these shapeless songs
Into fantasies
For the hungry ear
Pound these pale notes
Into bright bracelets
For the heart's wearing

"Swing It Brother Swing"

(Count Basie with Billie Holiday)

Deep rhythm captivates me, hot rhythm stimulates me
Can't help but swing it boy,
Swing it brother swing.
Don't stop to diddle-daddle.
Stop this foolish prattle.
C'mon swing me king,
Swing it brother swing.
Rarin' to go and there ain't nobody gonna hold me down.
Say, listen boy, hurry up and send me, let me go to town.
Stop this diddle-daddle, and this foolish prattle.
C'mon kill it boy.
Swing it brother swing.
Deep rhythm captivates me, hot rhythm stimulates me
Can't help but swing it boy,
Swing it brother swing.
Don't stop to diddle-daddle.
Stop this foolish prattle.
C'mon swing me Count.
Swing it brother swing.
Rarin' to go and there ain't nobody gonna hold me down.
Say, listen boy, hurry up and send me, let me go to town.
Stop this diddle-daddle, and this foolish prattle.
C'mon swing me Count, swing it brother swing.

This Is Paradise

I

Here is the peaceful postcard paradise
A considerate sun slaves overtime
The moon dances to a soft guitar
The champagne rain bubbles and warms
And June lasts a full twelve months;
Here live the bright prismatic people
Sun-washed, moon-dried,
Diamond set in the lava ring
Of brown-green mountain and rainbow valley
In the blue jewel case
Of the Pacific.

⌐⌐

The seven main islands of Hawaii
Born two thousand miles from California
Are inhabited by people, pineapple
Sugar cane and Pearl Harbor
Grown dependently together—
This much is in the travel folders.

The rich cruise here in winter
Planes bring the middle class in summer
(The poor see the sights any time
At their neighborhood movie or on T-V:
Who says there's no equality in America?)
With air above and water below
Subject to municipal regulations
And official boundaries
Afloat on the ocean,
You enter the City & County of Honolulu
A thousand miles
Before you reach

The City & County of Honolulu
(Discount any comments
From birds and fishes—
They have neither voting rights
Nor civic consciousness)
Bring along a blank paper mind
Until the Island of Oahu
Inflates from dime to dollar
And then a sack of bulging bullion
Split by the worried brow of Diamond Head;
See the languid palms
Dressing the shining coral shores;
Bright houses and slick buildings
Like quarters and dimes
In a pocket of greenbacks;
Come by luxury liner
And see the little welcoming boats
Like chicks around a mother hen;
Brown boys in bright trunks
Diving to spray tourists
With splashes of Local Color;
Hula dancers waving their hips
To conduct the Royal Hawaiian Band;
Come by air
And see the fly-speck mountains
Spring into gaunt giants
As the land reaches up
Like a friendly hand;
Come either way
And wear a lavalier of flowers
On that greeting drive through strange streets
Glowing with the bright prismatic people;
Now enter into the baited door
Of your tourist trap in Waikiki,
Pour your eager flesh and bone
Into a bathing suit,
Dash to the nearby beach
And sit;
Sit while barefoot boys bob by
Twanging ukes;

Sit while waves regularly report
Their quotas of spray and surfboard riders;
Sit for dinner under soft stars
Sit until the night grows confidential
And solicits for his scented woman, Sleep
Now take a postcard to your room
Write "Having wonderful time—"
And go to bed, murmuring
"It's really true!
This really is Hawaii!"

Tomorrow, long after the sun
Has wandered into your room
Sat awhile, and left his calling card
You will leisurely arise
Breakfast on papaya,
Guava jelly and Kona coffee
Then buy a gaudy Aloha shirt;
Now start your conducted tour
Of the island,
See for yourself the fabled sights
Leap to life from the guidebook;
Go to a luau and eat like the natives—
The quaint, friendly, childish natives;
Pinch the buxom bottoms of the island girls
While your wife makes eyes
At the sleek brown boys;
Loaf and live
By all means live;
Go to the Outer Islands
Visit the bubbling volcanoes on Hawaii
Huge Haleakala crater on Maui
Wonderful Waimea canyon on Kauai
Or stay in Waikiki;
This is Paradise
Any way you take it—
And so two weeks, a month slip by.

Now it is time to leave
Return as president of that Iowa bank

(Good old Iowa, the REAL U. S. A.)
Back as buyer for the Boston store
(Good old Boston, pride of New England);
You've had as good a time
As money could buy
At prevailing prices;
(That explanation
By the Hawaii Visitors Bureau
Was logical:
"Everything's shipped in, you know")
You'd like to come again
Not next year but sometime
But no matter
You've plenty to tell the folks back home,
You've seen the peaceful postcard paradise,
You've seen the bright prismatic people
And now you know Hawaii!

II

Pardon me, Paradise
But under your cool stylish frock
Designed by the Chamber of Commerce
Tailored by the Visitors Bureau
Your soiled slip shows . . .

Hawaii is more than pineapple and sugar cane
Tall mountains and green valleys
Grass shacks under pandering palms
Gleaming sands and green-blue ocean
Smoking volcanoes and cascading waterfalls
Gliding guitars and ripe red laughter—
For these
These are but props and a stage setting,
Painted scenery for continuous drama.

Pick it up at Scene I, Act the Second
Pick it up when old Captain Cook
Blasted the dam of silence
And the raging waters of missionaries
Roared through the widening breach

Sweeping over the old ways
Inundating the ancient gods
Flooding the sacred soil of custom and tradition
Leaving seeds of civilization in the thin silt;
Fruitful civilization bound to bless
The heathen sinners.

And the missionaries were magicians, too;
These magicians of missionaries
The conjure men of Christianity
Placed the vanishing cloth
Of Mother Hubbards on the women
Then Whoosh and Presto
Nudity into nakedness,
A factory-fresh set of morals
And a rise in illegitimate births.

Now that it was uncivilized
To kill by spear or club
Guns became a symbol of progress;
Guns with a silent sting
More poisonous than the bite of the scorpion
Sharper than the sudden kiss of the centipede—
Thus the natives advanced.

The missionaries beat holy drums for the good life;
People who had never heard of Satan
Were sold on the idea
That they had been bound for hell
That material things
Were bait in the devil's trap;
"Put ye the world behind you,"
Spake the come-on men for the church
"Now take the Word of God
As it is written in the Bible,
Believe,
And you shall find mansions in heaven."
The people heard and found salvation
Kings, chiefs, common people found salvation
And they turned their backs on the verdant islands

Lifted their eyes from the land that bore them
And began making reservations
For life eternal beyond the skies;
The missionaries came with Bibles
The heathen natives had the land
Now the natives are no longer heathen,
They have the Bible and Jesus
And in this equitable trade—
This oh so reasonable swap
The missionaries got the land:
End of the last scene of the Second Act.

(Maybe you've viewed this show before
Maybe you recognize this whitehaired plot
If that is the case I'm sorry
Nevertheless . . . anyhow . . . regardless
The drama still goes on)

III

Under the manure of the missionaries
Sprouted the Big Five
Monster all arms and mouth
Grabbing and gorging
Taking the best and the most
Packaging the crumbs
To sell at a price
Thus proving,
Say the public relations men,
The virtue of Free Enterprise
Which allows any man
To make a million.

God and the Big Five
(God ruled
Like the King of England
Tolerated
By the Aristocracy of the Dollar
If God got rambunctious
Out He went)

Time was
When the Big Five had God on their payroll
To care for the Sunday trade;
Weekdays they handled the people direct:
Sneeze, and they sold you handkerchiefs
Eat, and the food came by Big Five boat
Dress, and their stores peddled you cloth and clothes
Read, and the words had passed their censors
Die, and ride to glory in a Big Five box on a Big Five hearse
(One day the president of the largest bank
Delivered the commencement address
At the University of Hawaii:
"The best things
Yes, I say the best things in life
Are free.")

But that was before the Union
(Given free choice
Satan is preferable
The devil doesn't ask shorter hours, higher pay
Like Harry Bridges and his ILWU)
Men on the wide plantations
Those handling cargo on the waterfront
Hung hand-me-down hates in the closet
And organized
In one big union
Japanese, Chinese, Filipino, Portuguese, Puerto Rican, Hawaiian, Korean
And together
Raised their voices for a living share of the take
And treatment as men and women;
The Big Five sneered
Flexed its muscles
And hit—
But the Union stood and fought
Growing strong in struggle;
Then the onlookers
Seeing the Big Five no longer king
Themselves grew bold
Forming their own corporations
Biting the sweet apple of independence—

Nevertheless
Directors of Big Five firms
(Interlocking, naturally)
Take two full days each year
To count their annual profits.

In the old days
Those oh so good dead days
(Shed a tear for the pungent past)
When the Big Five decreed
Finis for the militantly articulate
They bought one-way passage
On the next outgoing ship;
But Time whistles a new tune
The plain people
Are no longer concubines of Fear.

No longer the hungry whip of the overseer
Eats soft flesh of the plantation hand,
No longer the boot of the waterfront boss
Underlines orders to the stevedore,
Still
The road to Heaven
In this island paradise
Is rough and long.

Behind the rows of rotting shacks
Herded together to leave more room
For growing pineapple and sugar cane
Rats and babies
Race for the privvies;
Seated in his office
Looking out into the lavender water
Of his private swimming pool
The plantation manager spoke
To the grievance committee
Of the union:
"It is your duty
As good citizens

To help preserve
Our American way of life."

During the big shipping strike
Somebody wrote to the stevedoring firms:
>   For those who know
>   The day they'll die
>   Moons whiz by
>   But minutes ride snail-back
>   For the anxiously waiting.

IV

America is more than white
America is more than extension of Europe
In Hawaii the pot melts and boils
Orient and Polynesia
Caribbeans and Philippines
Pour in their pounds
To blend with Europe and a dash of Africa
And we have the people of Hawaii—
The bright prismatic people—
Blonde to black
With the tan pastels
Of Japan and China dominant.

A haole* tourist from Birmingham
Went home after two days of his intended month:
"You can take these Goddamned islands,"
He told friends in Dixie
"And shove them up your ass
I don't like Hawaii—
Too many niggers there."

A Hawaiian dark as ginger root
Said to his new neighbor from Nebraska
(A Negro light as a lemon)
"We ought to get along real well—
During World War II

*Originally foreign, now means a white person.

■ 203

My best friend
Was a colored boy from Pittsburgh."

Koji Takemoto sells soap powder on television
Ching On Mau buys Mickey Mouse boots for his son
The corner grocery is owned by Calixto Balbag
Antonio Rezentes and Kaleo Fanane drink Milwaukee beer and argue
    about the Giants and Dodgers;
Yesterday Mun Ng the printer
Setting type for Epstein and Ellison, Ltd.
Laughed and said
"What funny kind names, these."

Mrs. Yoshiko Saito Hanks has returned from Texas;
She plans a trip to Tokyo
After she becomes plain Yoshiko Saito again;
Texas was all right
It was big and broad and hot in summer
But it grew lonely
At the cottage in Dallas,
Her haole in-laws could not climb the mountain
Of a Japanese in their family
And soon gave up trying;
Neighbors said to her husband,
It's all right to sleep with 'em
But for Christ sake
Why do you have to marry 'em
So after a year in Texas
With her soldier husband
Mrs. Yoshiko Saito Hanks
Has come home.

꒦꒷

Each Friday night brown John Keakana crams his wife and four kids into their
    sputtering jalopy and drives from Honolulu to the country to weekend
    camp and fish on a sandy beach
And the tourists from Topeka and Joliet riding around the island in the prancing buses smile pinkly and murmur: "How quaint, how carefree the Ha-

waiians are, not a worry in the world, nothing to do but loaf and fish just
like their ancestors"
Sunday afternoon John herds his Keakanas home and weighs his fish. Some
he sells and some he keeps to help stretch monthly pay within $40 of what
the social scientists call necessary for minimum health standards

⌐⌐

Four stood by the gaping grave:
Book reading priest in black
Woman poking wet eyes with bright apron
Husband silent and circumspect
Young boy aiming his curious gaze at the quiet home of the buried dead
    around him—
This was all
The old man's world was small;
Neighbors noted "Kawasaki has another mouth to feed"
    seventy years before in Kyoto
Two days ago somebody mentioned "Old Man Kawasaki kicked off
    last night" in the little lane in Honolulu;
Both main events in this history
Flattened to the casual;
Now four stood by the gaping grave—
This was all
The old man's world was small.

Outside a country church
I heard a young woman say:
"If it's true the good die young
My boy I lost at the age of eight
Must have been near perfect.
But think what a no-good bum
Methuselah must have been."

One delegate to Congress
In the first half of the century
Given the run-around on statehood for Hawaii
Left this final request:
        When I die
        Burn these brittle bones

Then take the thin ashes
Some blowy snowy day
And scatter them on the Senate steps
So those who stomped upon my living soul
May complete their act.

V

"Race prejudice? There's none in Hawaii"
Said blonde Bob Bowser
Driving from his beachside home in Kahala
(You'll love this exclusive section, said
      the realtor. No Oriental neighbors)
To an evening at the Outrigger Club
(Membership restricted to Caucasians)
"Never could understand why
The damn Japs always stick together
Unless maybe they're just clannish."

"We don't say nothin'
When those haole boys from the Mainland
Get in our high school
And act like they're better'n us,"
Grinned the clove-brown Samoan,
"We jus' sit tight 'n' wait
'Til they come out fo' football practice."

Moses, mud-black Hawaiian
Was fired as tour car driver
After socking that visitor from Denver
Who innocently asked
If Moses was Negro.

Three Oriental lads
Studying at the University
Stood at the bus stop
Drenched in grave sarcasm;
Bowing low
They spoke to the lone Japanese co-ed:
Who had twice dated a Canadian classmate:
"We salute you—

From now on
You're white man's meat
You haole-lover you."

"You gotta understan',"
Said the red-headed sailor from Savannah
To Anna Kahakapai
Nutmeg-toned bedmate
"You're better'n any damn nigger
So don't never
Even talk to 'em
If you can help it
Or none of us
Ain't gonna pay you no min'."
And the graduate from Ole Miss
Supervising at Pearl Harbor
Looked around his first day
At strange yellow faces
Ancestor-flung from Korea, Okinawa, Japan, China
And one lone mulatto
With the map of familiarity
Then he smiled
And he walked over and spoke
Confidentially:
"You and me
We have to stick together—
We understand each other."

One week in the country
And the navy wife phoned her landlord:
"Across the street
Lives a bunch of dirty Hawaiians;
Next door on our right
A family of lousy Japs;
On the other side
A house full of slant-eyed Chinks;
And in front of us
On our very same lot
A white bitch married to a nigger—
I want our rent money back."

After a lifetime
Of crusading for black causes
Outwitting three lynch mobs
And six shotgun sheriffs
Africanus White
At the age of sixty
Came to Hawaii
Only to die one year later
In the unfamiliar jungle of superficial equality
From mental malnutrition.

VI

The night
Slippery as a black eel in Kaneohe Bay
Slices softly down zig-zag mountains;
Hotels in Waikiki
Mark feeble protests
In neon and mazda;
White buttons of light
Fasten homes to high dark hills;
A gay full moon
Spills champagne bubbles
Bursting in dancing splashes
On the rambling waves
Of the ocean;
Stars wait
Like patient white lizards
On the dark rock
Of the sky;
Slowly the night sinks
Into the confusion of history
As the peaceful postcard paradise
Sleeps.

Moonlight at Kahana Bay

White as the flower of the pikake
A proud moon rides high
In the crinkled sky

Above Kahana Bay
As the rambling black edge
Of the slouching mountains
Slices the glowing clouds.

Tonight the sea is a lavish lover
Placing long leis of fragile foam
About the soft brown throat
Of the swooning shore;
Fingers of the wandering waves
Gently stroke the floating petals
Fallen from the pikake moon
In luminous streamers.

Lights from the little houses
Tinkle but a tiny tune
Against the strong sonata
Of moon and sky and singing sea
And the deep bass beat
Of the surging hills
Sounding the scented night
The flowered friendly night
Around Kahana Bay.

9 June 1949 ■

Tale of Two Dogs

Soothed by the yellow hand of the Hawaiian sun
The mountains drowsed like tired gray men
On the front lawn of the Old Folks Home.
Then the Strangers came;
They loosed their chained terriers
Of pineapple and sugar cane;
Sent them boldly into the yard
To sniff with eager green noses
At the sleeping old.

Long since
Pine and cane
Have taken over the front lawn.

Snapping impatiently at obstructing ankles;
They run between
The tall still legs of the motionless mountains
As if they originated here
And the silent ancients
Were usurpers.

Here in this cultivated place
Growing the soft brown rose
Of Polynesia
The dogs have scratched
Digging for the buried pot of cash returns
Killing the broken bush
Under the flying dirt
Of greed and grief.

Annoyed by the yapping pair
An old man turns in his slumber
And the land slides on Pine and Cane;
He sits tall in his chair
And the rains beat down;
He rises in explosive anger
And the lava breaks loose from its chains
The smoking monster subduing all
Who dare disturb the rest
Of Mauna Loa, Kilauea.

There is none so patient
As a tired mountain drowsing in the sun;
There is no wrath so great
As that of a mountain outraged
Destroying the nipping dogs
Loosed on the front lawn
By the Strangers.

Pacific Invasion

Silently the fog lands
Its gray army from the sea

And races on quiet feet
To lay a shifting siege
Around the light-guarded fortress
Of my home;
Tirelessly the fog hurls
Its wet gray shafts
Runs reconnoitering fingers over the walls
And presses an anxious nose
Against the clear calm cheeks
Of my windows;
Only the charging wind
Splits the ranks of the fog invader
Hurling the silent army
Back into the soft grave
Of the sea.

Winter 1950 ∎

Horizontal Cameos: 37 Portraits

1. Lani

Lani is at her best
Horizontal
No ponderous perpendicular prelude
Is essential
Unless one insists
Upon romance with love
But that is added expense
For as the slogan speaks
From the desk of the insurance executive
Time Is Money.

Lani, age 25,
Had distributed a fortune
Before she realized
There was gold in descent from the vertical
Lani, age 30,
Has 50 grand salted away
With no change in habits

And has had many husbands
Including two of her own;
But with success has come prejudice
Which never before existed—
Today she will not tolerate
Any man with less than $20
She is that rarity
Psychologists seldom find—
A woman working
At her best occupation
Without benefit of aptitude test.

2. Anne

In the gangling hours
Thin, adolescent hours
Before night runs softly
Away into the west
Anne rises wearily
From her tired bed
And sleeps
Sitting in a chair.

3. Mamie

Schoolin's all right, I guess
But I ain't seen a man yet
Who wanted to go to bed
With a college degree;
I stopped at the eighth grade
And I can buy and sell
Jus' about all the gals
I know what finished school;
Every other year
I buy a new T-Bird
My closet's full
Of eighty buck shoes
And you oughta see
My thousan' dollar stereo set!

Las' week I didn't feel so good
I saw my doctor

An' he sent me to one of them head shrinkers—
What the hell did he mean
When he said I needed
Emotional security?

4. Connie

Having once lived in Chicago
Cavernous with contempt
For the Upper Class
Connie christened
Her parlor for pointed passion
"The Pump Room."

5. Hazel

You want to know why
I'm in this racket?
That's simple—
I don't like men
All they want is one thing
It's been that way since I was a kid
I used to tell 'em no—and fight
Now I say yes—and collect
If the no-good bastards want it
They can have it
So long as they've got cash;
And I put their money to good use—
Why, I provide much better
For Alice
Than her husband ever did!

6. Mary

Undoubtedly
There are two me's
The living, being I
And the insensitive mass
Who works horizontally

Often have I watched
While the insensitive mass
Created the incongruity

Of intimate embraces
With strangers I never cared to know
Its voice
Repeating stock love phrases
Is as impersonal to me
As a recording in the next room

The living, being I
Looks in detached disdain
Until the job ends
And I herd the insensitive mass away
Like a trained seal from the circus
To rest and wait
Until the next show

Undoubtedly there are two me's
But since the living, breathing I
Depends upon the insensitive mass
For my daily bread
Which is the real master
And which the slave?

7. Mrs. ——

Because I have a built-in
Boudoir look
Many of my husband's friends
Made passes at me
When no one was watching;
One day I said
"Listen, I get all the loving
I want at home.
Furthermore,
My husband gives me 50 dollars
Anytime I ask for it.
Why should I treat you any better?"
The practical-minded
Have since been satisfied
With sex and no emotional obligation
But the others
Consider it outrageously immoral

To pay for the privilege
Of bedding a close friend's wife!

8. Lorna

Lorna tiptoes among spun-glass memories
Mind-fingers polishing to bubble brightness
("Sure, Honey, if that's what you want . . .")
Wonder what ever happened to Miss Blaine?
Could've been real pretty if she'd reduced
("Darling, everything you do sends me . . .")
Russell would've made a good lawyer
The way he used to argue
It's a pity he had to die
In Vietnam
("Ooh, Honey, oooh . . .")
We sure had a lot of fun
All through high school
Marge and I
Wonder how she looks now
Has she gotten fat with the three kids?
("Darling, I enjoyed it too
And you *will* come back
Real soon?")

9. Eloise

Doctors heal the sick
And win lasting honor,
Ministers soothe the soul
And the world calls them saintly,
Soldiers kill in battle
And their country terms them heroes,
Yet I satisfy needs men knew
Before the birth of doctors and priests
And the sanctioned slayers in uniform,
I burst the bombs of joy
In the arsenals of willing men
I perpetuate that pleasure
Men will not live without—
And for this
People look down on me!

10. Alma

Coppers, why ram
Me into the can?
This is no man—
    Between my thighs
    Ten dollars lies!

11. Maggie

Look upon me
As any other proprietor
Of a small business;
One observes my wares
Or hears of my services
From satisfied customers
Then, if one wishes,
One buys
It is as simple as that—
I defy you
To name anything
That better defines
Our national ideal
Of free private enterprise!

12. Betty

Having reached her goal
Of a hundred grand in cash
Betty quit the business and Boston
At thirty-five
And moved to California
Devoting her ample leisure
To a church Home for Wayward Girls
Winning the respect and interest
Of the director
Whom she married
Thus providing
(Unintentionally, of course)
Funds for her husband
On his business trips
To spend
In the whorehouses of San Francisco.

13. Frances

Last night I dreamed
Of a meadow of men
Naked, staked to the ground
In the long flowing grass
Faces flung to the sun
And I
Moving methodically along
With a power mower.

14. Lucille

I don't like repeaters
After a John comes to you
Four or five times
Trouble gets to be his twin
They act too familiar
Or they want credit
Or special privileges
Some even ask to marry you

I don't have to like 'em
Just because I lay 'em
And as for marrying
If I cared *that* much
I wouldn't want money
In the first place!

15. Agnes

I want men
To come back again;
As a college freshman
I flunked out
After two weeks as a waitress
I was fired
My husband ran off with a redhead
On our first wedding anniversary—
The way I see it
A gal needs to feel
She's a success at something!

16. Winnie

If there's one thing I hate
It's those no-good young chicks
Who flounce about
Giving it away!

17. Louise

Orphaned at fourteen
Pregnant at fifteen
Unwed mother at sixteen
And a pro at seventeen
Louise
As justification
Told herself and clients
There was no other way
To support her child

With a handful of sleeping pills
She ended it all at twenty-two
Nobody ever knew
Whether it was grief
Over the death of her daughter
From pneumonia six months before
Or the demise
Simultaneously
Of her excuse.

18. Flo

Each of the past ten years
I've made twenty grand
(Tax-free, of course)
And except for a few clothes
I've got nothing now
But experience;
Since you can't take it with you
And I don't know when I'm going
There's no use keepin' it—
So I raised twenty thousand
Worth of hell every year

When I die
Let my mourners be
Those who miss my spendin'.

19. Blondie

I always feel clean
After Bob beats me;
I know this is a dirty racket
I was taught
There's nothing lower than whores and niggers
So I became curious—
After I got used
To the easy money
I couldn't quit;
Big black Bob
Rounds it out
I'm as far down
As a white woman can get—
When he whams hell out of me
It's punishment for my sins
And I go forth purified

If the time ever comes
When he no longer beats me
I think I'll kill myself.

20. Wilma

In a way
I feel sorry
For my sister Blanche
But after three years
I couldn't take her contempt
Any longer
One day I said,
"That lawyer you work for
Pays me more
For one hour every two weeks
Than you draw in salary
As his secretary
Twice a month"

And I let her know when and where
Naturally
That brought her down
She was afraid to tell him
And couldn't afford to quit

I think
This has hurt her more
Than merely knowing
Her sister is a whore.

21. Madeline

Twice annually
Madeline shopped in Paris and Rome;
Each year
A new white Cadillac convertible;
Her penthouse apartment
Included four originals by Matisse
And had been the birthplace
Of six Broadway hits;
She was available by appointment
Only to select white Gentiles
Well rated in Dun & Bradstreet

She was hospitalized
For a year at thirty-two
Because of a nervous breakdown
When her maid
Angry at being fired
Called her a floozy.

22. Hannah

No, I ain't nothin' but a streetwalker
I seen times so tough
I'd settle for just enough
To dirty a plate
At Joe's Beanery;
One day a gal in the know
Pointed out Madeline

Downtown in her Cadillac
But I wasn't jealous
I just ain't cut out to be
No thousan' dollar woman
And anyway
Her trade is jus' like mine—
No matter how much bread they got
They still put on their socks
One foot at a time!

23. Charity

The old man said
Dejectedly:
    "These be
      My daughters three
      Faith, Hope
      And Charity"

I do not know why
My two older sisters
Look down on me
As a disgrace to the family
When they are the cause
Of my career;
Faith married
To get away from home
She has five kids, a cheatin' husband
And enough unpaid bills
To paper the Empire State;
Hope wed for convenience
Being quite willing
To trade bedding rights for security
And plays around secretly
With any man who strikes her fancy;
Seeing their examples
I chose a better route
To leave home
And harvest security
Attaining, in addition,

Independence—
What right have they to think
They're better than me?

24. Rose

In Chicago's Congo
Rose moves properly
In sundown society
Helping run two clubs
Of the near-elite
Sculpting a reputation
As prim and hard-to-get;
Four afternoons a week
She is available
On the North Side
For white men
Who-want-to-change-their-luck—
Is it any wonder
That she violently opposes
Full integration

25. Trudy

It's lonely there
In the sweating jungle
Of the hard white sheets
Last week
I screwed sixty men
And not one
Was a friend—
That's the reason
I took up with Mike
He's not a statistic,
He exists!
Mike understands my needs
And doesn't consider me
A lay for pay
And I am grateful
I want him to wear $200 suits
And carry folding money;
As I see it

A woman needs companionship
Even if she has to pay for it.

26. Arline

Once I tried
To buy food with pride
And it didn't work

It was then I swore
To arm with powder and paint
For I'd rather be a fallen angel
Than a dead saint.

27. Rita

One big difference
Between Hollywood and Honolulu
Is that in Hawaii
I know what I'm gettin'

In Hollywood
I put promises in my purse
And smiled as if content
Maybe this guy
Really had connections in films
(Who do you say "no" to?
How do you tell
Which shell
The pea is under?)
Gals like me
Are a dime a dozen
And for free

But in Waikiki
I'm something special
To the Midwest tourists
And the Oriental trade
I'm only a little busier
Use fewer Milltowns
And have more in cash
Than the average starlet

Anytime they ask
I'll be happy to contribute
Substantially
To the Hawaii Visitors Bureau!

28. Hilda

One such as I
Grateful for even a pale smile
Would be endlessly thankful
For bigger things

Why then
O city fathers
Do you deny my request
To erect a monument
In any public place
(Paid for by me)
To the discoverer
Of penicillin?

29. Bernice

I thought I had left
Merry-go-rounds
When I broke the chains of childhood
But today
I live on a spinning circle
For years now
I've been shootin' smack
I became a pro
To support my habit
I need a fix
To hustle
I need to hustle
To buy a fix—
How do you leave
A whirling carousel?

30. Jean

Let it be known
O my sisters of the street

That as of now
I am quitting this shacking scene
For I have brought disgrace
To our ancient profession
And I no longer deserve
Your comradeship

Some of you
Wrapped in compassion
Would willingly forgive
And I am grateful
But no more
Can I retain my self-respect—
Through some weird weakness
I have committed
The supreme sin—
Two nights ago
And again last evening
Sleeping with faceless nobodies
I never expect to see again
I came!

31. Patty

Some psychiatrists say
Call girls are emotionally ill—
I proclaim such statements
Reveal the sick prejudices
Of their authors
Unless they concede
The American dream itself
Needs healing;
Printed shouts of the press
Aural orders of radio and TV
Command buy this car, face cream
Spend for this food stuffed with vitamin Z
Invest for old age
This I have done most faithfully
And to thrice the extent possible
By the salaried slaves of secretaries—
Does this not prove

I am one of the very few
To be genuinely
One hundred per cent American?

32. Marjorie

Red-headed Marjorie was exclusive
Catering solely
To the soul trade
It pleased her esthetically
To see black on white;
Further
Believing all men equal
But knowing society
Herded blacks in the basement
And placed prostitutes
Maybe a step above
It eased her ego
To throw her earnings
In cool contempt
Before a white pimp
Thus emotionally shoving him
As a symbol of whiteness
Lower than either
Her profession
Or her tricks.

33. Olive

As a child
I had for brothers
Three big bullies
Who deluged me daily
With their acid flood of raucous contempt
For the weakness of my sex
I cried and wished
For size and strength
But even Nature himself
(Nature, too, must be a man)
Scorned me
Granting but a scant ninety pounds
Forcing me to use

Other means to compensate
For physical inferiority
Of women

I worked hard
To win a reputation
For a purpose
So that today
I can afford to be choosy:
I accept no man
Weighing under two hundred
It is my supreme satisfaction
The triumphant revenge
Of ninety pounds of weakness
To reduce
These burly brutes
To a moaning mass
Of quivering flesh.

34. Jessica

I do not mind
The act itself
To me
A body's a body
Logically
One area no more private
Than any other
Hands clasping
Or bellies rubbing
Are all the same
Flesh meeting flesh—
Why is it then
That afterwards
I sometimes feel
Like a lake of slime.

35. Josephine

Once I spoke to a John
Alone at the counter in Joe's Beanery
Scorn exploded in his voice

As he said
"I don't drink
From a community cup"
I smiled,
"This plate before you
Was it bought only for your use?
Is that a virgin glass
Never before placed
At another's lips?
I can assure you
Thanks to modern medication
I am at least as sanitary
As they
Even though you desire
That kind of contact"
He stared
As the curtain of understanding
Parted;
I turned and walked
Out on the street
Not knowing
Whether to thank God or Satan
For purse-size douche bags.

36. Verna

I stand ready
To shoulder a gun anytime
To help defend
Our system of free private enterprise
And individual initiative
From all enemies
At home or abroad
For I believe religiously
In open competition
And fewer government controls—
Where would I be
With rigid prices
And regimentation?

37. Essie Mae

I'm the friendly simple
Neighborhood whore
That's all I want to be
And if I do say so myself
I give fuckin' good fucks
To my working men trade
For a mere ten bucks;
Last night a strange dude
I ain't never seen before
Asks if I'll do something
He calls fellatio—
It didn't sound right
So I cussed him out
And chased him away
'Cause I ain't no freak
And I don't want no weirdo—
What the hell's fellatio anyway?

To Helen

The thin cool fingers of the wind
Caress your tall loveliness;
The wind kisses
Each shining strand of spun brightness
About your head
Then sends a shimmering waterfall
About the face of you;
I think the summer sun
Would be jealous of your hair,
O Golden Goddess,
Did he not know you.

As for me
I have known you through long yearning years;
Ages ago I built a home for you
Within my mind
A home where I have lived with you
So that when you came down to me
Tired of Olympus,
O Golden Goddess,
I already knew how you would be.

And yet I did not know—
For not even the clearest dream
Can equal the dazzling reality of you.
There is no way to think
The wedding of your lips with mine;
Imagination makes no magic
To match the roaring wonder
Of you close to me;
And now that you have come
My dream caught and clothed in flesh
I shall not let you go.

I shall make you part of me,
My darling,
Fundamental as heart
Primary as mind
And to you I shall become
As the blood in your veins
So that neither you nor I
Could survive
The mutilation of leaving.

Could we today
See the first atom created
Looking on as it grew into a universe
Suns burn and blossom, hurling off whole worlds
Spinning stars and planets grow tired, cold and die
Matter disintegrates
All that is become again one hapless atom
Then vanish
There still would not be time enough
To satisfy my love for you . . .

[In What Strange Place]

In what strange place
Have you hidden the key
To our treasure chest
Where we piled high
The rare talismans
Of our love?
The ebony and alabaster box
Guarding the treasure
That now we sorely need;
We must not force either lid or lock
For fear our fragile gems might shatter—
Thin platinum thread of our first kiss
A covered chalice holding
Fragrance of your first love for me
Tiny fragments of tender words
Cherished from honeyed nights—

These are precious things
I would keep them always . . .

Last night I plunged into the twin calm pools of your eyes
Eyes blue as an April sky;
I seared my soul searching among the flames of your lips
Lips red as a robin's breast;
I hunted in the fragrant forest of your hair
Hair golden as a field of ripened wheat
But still no key . . . still no key!

I listen to the ballet of your voice like a silver-robed dancing girl;
I feel the wondrous warmth of your pale flesh branding the bronze of me;
And I cry because you cannot enter and flow through my veins,
Cannot become the air I breathe for I have no life without you;
I have been jealous of sleep tiptoeing in to close your eyes with soft slum-
    ber fingers
I want to rain my love upon you, strong as a sudden summer storm
I want sometimes to be gentle as the welcome dew in the long lazy hours
    of night
I would be your food that strengthens when hunger comes

All that I have of love
Icons of all my dreams
Lie locked in our treasure chest;
Ah, beloved
Have you tired of my baubles
Have our gems so wondrous in the moon mist
Turned to poor pebbles in the morning sun?
Have you hidden the key
Only for these troubled days
O Golden Goddess
Or have you thrown it complete away?

To My Own

Today
My love for you
Burns with a fierce full flame

In the heart of me
And I would force its heat
Into the golden home
Of my beloved

All that's worthwhile
Of the man called me
My dimpled dreams of days to come
My final facts of what has passed
Of the joy of having you
Are fuel for my fire
And the flame leaps high

I know now how it was
Inside the golden house of you
On the cool winter nights
Of our being
You shivered in the chill air of neglect
And you wondered
"Has the fire died?
Is he so busy he doesn't know my needs?
Warmth!
I must have warmth
Or I shall perish of the cold!"
Then you looked around
Looked through the ice-mated windows
And you saw a blaze
Crowding night from the sky
And the red and blue banners of flame
Danced happily
And called to you with flame words
And you said
"This is what I want."
And you went to it.
The bonfire roars
It sears the face of you with its fierceness
But your back is still cold
For it cannot have
The even heat of home

My dear
My dearest dear
The fire that seemed to fail
On the cool winter night
Is now near to consuming the house
And I shall never again
Let the air grow chill
If you return
To its tender warmth

I want you back!
I want you back again!
I want my fire to warm the house of you!

The fierce full flame
In the heart of me
Is my pagan offering
To your loveliness
O Golden Goddess
To your flowered lips
To the shining blue stars of your eyes
To the shimmering silk of your hair
To the happy warmth of your soft, full breasts
To the tall temple of your young body
And to its secret shrine—
Hot, moist—
Where I worship the womanness of you
With the delirious passion of me
I would burn candles
Tall, thin and amber
To that part of your mind
That still loves me—

You are my own
You are my universe now
Should you go
I would float alone
A homeless atom
In the dark and formless void

There is nothing
Without you
And there are so many dimpled dreams
We have not used
So many final facts of what has passed
Still to be gathered
To feed the fierce full flame
In the heart of me
The flame that would send its heat
Anew
Inside the golden house
Of you
My beloved—

She

I said goodbye to you
Before we ever met—
Long hard-hammering years
Drum soft dreams to dust.

I created you
Sweet woman born of mind
When I summed my years
On fingers and toes
And you lived with me
Unchanging
For five decades
Surviving two wives
And much warmly wanting flesh
Until at last
Believing you would never be
I tossed the pounded dust
Of your soft dream
Into tired oblivion
Then one day
Walking slowly down the street
I met you
My dream flesh-clothed and real

Hair, face, body
And your way of moving
All ageless as tomorrow
Created precisely
According to my private plans
(At such moments
Reality explodes
Time tumbles topsy turvy
And truth grabs a mask)
You smiled at me
Impersonally
Without recognition
Yet respectfully
For my painful pack
Of sawdust years
Then turned with yearning arms
To one still young
As I walked away
Wordlessly
On old man's legs
Remembering
I had already said
Goodbye to you
Before we ever met.

Alpha-Omega

Now we shall remove
Clothes and distilled customs
Called civilization
    any civilization
    Boston, Bombay
    Moscow, Accra
And return flesh-free
To the day when time awoke
In the brain of man
And he felt around in his casual cave
Cave dark as a month of moonless midnights

And with his hands he saw his woman
And his cave became bright as the dancing sun.

This is the careful cavern
Home where no one may enter
But He and She
The Man and Woman place
Unchanged by the crumbling ages
Unmarked by the paint of progress

Woman, lie close to me in the dropping dusk
Let each body foreclose
Its mortgage on the other
As the black stream of night
Flows over us
And the world shrinks
To the warm edge of You and Me

Tomorrow
When day runs in for a visit
We shall awaken
And I shall leave for a little while
I will turn
And you will wave from the welcoming cavern
As I go to find meat for our eating
In the valley below
But I'll be back before the sun goes—
Back to this safe hole in the cliffs
Back to where our world is
A Woman and a Man . . .

The Search Ends

I look into your face
My darling
And the ponderous puzzle of the universe
The whyfore of existence
Stands solved before me;
I hear stars sing

Planets waltz around our sun
Because there is you
And creation at last has meaning

I loved you darling
Before we ever met
I have wanted you
Since my atoms were first assembled
And I had grown bewildered
Wondering why the universe
Had ignited my flaming desire
For you
And then through endless hungering years
Had denied me
Your soul and body

You smile
And it is as I had always dreamed
Morning glories opening ripe petals
To the rising sun—
There is the taste of flame and honey
On your lips—
The silent whir of rising robin's wings
In your eyes—
And when I touch the sweet velvet
Of your face
Feel the warmth of your electric body
Like a sun crashing through cold clouds
I plunge into a fragrant pool
Of luminous love for you

I could float eternally
In the flowing waterfall of your hair;
Your voice is gentle fingers
Caressing my ears
And when I am near you
Time sleeps

All too soon you will go from me
But knowing there is you

That your soul and body are real
I shall love you
With every yearning atom
Until they cease to be;
And I am grateful
For even this passing whisper
Realizing I am one of the fortunate few
To see and touch a dream incarnate—
I thank you
For being
And I love you
For being you.

Alone

1

Limping seconds stumble
Along string-thin nothing nights
Clocks shout their tick tocks
Sleep looks in with frightened eyes
Then flees silently into the endless dark
And I lie restlessly alone
Endlessly counting my collection
Of worn memories

2

I live in a world
Peopled only by you
You are near
And the very air sings
The blood whistles in my veins
And the jigsaw puzzle
Of why am I here
Assembles itself

3

When you are gone
I talk low with ghosts

And none of us
Has very much to say

4

Tomorrow steps surely into the room
Shouldering a new sack of hopes
Eagerly I open each gay box
And peer excitedly inside
Sometimes I find a shining jewel
Precious as a new love's mouth
But mostly
My room is littered with disappointments
To be gathered
And burned with the trash at midnight

5

On that day
When I shall no longer await
The bag of promises
Brought by tomorrow
I shall arrange to die.

1984 ∎

War Quiz for America

(To Be Read Aloud by Eight Voices)

Leader: Who am I?

1st Voice: I am Crispus Attucks in Boston dying to give birth to America
             I am Peter Salem stopping Major Pitcairn at Bunker Hill
             I am John Johnson at Lake Erie, my lower limbs shot away, shouting,
                 "Fire away, my boys, no haul a color down!"
             I am 109 black sailors on whom Commodore Perry staked full trust

2nd Voice: I am Robert Smalls delivering my boat from the vest pocket of the Con-
                 federacy to the Union and Freedom
             I am the Tenth Cavalry rescuing Teddy Roosevelt at San Juan Hill in
                 Crimson Cuba
             I am Needham Roberts and Henry Johnson first of the battling Yanks
                 decorated by France for bravery under fire.

3rd Voice: I am Dorie Miller at Pearl Harbor shooting down four Jap planes with
                 a machine gun you never let me fire before
             I am that one American in ten you have always depended on when trou-
                 ble batters down the front door

Leader: Surely you remember me

Chorus: I am Roland Hayes slugged by police on the streets of Rome, Georgia

I am four of nine Scottsboro boys still rotting in Kilby prison in Alabama

I am Cleo Wright lynched at Sikeston, Missouri, while you cried for national unity in the face of Jap savagery

I am men and women murdered by police in Detroit, chased from my shipyard jobs in Mobile, creeping back by morn to my burned and looted homes in Beaumont

I am soldiers wearing your uniform beaten and killed down South without a chance to leave the fatherland and fight for continuation of this same American way of life

1st Voice: I am Paul Robeson singing "Ballad for Americans" through loudspeakers of radios all over the nation

A Woman: I am Marian Anderson, denied the use of Constitution Hall, thrilling Washington with "The Star Spangled Banner" in the open air at the Lincoln Memorial

Leader: You have seen me barred from the polls in ten thousand towns and have given me nothing but tissue paper words

You have seen me crowded six to a room in the covenant-fenced ghettoes of Chicago and denied the right to live in homes my taxes built in Detroit

1st Voice: When you cried aloud for more workers, I rushed to your factory doors armed with Executive Order 8802 and escorted by the Fair Employment Practice Committee but still I have been turned back by those who would rather fight me than whip the Axis

Chorus: I am the American Negro

I send my soldier sons proudly into a Jim Crow army for America is the only home I know

My young die to restore freedom to oppressed people of the world for who understands better than I the hurt of the aggressor's heel ground into the face

I am he who traditionally gives you hundred percent support from fifty percent citizenship

⌐⌐

Leader: Are these the Four Freedoms for which we fight? Freedom from want

Voice: ("So sorry but we don't hire Negroes. Our white employees won't work with you. The union, you know")

Leader: Freedom from fear

Voice: ("Nigger, take off yo' hat and say 'sir' when you speak to a white man
             in Arkansas. A smart darky down here's a curiosity—and sometimes
             we embalm curiosities")

Leader: Freedom of religion

Voice: ("Of course you can't come in here! This is a white church")

Leader: Freedom of speech

Voice: ("We gits along with ouah niggers, so unless you want to leave here feet
             first don't be putting none of them Red social equality ideas in their
             minds")

⌐⌐

Leader: Have you heard about regimentation in Washington?
             Ten men to run the war
             A hundred to ration black participation

⌐⌐

1st Voice: Uncle Sam, Uncle Sam
             Why send me against Axis foes
             In the death-kissed foxholes of New Guinea and Europe
             Without shielding my back from the sniping Dixie lynchers in the jun-
             gles of Texas and Florida?

Leader: Down in Georgia a soldier said:

2nd Voice: "Me? I'm from Paine County, Alabama
             "Born black and I'm gonna die the same way
             "Went t' school three yeahs befo' it rotted down. By the time the white
             folks got around t' fixing it my first wife had done died.
             "But you oughta see my brothah. Finished State Teachuh's College an'
             now he's making forty dollah uh month back home. That's ovah half
             uh what they pays white teachuhs
             "Been helpin' Pappy work the same fifty acres for Mistuh Jim his own
             pappy had. Pappy bought a single barrel shotgun from Mistuh Jim
             five yeahs ago. Paid ten dol'ahs down an' a dollah a week an' he still
             owes twenty mo'

"Sheriff came 'round and tol' me they wanted me in the Army. Came heah to Fort Benning an' they give me a gun and a uniform an' three good meals a day. Fust time I evah knowed a white man to give me anything

"This mawnin' I heard somebody on a radio say we was all fightin' fo' democracy

"Democracy? What's democracy?"

Leader: Nothing is so final as a bullet through the heart or head
And a correctly thrust bayonet is an unanswerable argument
For democracy against fascism
For Four Freedoms against oppression.
This you taught me in camps from Miami to Seattle
To use against Nazi, Jap
And it works;
It works in the Pacific Islands
In Africa, in Europe,
Everywhere it works
You have convinced me completely
Even as I have become expert
In killing the mad dogs
Leaping to tear
Democracy's soft throat—
And if that's the technique
If it works in lands I never saw before
Against strangers with faces new to me
Then it must be the right thing to use
Against all foes of freedom
Against all apostles of fascism
Against some people I know
Right here in America.

Voice: I know more about Bilbo than I do about Tojo

Voice: I've read about Hitler but I have also lived in Georgia when Talmadge was governor

Voice: Talk about Mussolini if you want to, but did you ever hear Rankin rave in Congress?

Voice: To me the Black Dragon Society is just a foreign nightmare but I have been beaten and murdered by the Ku Klux Klan

Leader: So if I'm going to clean up the Rhine—
I might as well include the Mississippi—
With the understanding
Of course
That it will be only
For democracy against fascism
For Four Freedoms against oppression—
Say, Uncle Sam,
Are you sure you want me to have a gun?

⌐⌐

Chorus: Do you get it, America?
If you take my brown sons to fight abroad for democracy then I have a
right to expect it here
If you're going to carry the Four Freedoms all over the world you may
as well start at home
If you want me to help crush fascism and oppression I want no distinc-
tion between foreign and home grown brands

Leader: I know the glib guys are selling slogans
I know some top Britishers say this is a war to keep their empire intact
I know some people want to whip the Japanese for ever daring to think
they are as good as whites
I know some heavy investors side with China because they'd like to keep
'em handy to exploit
I know some big shots are fighting to restore a 1930 world
I know some loudmouths rattle off sweet talk about human rights and
world brotherhood and intend it as hogwash
And I know there are some who see me working and sweating and bleed-
ing and dying and they say "You'd better you black bastard if you
know what's good for you"
And it's up to the rest of us to set 'em right

Chorus: Do you get it, America?
Do you get it, Congress?

Voice: Say, Mister, you with the white face, are you an American?
Where did you come from and when? France, Poland, England, Russia,
Spain, Italy? Oh yeah? And how do you know somebody from Sene-
gal never got mixed up in your family?

Leader: I know there are white Americans who want to be Americans, disciples of the square deal, lovers of the Constitution, believers in raceless justice, equality.

I've praised all 57 varieties of gods for Wendell Willkie, Henry Wallace, Pearl Buck, Eleanor and Franklin D. Give us enough guys like Phil Murray and R. J. Thomas and we'll disintegrate Father Coughlin and Gerald L. K. Smith into friendless atoms

Voice: I know also that I have my dark Dillengers, my tinsel Tojos, my hybrid Hitlers for I have seen them loot stores in Detroit and Harlem, heard them hymn hate in Chicago's Congo, watched as they lynched opportunity in new jobs and public places, and I love them no more than you love your own pale troublemakers

Chorus: But what of the others, the worthy ones, millions of whites, millions of blacks, the common people, the workers, the doers, born under the same flag, dreaming the same dream of liberty and security, marrying and bearing children swaddled in similar dreams?

Leader: These common people, the strugglers, why do they duel each other? Why do they fight among themselves when there are bigger enemies? Why do they shoot and maim and kill in Mobile, Los Angeles, Beaumont when their foe bristles in Berlin, Tokyo? And why did the Detroit casualty list yield none but the names of the common people?

Voice: When white sharecropper rips the flesh of black sharecropper, who laughs and steals the shirts of both?

Who gains when white laborers bolt their urban doors in the face of their black brothers in toil?

Who loosed poison arrows at the Congress of Industrial Organizations, for daring to recruit all workers in a raceless fraternity?

Does anybody clip bigger dividends in Wall Street when workers walk their separate ways?

Chorus: In a democracy the people run the country!

2nd Voice: What millionaire newspapers paint an idea Red because it would help the common people?

How much taxes go for costly sacrifices to the graven god of race prejudice?

Who walks to Congress across bowed backs of the quarreling masses?

3rd Voice: Who sold scrap iron to Italy to dump on Ethiopia, oil to the Japs to wing war planes over China?

How did "U. S. Steel Corporation" get on shrapnel extracted from Corporal Berowitz at Guadalcanal?

Chorus: In a democracy the people run the country!

Leader: Ideas slip together and a pattern forms. Hitler wrote:

Voice: "America is a pushover. Get the races fighting among themselves and I can step in any old time"

Leader: And Standard Oil in Texas gave pamphlets to white workers saying to join the CIO would mean social equality
And Hirohito sent word to black men:

2nd Voice: "Japan is the champion of all colored people. Stand ready to rebel"

Leader: And a vice president at Packard got white labor to strike when Negroes were upgraded on assembly lines
Who snipped this pattern? The common people?

Chorus: In a democracy the people run the country!

Leader: That's it!
In a democracy the people run the country!
Say, Mister, you with the white face, you toiler
Come over here and let's talk.
Maybe we both got the same disease
But different symptoms;
Mine pops out in humiliating race discrimination
Yours is a rash of class distinction and poverty coming from the same infection.
Fascism and profit grabbing
And we're both tired steppers to a dollar jazz

Chorus: In a democracy the people run the country!

Leader: Who says we can't get along!
We are the people
We are the black workers and the white workers and all the workers
We are the marching sweating fighting people
We are the builders of America
We are the keepers of America
We are the breathing facts of democracy
We are the people
And in a democracy the people run the country

Chorus: Shout a factory fresh slogan, streamlined and strong:
            "A people's peace in America to win a people's war"

Leader: Shout it in the cabins and cotton fields down South
            Shout it in the tenements and business plants up north
            "A people's peace in America to win a people's war"

Chorus: Shout it in Harlem and Hollywood
            "A people's peace to win a people's war"
            How about it, America?

Black Man's Verse (1935)

Introduction

4   "Duskymerican": Davis combines *dusky* and *American* to create this nonce phrase describing African Americans. He follows in the wake of writers like James Weldon Johnson and George Schuyler, who both used "Aframericans." Schuyler, it should be noted, made his use satiric.

Chicago's Congo

5   "Congo": Davis refers to the former Belgian colony, which is the second-biggest country in sub-Saharan Africa. Because the poem is set in Chicago, he calls attention to the sharply delineated Negro ghetto, separated from the white community by a high though unofficial wall of segregation and discrimination. Here, nearly a half million Black Chicagoans maintained a community life that, on the surface at least, seemed virtually independent of white Chicago's.

6   "Transvaal": Before Black South African independence, the Transvaal Province was the most populous and wealthiest of South Africa's four provinces. The area was designated for Bantu homelands as well as the provincial territory reserved for whites.

6   "Wagner": The German composer Richard Wagner (1813–83) wrote operas and symphonies that had a revolutionary effect on the course of Western music.

7   "L train": Also called an "el train," this is short for "elevated train," a major form of public transportation in Chicago.

What Do You Want America?

9   "Medusa's head": One of the three Gorgons in Greek mythology, Medusa was a beautiful maiden whose hair the goddess Athena transformed into snakes because she violated Athena's sanctuary. Generally her glance alone had the power to petrify mortals. After she was decapitated by Perseus, her head had the power to turn those who looked at it into stone.

9   "Scottsboro, Alabama": In 1931 nine Black youths were accused of raping two white women of dubious reputation on a freight train near Scottsboro, Alabama.

9   "Chain gangs": This form of forced labor arose during the postbellum era. A group of convicts was chained together and made to work on stone quarrying, road building, and bridge constructing.

10   "Crispus Attucks": Of at least partial African American descent, Attucks (1723–70) was acclaimed as the first martyr of the American Revolution when he and four others were killed by British soldiers in what became known as the Boston Massacre.

10   "Peter Salem and . . . Pitcairn on Bunker Hill": Major John Pitcairn (1722–75) led the British troops at the Battle of Lexington on 19 April 1775. He was fatally wounded in the Battle of Bunker Hill on 17 June 1775 by Peter Salem (1750–1816), one of five thousand African Americans who fought in the American Revolution. Had Salem remained a slave he would have been unable to participate in the war because only freed blacks could serve in the army.

10   "Perry on Lake Erie": In the War of 1812, many Blacks were allowed to enlist in the navy despite their race. After the battle of Lake Erie, Captain Oliver H. Perry gave unstinting praise to Black members of his crew and declared that danger did not seem to affect them.

10   "at Gettysburg, on San Juan Hill, in the Argonne, and at St. Michel": The Battle of Gettysburg (1–3 July 1863) was a major and bloody engagement in the American Civil War fought near Gettysburg, Pennsylvania. San Juan Hill, near the city of Santiago, Cuba, was a site where the Black contingents of the Tenth Cavalries saved Theodore Roosevelt's Rough Riders from complete annihilation in July 1898. The Battle of Argonne in September 1918 gave Allies ample evidence of the courage of the all-Black 369th Infantry. Later in 1918, the Battle of St. Michel afforded members of the 369th Infantry another opportunity to prove their courage.

10   "Phillis Wheatley . . . McKay": Davis lists here a few of the most distinguished names in African American poetry: Phillis Wheatley (1753?–1784), the slave prodigy who wrote *Poems on Various Subjects, Religious and Moral* (1773); Paul Laurence Dunbar (1872–1906), who was the first to use distinctively Black dialect within a formal poetic structure; James Weldon Johnson (1871–1938), arguably the most cosmopolitan of the group since he enjoyed careers as poet, novelist, dramatist, teacher, critic, diplomat, and NAACP official; Countee

Cullen (1903–46), who, because of his appeal to whites and Blacks, emerged as the archetypal New Negro Renaissance poet; Langston Hughes (1902–67), for whom blues and jazz provided deep and abiding sources of poetic inspiration; and Claude McKay (1890–1948), who explored the relationship between art and politics in a complex array of writing, none more successful than his experiments with the English sonnet.

10   "Tanner": Henry Ossawa Tanner (1859–1937), a world-renowned painter at the turn of the twentieth century, won prizes at the Paris Exposition of 1900, the Pan American Exposition of 1901, and the St. Louis Exposition of 1904.

10   "Hayes and Robeson": Roland Hayes (1887–1977) was an internationally renowned tenor whose rich, delicate voice was used to good advantage in programs blended from spirituals, folk songs, operatic arias, and German *lieder*. Paul Robeson (1898–1976) was an actor whose leading roles in such plays as *Othello* and *The Emperor Jones* won for him wide dramatic acclaim and whose singing also made him one of the greatest artists of his time. Because of his developing Leftist political views, he became a subject of controversy and governmental investigation.

10   "Bert Williams, Miller, and Lyles": Williams (1876–1922), a legendary comedian, was considered by many to be the greatest Black vaudeville performer in the history of the American stage. Flournoy E. Miller and Aubrey Lyles took Broadway by storm with such musical hits as *Shuffle Along* (1921) and *Runnin' Wild* (1923).

10   "Handy": William Christopher Handy (1873–1958) is generally regarded as the "Father of the Blues" because he was the first musician to publish the folk blues.

10   "Carver": A nationally renowned agricultural scientist, George Washington Carver (1864–1943) devoted his life to researching the peanut, the sweet potato, and the soybean, products that revolutionized the economy of the South by liberating it from an excessive dependence on cotton.

10   "Washington and DuBois": Booker Taliaferro Washington (1856–1915) was the founder and president of the famous Tuskegee Institute and was considered, in his day and time, the most influential African American. His educational and political goals of accommodation and conciliation were most thoroughly critiqued by W. E. B. Du Bois (1868–1963) in *The Souls of Black Folk*. Armed with a Harvard Ph.D., Du Bois opposed Washington's vocational training and advocated a liberal arts education and a Talented Tenth to formulate solutions to African American racial problems. In Du Bois's model one-tenth of the Black male population would be supported in efforts to obtain a liberal arts education, which these men would then use to provide intellectual guidance for the race as it sought liberation from the debilitating effects of post-slavery life. By his own admission later, the theory was flawed since it failed to account for self-interest, having no way of compelling this educated elite to work on behalf of the race, and because it ignored the ability of women to provide leadership.

10   "Benjamin Banneker": A Boston inventor, mathematician, and almanac maker, the African American Banneker (1731–1806) constructed in 1761 what was probably the first clock made in America—a wooden "striking" clock so accurate that it kept perfect time and struck each hour unfailingly for more than twenty years. As a field assistant to Andrew Ellicott, Banneker surveyed the land that became designated as the District of Columbia.

10   "Jack Johnson": Johnson (1878–1946) was the first African American heavyweight boxing champion of the world, winning the crown in 1908. His mythic reputation in American popular culture was enhanced and ultimately undermined by his violation of the social mores of his time by dating and marrying white women.

10   "Eddie Tolan": In the 1932 Olympics, Tolan (1908–67) won the distinction of being the fastest human being when he ran the 100 meters in 10.3 seconds and the 200 meters in 21.2 seconds.

10   "Dehart Hubbard": With his jump of 24'5 ⅛" at the 1924 Paris Olympiad, Hubbard (1903–76) became the first African American to win an Olympic gold medal.

10   "Bessie Coleman": Coleman (1892–1926) was the first African American female aviator. Because of American racial bias against training Black pilots, she went to Paris in November 1920 and attended an aviation school in Le Crotoy.

10   "Amelia Earhart": Earhart (1897–1937?) was the most celebrated female American aviator of her time. After many notable "firsts," she disappeared after taking off from New Guinea for Howland Island in the Pacific on 1 July 1937.

10   "Fritz Pollards, Duke Slaters": Frederick Douglass "Fritz" Pollard (1894–1986), in the 1916 season, was an all-American football player at Brown University. Frederick W. "Duke" Slater (1898–?) was the University of Iowa's first Black all-American football player in 1921.

11   "the Kaiser": Kaiser Wilhelm, or William II (1859–1941), was the king of Prussia and the German emperor from 1888 to 1918.

11   "the Rome of Caesar": Julius Caesar (100–44 B.C.), the great Roman general and statesman, ruled in a dictatorship that led inevitably to Rome's transition from republic to empire.

I Sing No New Songs

11   "Milton": John Milton (1608–74) cast a long shadow in English literary history because of such canonical works as *Paradise Lost* and the argument for freedom of the press in *Areopagitica*.

11   "Lindsay": Vachel Lindsay (1879–1931) was an American poet who believed that art was a regenerating force in life. When he embarked upon several tramping journeys to preach the gospel of beauty, he traded his verses for food and lodging. His most famous collection was *The Congo* (1914), which broke new ground stylistically although it furthered many Black stereotypes.

11   "Jim Colosimo": Big Jim Colosimo, who emigrated from Italy, got his first job in America as a water boy for a railroad construction gang. In 1902, Colosimo married the owner of a popular Chicago house of prostitution. From there, by easy stages, he rose to the top of Chicago's underworld society. There are conflicting accounts of his death, but it appears that he died in 1921 at the hands of his nephew Torrio and a lieutenant, Al Capone.

Gary, Indiana

18   "Gary, Indiana": The city is located in the northwest corner of the state, on Lake Michigan. Laid out by the U.S. Steel Corp. in 1905, it became a major steel-producing center.

19   "Babel": In the Bible, the Tower of Babel was erected by the descendants of Noah in an attempt to reach heaven. God showed his displeasure at their audacity by making the people's many languages mutually unintelligible. Davis refers to the workers who came from Europe, Asia, and Central America and the many different languages they spoke.

20   "old Judge Gary": E. H. Gary was a lawyer and prominent figure in the steel company that founded the city. He stood for stability and centralization in business. He insisted that his directors be men of honor and probity, and he developed an extensive system of pensions and other benefits for steelworkers. He resisted unions and opposed antitrust legislation, which he considered destructive and reactionary.

Jazz Band

21   "Dios, Jehovah, Gott, Allah, Buddha": These words are all names for God. *Dios* is Spanish; *Jehovah,* which means "creator," has largely replaced *Yahweh* in English-speaking Christian churches; *Gott* is German; *Allah* is the god of Islam, founded by Muhammad (567?–632); Siddhartha Gautama, known as the Buddha, was an Indian philosopher who founded the religion that bears his name during the sixth century B.C.

21   "cake walk": This promenade or march originated in slave culture but by 1895 had become a mass cultural phenomenon, when it was incorporated into Broadway productions. It consists of couples performing intricate or eccentric steps and takes its name from the cakes contestants originally received as prizes.

Returned

25   "Hannibal and Michaelangelo": Leader of the Carthaginian forces, Hannibal (247–183 B.C.) was regarded by many as the greatest general of antiquity. Michelangelo Buonarotti (1475–1564), the Italian sculptor, painter, architect, and poet, is generally considered the most masterful artist who has ever lived.

Five Portraits of Chicago at Night

27   "Lake Michigan Chicago's Loop": The term *Loop* became synonymous with downtown Chicago fifteen years before the completion of the elevated railway system around the central business district. It remains a defining Chicago landmark.

27   "Chinatown . . . The Gold Coast": Davis lists neighborhoods in Chicago including the Gold Coast, a wealthy white residential area along the shore of Lake Michigan.

27   "Flivver": This is a slang term for an automobile, especially one that is small, inexpensive, and old.

Hands of a Brown Woman

30   "Pharaohs . . . Cheops": The pharaohs were the kings of ancient Egypt. Cheops, one of these royal figures, began a fifty-year rule about 2650 B.C. and ordered the building of the largest pyramid at Giza.

30   "Golgotha": Golgotha was the site where Christ was crucified.

30   "Columbus, Cortes": These two explorers were credited with "discovering" the New World. Christopher Columbus (1451?–1506) was the Italian-born Spanish navigator who directed four round-trip transatlantic voyages to North America. Hernando Cortes (1485–1547) was the Spanish conqueror of Mexico.

Creation

31   "Beast of Mythology": Davis probably refers here to the minotaur, the monstrous offspring of the union between the Cretan Bull and Pasiphae, wife of Minos, who had lain with the animal while she was inside a wooden cow built for her by Daedalus. It is usually depicted as a horribly disfigured creature having a bull's head and a man's body.

Which One?

31   "Muhammed": See the note to 21 for "Dios, Jehovah, Gott, Allah, Buddha."

Lullaby

32   This poem was first published in *Crisis* 35.11 (Nov. 1928): 372. Its original subtitle was "For a Flute and Violin." Before he included it in *Black Man's Verse*, Davis modified the poem substantially. Line nine, for instance, originally read: "Kiss me with sugar lips." Line fifteen first read: "My soft body's baby." Line eighteen originally read: "I will bring the gold of rich perfumes." The whole last stanza was changed from this original statement:

> A blanket of black silk for your crib, baby
> A blanket of silk embroidered with stars

The sky for your blanket, the world for your crib
The night for your nursemaid, baby.

In two ways, this second version is superior to the first. There is a more racialized notion of love in changing "sugar lips" to "soft, dark lips" as well as in the change from "soft body's baby" to "black body's baby." The imagery of the last stanza in the original version is bogged down in rhetoric and inconsistency. The revised poem transforms this stanza into a more sensuous, suggestive expression of love, one more in keeping with the feeling the poem attempts to project.

Georgia's Atlanta

36 "Black Shirts": The Italian militarist Benito Mussolini (1883–1945) used the pretext of saving the country from bolshevism, which had already ceased to be a threat, to launch his rise to power in the winter of 1920–21 with the help of his militia, the Black Shirts.

36 "B.Y.P.U.'s": The Baptist Young Peoples' Union emphasized spiritual training for youth in the Baptist church.

36 "Ku Klux Klan": This refers to either of two distinct secret U.S. terrorist organizations; one was founded immediately after the Civil War and lasted until the 1870s and the other began in 1915 and continues its focus on white supremacy to the present.

Portrait of an Old Woman

38 "Leavenworth": This is a federal prison located in Kansas.

To You

43 "Aria": An aria is an elaborate melody sung solo with accompaniment, as in an opera or oratorio.

Love Notes at Night

44 "Zither": A German musical instrument, the zither consists of a flat sounding box with thirty to forty-two strings stretched over it and is played with a plectrum, or pick, and the fingertips.

44 "Acropolis": This is the citadel or central upper fortified part of an ancient Greek city, a site chosen for defense because it was elevated and inaccessible. Best known is the structure in Athens, whose buildings are models of perfection.

The Story Ends

46 "Olympus": Mount Olympus was the fabled home of the Greek gods, who lived in the pure upper air beyond a cloud gate.

46   "Zeus": The supreme god of the Greek pantheon, Zeus was later equated with the Roman god Jupiter.

47   "Fates": The three Greek goddesses known as the Fates assigned necessity or determined destiny.

47   "Betelguese": The brightest star in the constellation of Orion, Betelguese is yellowish-red and is therefore easily distinguished from the other important stars in the constellation, which are white.

Robert Whitmore

50   "Elks": This fraternal organization is one to which many African Americans belong.

50   "apoplexy": No longer in use, this term means a stroke caused by a blockage or a blood clot in the blood vessels of the brain. As used poetically here, it refers to embarrassment, chagrin, and hurt feelings.

George Brown

51   "disfranchised": African American men were not granted the right to vote, or the franchise, until passage of the Fifteenth Amendment in 1870. Well into the twentieth century, many trying to vote were either given qualifying "literacy tests"—which were never intended to be passed—forced to demonstrate an understanding of arcane clauses from their state constitutions, assessed a discriminatory poll tax, or simply turned away.

Roosevelt Smith

52   "Carl Sandburg, Edgar Lee Masters": Carl August Sandburg (1878–1967), an American poet, biographer, lecturer, and folk singer, was world-famous as a writer of free verse that commented on the people and places of modern American life. Edgar Lee Masters, an American poet (1869–1950), was best known for his *Spoon River Anthology* (1915). Employing the convention of having the dead in a local graveyard discuss the lives they really lived, Masters presented an honest though stern portrait of life in an American community.

52   "Aframerica": See the note to 4 for "Duskymericans."

52   "'Ships That Pass In The Night'": This poem by Paul Laurence Dunbar first appeared in his *Lyrics of Lowly Life* (1896), the collection made famous by the renowned literary critic William Dean Howells. In his introduction to this collection, much to Dunbar's chagrin, Howells wrote: "So far as I could remember, Paul Dunbar was the only man of pure African blood and of American civilization to feel the negro [sic] life aesthetically and express it lyrically" (rpt. in *The Life and Works of Paul Laurence Dunbar*, ed. Lida Keck Wiggins [Naperville, Ill.: J. L. Nichols, 1907], 15).

52   "Gertrude Stein or T.S. Eliot": Stein (1874–1946) was an American author known for her experiments with language and for her influence on such

American writers as Sherwood Anderson and Ernest Hemingway. Thomas Stearns Eliot (1888–1965), the American-born poet, dramatist, and critic, became a British subject after 1927. Many have regarded him as the greatest poet of the twentieth century.

52 "Keats, Browning": John Keats (1795–1821) was the youngest of the major poets of the Romantic period in English literature. His experiments with form, particularly the sonnet, not only distinguished him among his contemporaries but also established poetic models for later generations to follow. Robert Browning (1812–89) was an English poet of the Victorian era famous for his dramatic monologues and his psychological epic *The Ring and the Book* (1868). In his *World's Great Men of Color* (1946), J. A. Rogers created a controversy by claiming Browning's ancestry was African.

I Am the American Negro

Forewarning

57 "Pollyanna": In the 1913 American novel *Pollyanna* written by Eleanor Hodgman Porter (1868–1920), the child heroine is an expert at the "Glad Game" of always looking at the bright side during her numerous tribulations. *Pollyanna* has become a synonym for a fatuous, irrepressible optimist.

57 "Venus": She is the Roman goddess of beauty and love.

I Am the American Negro

58 "Mandingo, Benin, Yoruba": Mandingo is the linguistic and cultural designation for one of the most important groups in western Africa, whose commerce and politics were vastly developed before the European commercial revolution of the midfourteenth century. In precolonial western Africa, Benin was noted for its impressive bronze, ivory, copper, and brass sculpture. Yoruba is a linguistic, cultural, and religious designation for certain of the Ife, Ibadan, and Egba peoples who lived in parts of Nigeria, Benin, and northern Togo.

58 "Timbuktu, Kana, Zimbabwe, Zegzeg": Timbuktu is a town in northern Mali that became a crossroads for commerce and an international center for intellectual advance during the fifteenth and sixteenth centuries. Kana is the language spoken in the northeastern fringe of Ogoniland in southeastern Nigeria. As used here, *Zimbabwe* probably refers to the ruins indicating the existence of a past civilization in southeast Africa, in what is now Zimbabwe. This term derives from the Bantu *zimba*, meaning houses, and *magbi*, meaning stones, and preserves a long heritage that extends possibly back to the Stone Age. The ancient state of Zaria, also called Zeg-Zeg by the geographers and historians of the Middle Ages, was one of the original and most dominant states of the Hausa people.

61 "Spottsylvania Courthouse, / Bull Run": During the Civil War, a series of

engagements broke out below the Rapidan River near Spottsylvania Court House, Virgnia, in 1864. The Battle of Bull Run, or the Battle of Manassas, took place near Manassas, Virginia, on 21 July 1861.

61   "three Constitutional Amendments": In 1865, Congress ratified the Thirteenth Amendment to the Constitution, abolishing slavery in the United States. This was followed in 1868 by the Fourteenth Amendment, granting African Americans full civil rights. The Fifteenth Amendment, forbidding the denial of voting rights on the basis of "race, color, or previous conditions of servitude," was ratified in 1870.

62   "Howard, Atlanta, Tuskegee; at Harvard, Oxford, Berlin": Davis lists colleges and universities that have nurtured an important number of Black scholars. Howard University, known as "the capstone of Negro Education," is in Washington, D.C.; Atlanta University, later the first all-black American graduate school, is located in Atlanta, Georgia. Booker T. Washington opened the famed Tuskegee Institute in Alabama on 4 July 1881. Scholars such as W. E. B. Du Bois and Alain Locke have benefited from graduate and postgraduate studies at Harvard, Oxford, and Berlin Universities.

62   "Plato and Einstein": Plato (ca. 427–347 B.C.), the second of the great trio of ancient Greek philosophers (Socrates, Plato, and Aristotle), was known for such influential philosophical works as *The Republic* and *The Sophist*. Albert Einstein (1879–1955) was the German-American physicist who, beginning in 1905, developed the special and general theories of relativity, the equivalence theory of mass and energy, and the photon theory of light.

Dancing Gal

64   "Tanganyika": In 1961, Tanganyika gained independence from the British and in 1964 merged with Zanzibar to form the east African nation now known as Tanzania.

64   "Hindustan": Originally a designation for the region and dialect of the Hindi-speaking people in northern India, Hindustan later came to designate the trade language for the entirety of India.

They All Had Grand Ideas

66   "Alexander": Alexander the Great (356–323 B.C.), by way of his conquests, spread Greek culture widely throughout the Middle East and central Asia. Some historians believe that he hoped to create a multiracial state and may have conceived of the essential unity of humankind, though whether he saw himself as a universal monarch is still debated.

66   "Judas": In the New Testament, Judas Iscariot was one of the original Twelve Disciples; his betrayal led to the crucifixion of Jesus.

66   "Monroe Doctrine": On 2 December 1823, President James Monroe used his annual message to Congress for a bold assertion: "The American continents . . . are henceforth not to be considered as subjects for future coloni-

zation by an European power." Known as the Monroe Doctrine, this statement became a cornerstone of American foreign policy.

66　"Lenin and Trotsky": Lenin, the adopted name of Vladimir Ilyich Ulyanov (1870–1924), was a Russian revolutionary and founder of the Soviet Union; with the aid of the Bolshevik-organized Red Guard, he overthrew the czarist government in the 1917 October Revolution, seizing power in the name of the people. Leon Trotsky, whose original name was Lev Davidovich Bronstein (1879–1940), was the second most powerful man in the Soviet Union from the October Revolution to the death of Lenin. He lost ground to Josef Stalin after Lenin's death and was assassinated in exile.

66　"Stalin": Josef Stalin (1879–1953) moved away from the collectivist vision of Lenin and Trotsky and became the dictatorial ruler of the Soviet Union in 1925. Following World War II, he instigated a foreign policy that largely determined the configuration of postwar Europe.

66　"Napoleon": Napoleon Bonaparte (1769–1821), born in Corsica and educated in French ways, was nevertheless no native Frenchman. His rise to power was accomplished via his military conquests of the French monarchy and culminated in his position of emperor in 1804. His downfall was recorded at the Battle of Waterloo on 18 June 1815, which is still considered by some as the most famous battle of modern history.

66　"an actor / slipped Lincoln the last curtain call": On 14 April 1865 President Abraham Lincoln (1809–65) was shot by the actor John Wilkes Booth at Ford's Theater in Washington, D.C. He died the following day.

66　"Men dream and die . . .": Here Davis expresses the theme of "no new ideas" by presenting a succession of thinkers who built on the works of their predecessors: Muhammad followed Jesus Christ; Kaiser Wilhelm followed the lead of Hannibal in building his empire; Einstein's theories of physics built on those of the seventeenth-century philosopher-scientist Sir Isaac Newton (1642–1727); and the distinguished Irish playwright George Bernard Shaw (1856–1950) stood in the long shadow cast by William Shakespeare.

Christ Is a Dixie Nigger

67　"New White Hope": Boxing Hall of Famer Jack Johnson, the first Black World Heavyweight Champion, dominated the sport for seven years during the early 1900s. In an effort to restore the crown to a white boxer and therefore white hegemony, the most likely white candidate to defeat Johnson was referred to as the "great white hope." On 15 April 1915, the white boxer Jess Willard was awarded the crown when Johnson "took a dive" during their match.

67　"Rosenwald money": Between 1913 and 1932, The Julius Rosenwald Fund helped to establish 5,357 grade or high schools in the South for black children. In 1937, before he published this collection, Davis received the first Julius Rosenwald Fellowship for Poetry.

68   "Pilate": Pontius Pilate was the Roman governor of Judea who presided at the trial and condemnation of Jesus.

68   "Gethsemane": This is the place on the Mount of Olives where Jesus went after the Last Supper, prayed in agony, and was arrested.

Washington Park, Chicago

68   "Washington Park": This neighborhood was once an exclusive area of Southside Chicago bounded on the east by Cottage Grove Avenue and the west by Grand Avenue. It stretched from Fifty-first Street on the north to Sixtieth Street on the south.

68   "Dearborn Street": An early fashionable residential street, Dearborn had elegant brownstones that were converted into rooming houses by the 1940s.

68   "South Parkway": As its name suggests, this was an important north-south residential street with, at times, broad grassy medians. It was known for its mansions and large townhouses.

69   "mazda": In the same way *xerox* has entered our vocabulary to mean "photocopy," *mazda* refers to incandescent lighting. Appropriating the religious significance of light from Zoroastrian religion, the General Electric Company named its new tungsten filament lamp Mazda around 1909.

70   "Martha, the Love Murderess": Of several Marthas who bore this nickname, Davis probably intends Martha Wise, a thirty-nine-year-old widow from Ohio. In 1924–25, she devised a plan to kill members of her family who refused to indulge her request to marry a younger man. In these two years, she poisoned three family members before other relatives became suspicious and reported her to authorities. She later confessed, claiming, "the devil made me do it."

73   "Edison, Marconi, Einstein, Darwin": Thomas Alva Edison (1847–1931) patented more than one thousand inventions, including the incandescent electric lamp and the phonograph. Guglielmo Marconi (1874–1937) was an Italian electrical engineer and pioneer of the radio. Charles Darwin (1809–82), in 1859, published his *On the Origin of Species by Means of Natural Selection*, in which he posited his theory of evolution.

Note Left by a Suicide

74   "Potter's Field": This public burial place, especially in the city, was for paupers, unknown persons, and criminals.

74   "Socrates, Espinoza, Kant": Socrates (ca. 470–399 B.C.) of Athens established a philosophical presence in the last half of the fifth century B.C. with his Socratic method of intellectual inquiry, in which, inductively, a series of questions lead point by point to establishing a general truth. Baruch Spinoza (1632–77) became known as "the prince of rationalists" by arguing that nothing is capricious or contingent but everything proceeds in an orderly manner according to law. Immanuel Kant (1724–1804) was a German phi-

losopher and the foremost thinker of the Enlightenment; he has recently come under extreme scrutiny for advancing a philosophy that argued Africans and their descendants were irrational and uncivilized and therefore were inhuman.

75   "will-o'-the-wisp": A will-o'-the-wisp is anything that deludes or misleads by luring on.

To One Who Would Leave Me

76   "Bernhardt": Sarah Bernhardt (1845–1923), a French woman, was one of the most famous actresses in theater history. She made a triumphant return to the stage following the amputation of one leg. Eleonora Duse (1859–1924), an Italian actress, achieved fame playing the same role in *La Dame Aux Camelias* that Bernhardt had made famous earlier. She had a serious illness yet continued her spectacular career.

76   "Circe": In Greek legend, she was a famous sorceress who managed to lure men to her island, where she turned them into swine.

76   "Midas": King Midas of Greek mythology was known as the richest man in the world. He developed such a wish for gold that everything he touched turned to gold—thus, "the Midas touch."

'Mancipation Day

77   "'Mancipation Day": This day commemorated the anniversary of the Emancipation Proclamation, which went into effect 1 January 1863. By law, slaves held in states that had seceded from the Union were declared free. It did not cover, however, those slaves in the border states that did not secede.

77   "Sing Sing, Joliet, Leavenworth, San Quentin": Davis cites here notorious prisons: Sing Sing, a state penitentiary in New York; San Quentin, the oldest and most famous prison operated by the state of California; and Joliet, a state facility in Illinois.

77   "Jim Crow": The term dates back to at least 1828, the year Thomas D. Rice discovered how the antics of a Black youth could be made the source of humor on the American stage. What emerged from his appropriation was a full-scale production called the "Minstrel Theatre." Jim Crow came to signify the host of laws supporting racial segregation.

Notes on a Summer Night

78   "Kankakee": A city in northeastern Illinois, Kankakee is about fifty-four miles south of Chicago.

Awakening

81   "spring zephyr": Here Davis employs a conventional poetic reference to the Greek name for the west wind.

Modern Man—the Superman

83   "Hearst, Hitler, Mussolini": William Randolph Hearst (1863–1951) was the American newspaper and magazine publisher who raised sensationalist journalism to unprecedented heights. Here Davis connects Hearst to early twentieth-century dictators. Adolf Hitler (1889–1945), Nazi party leader from 1919 to 1945 and dictator of the Third Reich from 1933 to 1945, was the architect of the German racist state, the proponent of enslaving non-Aryan peoples, and the central figure behind the instigation of World War II. Benito Mussolini (1883–1945) was Italian dictator from 1922 to 1943 and founder of Italy's Fascist party.

83   "Dumdums": These hollow-nosed or soft-nosed bullets expand on impact, inflicting severe wounds.

85   "Chrysler Tower": Designed by William Van Alen, this building competed with the Empire State Building for the distinction of being the world's tallest structure in the early 1930s.

"Onward Christian Soldiers!"

87   "Onward Christian Soldiers": This Christian hymn was written by Sabine Baring-Gould and A. S. Sullivan in 1872.

Moses Mitchell

88   "Blonde Victoria Bates": Davis combines the names of the two white women who accused nine Black boys of raping them on a train near Scottsboro, Alabama, in March 1931. Their actual names were Ruby Bates and Victoria Price.

Benjamin Blakey

91   "Odd Fellows Temple": The Fraternal Order of Oddfellows was a secret benevolent and social organization of men.

Frank Marshall Davis: Writer

94   "his wine / He brews from wormwood": Wormwood is an herb yielding a bitter oil and has come to signify anything grievous or extremely unpleasant.

94   "seasoned with gall": Gall or bile comes from the gall bladder and connotes bitterness of spirit, rancor, or deep resentment.

47th Street: Poems

Foreword

100   "Karl von Linne": Davis's views on the concept of race have a remarkably contemporary feel and resonance. Beginning with Carolus Linnaeus, Davis retraces efforts by biological scientists to categorize the human species into

different varieties or types (Negroid, Mongoloid, Caucasoid) and briefly explores how this typology is used to justify the domination of a "superior" group over an "inferior" one. He also lists Unna, Wedding, Charcot, Finsen, Sambson, and Bailey as those who sought to disprove Linneaus by demonstrating a determining relationship between skin color and environment. The history Davis writes, though, takes us through a fairly arcane world, inasmuch as these names have virtually disappeared from the scientific discourse on the subject. Ultimately, of course, Davis is less interested in writing a treatise on racial classification than he is on disputing the fallacy of the concept. As his introduction reveals, an idea of race rooted in biological fact is faulty thinking. Echoing fictionist Richard Wright, Davis posits: "America will have Negro writers until the whole concept of race is erased."

102 "Pushkin of Russia, Dumas of France": Born into nobility in Russia, Alexander Sergeyevich Pushkin (1799–1837) became one of the foremost poets and prose writers in Russian literature. His mother's grandfather was Abram Hannibal, the Black general of Peter the Great, which has been used to document Pushkin as a writer of color. Alexandre Dumas, Pere, (1802–70), was a French novelist and dramatist. His father, an illegitimate son of the Marquis de la Pailleterie and a Black woman, Marie Cosette Dumas, was a general in the French Revolution. Dumas delighted many generations of readers with his highly romantic novels immortalizing the adventures of the Three Musketeers and the Count of Monte Cristo.

102 "Senator Bilbo": Theodore Gilmore Bilbo (1877–1947) served as U.S. senator from Mississippi from 1935 to 1947. His reputation for being a demagogue and arch-segregationist made him one of the most feared opponents of Black racial causes.

47th Street

103 "'Orphan Annie,' 'Popeye'": "Orphan Annie," starring the most famous and most successful waif in comics, was created by Harold Gray on 5 August 1924. The character began as a composite of the most famous roles Mary Pickford played on film: tough, back-talking, and honest. Soon, she embodied a political stance, and the strip reached its height of popularity during the Great Depression, when it addressed and assuaged the fears of the period. "Popeye" was another comic strip, this one created by E. C. Segar in 1929. When Popeye the sailor walked in, his direct approach to correcting injustice made him an overnight sensation.

105 "Helen, Venus, Cleopatra": Helen of Troy, in Greek lore, was so beautiful that it is said she indirectly caused the Trojan War. Venus, in Roman mythology, was the goddess of beauty and love. Cleopatra (69–30 B.C.), the beautiful queen of Egypt, was one of the greatest romantic heroines of all time.

106 "Don't Spend Your Money Where You Can't Work": This slogan of the civil rights movement was first used to good effect by Joseph D. Bibb, editor of

the *Whip*, Chicago's most militant journal, which tried to cut into the much larger *Chicago Defender* newspaper circulation.

108 "policy writer": In *Livin' the Blues*, Davis describes policy, a game of chance, in this way: "In policy, the numbers are usually inserted in small capsules, placed in a wheel-like drum, which is turned for mixing. The first selected (at random, theoretically) are the winning combination. After the drawing, they are printed on slips of paper, distributed at various stations and given to writers. A wheel may have three or four drawings a day, often known as 'classes,' thus giving the operators a triple or quadruple shot at the public's money" (206–7).

109 "Louis Armstrong": Daniel Louis "Satchmo" Armstrong (1900–1971) was an American jazz trumpet virtuoso, singer, band leader, and actor. His early playing was noted for its improvisation and his reputation as a vocalist was quickly established. Armstrong was a major influence on the melodic development of jazz in the 1920s; because of him, solo performance attained a position of great importance in jazz music.

109 "Leopold Stokowski": Stokowski (1882–1977), a British-born conductor, was known for his flamboyant showmanship, the rich sonorities of his orchestras, and his influence as a popularizer of classical music. He gained international reputation as musical director of the Philadelphia Orchestra from 1912 to 1936 and continued to conduct the group in guest appearances until 1941. Organizer of the All-American Youth Orchestra, he conducted the NBC Symphony (1941–44) with Toscanini and founded low-priced concerts at the New York City Center (1944–45). He directed the New York Philharmonic (1946–50) and the Houston (Texas) Symphony (1955–62) and in 1962 formed the American Symphony Orchestra in New York City.

109 "A dozen Paderewskis": Ignace Jan Paderewski (1860–1941) was a Polish pianist, composer, and statesman. His brilliant, sensitive playing won him worldwide popularity exceeding that of any performer since Franz Liszt. In 1891 he made the first of many concert tours of the United States. An ardent patriot, he briefly headed Polish governments in 1919 and 1940–41 (the latter in exile).

109 "Le Miserere": This is an aria from the opera *Il Trovatore* by Giuseppe Verdi.

110 "Blackstone Hotel, Park Avenue, Piccadilly Circus, Hong Kong": For Davis, these sites represent wealth, prestige, prominence, and privilege. The Blackstone Hotel, built at Michigan Avenue and Seventh Street in Chicago, routinely housed celebrities. In New York, Park Avenue, for most of the twentieth century, smacked of money—old, new, inherited, married-into, self-made, or ill-gotten. Piccadilly Circus is London's center of traffic and amusement. Hong Kong, until a lease with China ran out in 1997, was a British colonial center for finance, trade, and industry.

111 "WPA": The Works Progress Administration was created in 1935 by President Franklin Delano Roosevelt (1882–1945) to provide useful public work for needy persons left unemployed by the Great Depression. It was renamed the

Notes to the Poems ■ 265

Work Projects Administration in 1939 when it was placed under the Federal Works Agency. In its eight years of operation, it employed about 8.5 million individuals at a total cost of nearly $11 billion. World War II brought increasing employment and on 30 June 1945, the agency was terminated.

111   "black boys at Pearl Harbor": On 7 December 1941, Japanese planes launched a surprise attack on Pearl Harbor, eventually sinking the battleship *Arizona* and compelling the United States to join World War II. Several Black seamen stationed on the ship were killed.

Snapshots of the Cotton South

116   "Co'n pone": Native Americans taught the early settlers how to make flat breads, such as corn pone and ashcake, from cornmeal. By adding various ingredients, the settlers created Johnnycake, cornbread, spoon bread, and hush puppies.

118   "Southern Tenant Farmers Union": This interracial labor organization emerged during the 1930s. Despite the forces arrayed against it, the STFU continued to grow, peaking at an estimated thirty-one thousand members in 1938. In the fall of 1935 the union called its first strike, demanding payment of $1.00 per 100 pounds of cotton (the prevailing rate was $.40 to $.60) but privately agreeing to accept $.75.

119   "Manual Arts": Also known as industrial training, the manual arts curriculum includes automobile mechanics, electronics, graphic arts, industrial crafts, industrial drawing, metal working, photography, and woodworking.

Tenement Room

127   "Tenement room": In his book *Livin' the Blues,* Davis also castigated the practice of owners dividing their houses into small units or apartments and renting them out to individuals or whole families. This division led to huge profits for owners and cramped living conditions for tenants.

To Those Who Sing America

129   "Sacco and Vanzetti in Boston, Tom Mooney in California": Nicola Sacco and Bartolomeo Vanzetti, both anarchists, were tried and convicted of the 15 April 1920 robbery of a shoe company paymaster in South Braintree, Massachusetts, during which a guard was shot and killed. Their execution on 22 August 1927 was preceded by worldwide sympathy demonstrations because their conviction was thought to stem from political reasons rather than evidentiary ones. Thomas J. Mooney (1883–1942) was an American labor activist involved in several violent labor struggles in California before 1916. He was convicted as a participant in the bomb killings at the San Francisco Preparedness Day Parade in 1916 and sentenced to death. Because of widely held beliefs in his innocence, his sentence was commuted to life imprisonment in 1918 and he was later pardoned unconditionally.

129   "Daughters of the American Revolution, Ku Klux Klan, American Legion and
       Boards of Censors": Davis brings together four very different organizations
       that shared, in his view, a hypocritical vision of America. The Daughters of
       the American Revolution (DAR), formed by supposed descendants of the
       Revolutionary War, were notorious in their efforts to preserve patriotism in
       the United States. Their refusal to permit the celebrated Black opera singer
       Marian Anderson (1897–1993) to perform at their Constitutional Hall led to
       her famous outdoor concert at the Lincoln Memorial on 9 April 1939. The
       American Legion, founded in 1919 in Paris, was infamous for supporting
       efforts to build up the military strength of the United States and for attack-
       ing so-called subversive or anti-American teachings and organizations.
       Formed in 1909 and renamed two times, the Board of Censorship purport-
       edly opposed the depiction of crime or violence for its own sake, indecency,
       and immoral suggestiveness in artistic works. However, when its members
       had the opportunity to oppose the showing of the infamously racist movie
       The Birth of a Nation (1915), they refused to do so.

129   "Mistermorgan, Misterdupont, Mistermellon": Here Davis refers to the
       financial and industrial empires founded by Junius Spencer Morgan, E. I.
       DuPont de Nemours, and Andrew W. Mellon.

Peace Quiz for America

131   "John Johnson": In the War of 1812, Nathaniel Shaler, the commander of the
       Governor Tompkins, said that the name of John Johnson, an African Ameri-
       can seaman on his ship, should be registered in the book of fame. As Johnson
       lay dying after he had been struck by a twenty-four-pound shot, he suppos-
       edly exclaimed, "Fire away my boys; no haul a color down."

131   "Needham Roberts and Henry Johnson": Roberts and Johnson were the first
       two African American war heroes of World War I, both from the 369th In-
       fantry unit. Despite being wounded, they were successful in fending off the
       Germans, for which they received the French Croix de Guerre.

131   "Dorie Miller": Dorie Miller (1919–43) was assigned as a messman on the
       battleship *Arizona* in World War II. On 7 December 1941, during the Japa-
       nese surprise attack on Pearl Harbor, Miller was briefly knocked down by the
       force of an explosion but pulled the *Arizona*'s mortally wounded captain
       from the line of fire and took up a position at an antiaircraft gun. He had
       never been taught to fire a gun, but he shot down four Japanese planes be-
       fore being ordered to leave the badly damaged ship.

131   "Roland Hayes" (1887–1977): When this renowned tenor returned home to
       Georgia from traveling the world, he met with the unreconstructed social
       mores of Jim Crow. His wife went into a local shoe store and demanded the
       service she had become accustomed to in Europe, but the white clerk insulted
       her. Hayes came to her rescue, was beaten by the white clerk, and was thrown
       in jail by the police.

131   "Kilby Prison": This was the site of incarceration in 1931 for the nine Black youths known as the Scottsboro Boys.

131   "Cleo Wright": Davis refers here to the 20 January 1942 lynching of twenty-seven-year-old Cleo Wright in Sikeston, Missouri. Wright had apparently attacked a white woman with a knife. In the struggle with the police, he was brutally beaten and had to be hospitalized. The mob broke into the hospital, forcibly removed him, and dragged him through the streets before burning him alive.

131   "Marian Anderson": An American contralto, Anderson (1897–1993) was the first Black woman to be named a permanent member of the Metropolitan Opera Company. Her rich wide-ranged voice was superbly suited to both opera and the Negro spirituals that she included in her concerts and recordings. In 1939, the Daughters of the American Revolution refused to let her perform in a concert at Constitution Hall because of her ethnicity, so she performed outside the Lincoln Memorial.

132   "Executive Order 8802": On 25 June 1941 President Roosevelt issued Executive Order 8802 in which he wrote, "There shall be no discrimination in the employment of workers in defense industries or government because of race, creed, color or national origin . . . and it is the duty of employers and of labor organizations . . . to provide for the full and equitable participation of all workers in defense industries without discrimination because of race, creed, color or national origin."

132   "Fair Employment Practices Committee": In pursuance of the executive order, a committee on Fair Employment Practices was set up to receive and investigate complaints of discrimination in violation of the order.

132   "Four Freedoms": Roosevelt announced these worldwide social and political objectives in the State of the Union message he delivered to Congress on 6 January 1941. Roosevelt declared that all people should have the freedom of speech and expression, the freedom to worship God independently, the freedom from want, and the freedom from fear. He called for the latter through "a world-wide reduction of armaments to such a point and in such a thorough fashion that no nation will be in a position to commit an act of physical aggression against any neighbor anywhere in the world."

134   "Tojo": Hideki Tojo (1884–1948) led Japan's war efforts after the attack on Pearl Harbor on 7 December 1941. Buoyed by his military victories, he then assumed virtual dictatorial powers by taking over as chief of the general staff. On 16 July 1944, he was removed from this post and on 18 July his entire cabinet resigned. On 26 April 1946, he was indicted and tried as a war criminal before the international military tribunal for the Far East. He was found guilty and hanged.

134   "Talmadge": Eugene Talmadge (1884–1946) was a governor of Georgia who represented well the Southern agrarian philosophy of fiscal and racial conservatism. His magnetic personality and great talent for leadership made him

a popular political figure among white voters. He used the National Guard to break textile mill strikes and he interfered when educators at the University of Georgia advocated racial equality.

134   "Rankin": John Elliot Rankin (1882–1960) of Mississippi served in the U.S. House of Representatives from 1921 to 1953. A committed segregationist and states' rights advocate, he was consistently vituperative when denouncing efforts to accord Blacks their constitutional rights. During the mid-1940s, he often found conspiracy theory to be an effective means for attacking racial integration.

134   "Black Dragon": The Black Dragon Society was an ultra-nationalist Japanese secret organization. One of its avowed objectives was to create unrest in Manchuria, which had large Chinese, Japanese, and Korean populations.

135   "Wendell Willkie": Willkie (1892–1944) was defeated by Roosevelt in the 1940 presidential election. As a special envoy to Roosevelt, he embarked on a worldwide goodwill trip in which he reassured foreign nations of a swift, secure end to the war. In his enormously popular book *One World* (1943), he predicted a postwar coalition that included China, Russia, and possibly the Middle Eastern nations.

135   "Henry Wallace": Wallace was elected vice president in 1940 and served in this capacity during Roosevelt's third term in office. In 1948, Wallace was the choice of the Progressive party for its presidential candidate. His motto, "This is the century of the common man," combined labor rights, civil rights, and international human rights. About Wallace, Davis wrote in his *Livin' the Blues*: "When it seemed thousands of black Democrat voters would desert [Harry] Truman for the more appealing Wallace program, the Missourian astutely came out in support of bold new civil rights legislation. Like a magnet, this political move drew back enough Afro-American voters to win Truman an upset victory at the polls that November" (299).

136   "Father Coughlin and Gerald L. K. Smith": Charles Edward Coughlin (1891–1979) was a Roman Catholic priest, who, in the 1930s, made frequent radio addresses in which he assailed American financial leaders for having caused the Great Depression. He seemingly directed his most pointed barbs at the Jewish members of Wall Street and by World War II exhibited some sympathy for the Nazis. Gerald L. K. Smith (1898–1976) headed the ultra-right-wing, isolationist America First party and loudly opposed communism.

136   "Congress of Industrial Organizations": The CIO was a body of unions formed in 1935 to organize mass production industries. From the beginning, the CIO made it clear that it sought to organize workers regardless of race, and in its early campaigns, it made a special appeal to African Americans. The CIO merged with the American Federation of Labor in 1955 to form the AFL-CIO, which became the most powerful labor organization in the United States.

137 "Hirohito": Hirohito (1901–89) became the 124th emperor of Japan on 25 December 1926. His call was intended to appeal to African American dissatisfaction with Jim Crow laws and to subvert American democracy from within.

For All Common People

138 "Salamua": A small settlement, Salamua is located on the northeast coast of New Guinea. During World War II, the village fell to the Japanese on 8 March 1942, but U.S. forces under General Douglas MacArthur recaptured it on 16 September 1943.

Nothing Can Stop the People

142 "Chamberlain": (Arthur) Neville Chamberlain (1869–1940) was British prime minister from 28 May 1937 to 10 May 1940. His name is identified with the policy of appeasement toward Adolf Hitler's Germany in the period immediately preceding World War II.

143 "Chiang Kai-shek": (1887–1975): A Chinese military leader, Chiang Kai-shek (1887–1975) became the first constitutional president of the Republic of China.

Alone

153 Davis would use this title again for a poem that was published for the first time in *Blind Alleys: A Journal of Contemporary Literature* 2.1 (Summer 1984): 25–26. For that poem, see 239.

You Are All

153 "Baffin Land": This island, the fifth largest in the world, is situated in the Canadian Arctic Archipelago in the Baffin region of the Northwest Territories. Its eastern mountains have glaciers and icecaps, and some elevations are over eight thousand feet.

I Have Talked with Death

161 "replevin": This is the recovery of goods or chattels wrongfully taken or detained.

Self Portrait

163 "Tenth American": See the note to 10 for "Washington and DuBois."

163 "Hoover and Browder": Herbert Hoover (1874–1964) was president from 1928 to 1932, during the onset of the Great Depression. His fiscal policies generally favored the banking community and big business, while he left the states and local communities to provide relief for jobless workers. Earl (Russell) Browder (1891–1973) was a U.S. Communist party leader for almost twenty-five years until his split with official Party doctrine after World War II. When

he declared in 1946 that capitalism and socialism could peacefully co-exist, he was expelled from the Party and three years later was named in "treason trials" in Budapest and Prague as the originator of the heresy known as "Browderism."

164   "Stardust or Shostakovich": Now a standard, "Stardust" was a popular song written by Hoagy Carmichael in the 1920s. Dmitri Shostakovich (1906–75) was a Soviet composer whose music, much of it inspired by Soviet history, gained recognition throughout the world and placed him high among the foremost creators of Western music in the twentieth century.

Peace Is a Fragile Cup

165   "Pithecanthropus erectus to homo mechanicus": In this phrase, Davis reconstructs the development of humankind: *Pithecanthropus* is a former genus of an extinct primate, apparently intermediate between humans and the existing anthropoid apes; "homo mechanicus" is Davis's Latinized expression for "mechanical man," one who is devoid of feelings and emotions. This anthropological history, in which humankind has "evolved" beyond *Homo sapiens,* parallels the development of humankind's ability to invent new and more horrible weapons of war.

165   "Nazi gas chambers at Lublin": Lublin, a city in southeastern Poland, about one hundred miles from Warsaw, was the site of the infamous Majdanek concentration camp. An estimated 500,000 passed through this camp, and over 350,000 perished there.

165   "Belgrade": For its refusal to join the Axis Powers, this city in Yugoslavia was the target of Operation Punishment on 6 April 1941, in which seventeen thousand people died during German bombing raids.

165   "Thermopylae, Gettysburg, Bataan": Thermopylae was the site of a 480 B.C. battle in Greece in which a small group of Greeks under the Spartan king Leonidas fought to the death and heroically delayed the conquest of Athens by perhaps 180,000 Asiatics under Xerxes. In the Civil War, the Battle of Gettysburg resulted in heavy casualties on both sides: Union forces lost 23,000 out of 88,000 while Southern troops lost 20,000 out of 75,000 soldiers. The Bataan Death March was a forced march of 70,000 American and Filipino prisoners of war captured by the Japanese in the Philippines in the early stages of World War II. Starting out on 9 April 1942, they were forced-marched fifty-five miles to San Fernando, then taken by rail to Capas, from which they walked the final eight miles to Camp O'Donnell. They were starved, mistreated, and often kicked or beaten on their way, and many who fell were bayoneted. Only 54,000 reached the camp; 7,000–10,000 died on the way; the rest escaped to the jungle.

Uncollected and Unpublished Poems, 1948–84

Lady Day

193   "Her rum-brown rope of a voice": Although this text appears as a stanza in "Billie Holiday," it is clear from his papers that Davis intended it to stand as a separate poem as well.

This Is Paradise

195   "Big Five": In the Hawaiian Islands, the sugar and pineapple plantations were controlled originally by five parent companies: American Factors, C. Brewer, Alexander and Baldwin, Castle and Cooke, and Theo H. Davies and Company. Many of these families were direct descendants of missionaries who came to Hawaii between 1830 and 1837.

201   "Harry Bridges and his ILWU": The International Longshoremen and Warehousemen's Union came about largely through the efforts of its first president, Harry Bridges. Born in Melbourne, Australia, Bridges joined the San Francisco local of the International Longshoremen's Association in 1924. In 1934 he helped organize an important strike and from this experience gained the stature to break off from the ILA in 1937. Charters were issued to longshoremen in Hawaii and the ILWU became dedicated to the ideal of democratic unionism. Its house organ was the *Honolulu Record,* for which Davis reprised his column "Frank-ly Speaking" in 1949. The union's activism earned it a subversive designation by the FBI and other governmental agencies charged with ferreting out communism in the late forties and early fifties.

Moonlight at Kahana Bay

208   "pikake": The pikake is a delicate scented flower—a white jasmine.

INDEX OF TITLES

John Edgar Tidwell is an associate professor of English at the University of Kansas. Grants from the National Endowment for the Humanities and the American Council of Learned Societies, among other organizations, have enabled him to publish widely on African American literature and to focus particularly on Sterling A. Brown and Frank Marshall Davis. He has edited Davis's autobiography, *Livin' the Blues: Memoirs of a Black Journalist and Poet,* and is currently at work on a biography of Brown.

The American Poetry Recovery Series

The University of Illinois Press
is a founding member of the
Association of American University Presses.

Composed in 10.5/13 Minion
with Helvetica Neue Extended display
by Jim Proefrock
at the University of Illinois Press
Designed by Paula Newcomb
Manufactured by Thomson-Shore, Inc.

University of Illinois Press
1325 South Oak Street
Champaign, IL 61820-6903
www.press.uillinois.edu